T0288168

The Making and Unmaking of a Zionist

In loving memory of my mother and father
Rachel and Abraham

Hereby then are all admonished that none hold converse with him by word of mouth, none hold communication with him by writing; that no one do him any service, no one abide under the same roof with him, no one approach within four cubits length of him, and no one read any document dictated by him, or written by his hand.

Rite of expulsion from the Jewish community, in Robert Willis,
Benedict de Spinoza: His Life, Correspondence, and Ethics (1870)

He who lives according to the guidance of reason strives as much as possible to repay the hatred, anger, or contempt of others towards himself with love or generosity ... hatred is increased by reciprocal hatred, and, on the other hand, can be extinguished by love, so that hatred passes into love.

Spinoza, 'Of human bondage or the strength
of the emotions', *Ethics* (1677)

CONTENTS

PREFACE

The Israel-Palestine conflict often seems irreconcilable. The clash of political and ideological positions is bitter and polarised. The historical narratives of the two sides profoundly contradict each other. Violent actions to which Israelis and Palestinians have resorted plumb the depths of cruelty and callousness and are likened to the worst evils in history. Two religious traditions seem to be engaged in a Manichean life-and-death struggle. Competing nationalist claims are so fiercely asserted that territorial compromise appears unreachable. When described in these terms, it's no surprise that there is such despair as to whether a peaceful and just resolution can ever be reached; that what drives Palestinians and Israelis, and all who are wrapped up in the conflict, is too large and difficult to comprehend.

I can sympathise with anyone who feels this way. Listening to discussions that all too easily fall back on partisan posturing and trading of insults is enough to drive even the most well-meaning observer to distraction. But it is a false and counterproductive view implying an equivalence of power and status between the two sides that does not exist and encouraging onlookers to adopt an ultimately destructive, 'plague on both their houses' mentality. The problem is how to get people to see the conflict differently; to get beyond the headlines and the oversimplified, fight-to-the-death imagery.

What is so often overlooked, or perhaps even deliberately avoided, is the human dimension. Every Zionist and Palestinian nationalist, soldier and militant, perpetrator and victim – indeed, every individual enmeshed in the conflict – has a personal story. Knowing and understanding more about these individual stories, about how people came to be what they are or were, might help us to find new ways of reconciling differences and thereby rediscover our common humanity. A primary motive for writing *The Making and Unmaking of a Zionist* was to make a contribution to this objective by telling just such a personal story.

The book takes as its premise the belief that small details can illuminate the larger picture. In this case, the small details of a life in which Zionism and Israel have played a large part from an early age. The idea of writing such an account came to me initially in 2005, but it was only in 2009 that I finally felt free from external or self-imposed constraints and could fulfil a desire to retrace my personal and political journey over the last 50 years. In addition to demystifying some of the sources of the Israel-Palestine conflict, the story of my professional life may throw light on the internal history of a minority community in the UK as it sought to come to terms with a burgeoning of dissenting Jewish views on Zionism and Israel.

I became a Zionist in my early teens. I wanted to live on a kibbutz and build a socialist society in the new Jewish State of Israel. In 1970, when I was 24 years old, I realised my dream and went to live there. After two years I returned to England, studied for a university degree and worked briefly as a history lecturer. In 1979 I began working as a researcher, writer and editor for an institute dealing with contemporary issues affecting Jews worldwide. Over the next 30 years, both as an observer and a participant, I became ever more deeply engaged in communal and global Jewish politics, of which my involvement with Zionism and Israel was an integral part. I founded a Jewish policy think tank and subsequently established a multi-million pound grant-making foundation supporting Jewish life in Europe. In 2006 I returned to head the think tank and found myself at the centre of polemical debates over the danger of antisemitism and the policies of the State of Israel. After a three-year struggle with individuals and organisations within the Jewish and pro-Israel establishment, I resigned from the directorship in 2009.

During these years my understanding of the meaning of my engagement with Israel and the political ideology that inspired it has changed dramatically. But that change came about very gradually and unsystematically.

Without a day-by-day record, writing about one's past involves a great deal of both retrospection and re-imagination. This makes it easy to filter events and ascribe to some of them a significance they did not have at the time. And when you are describing how you arrived at views that you later repudiated, the temptation is very strong to use hindsight to show that even then you had doubts. Nevertheless, I have tried to tell my story with as little use of hindsight as possible and have added context and explanation only where it is necessary for understanding. My intention is to take the reader with me on my journey, exposing the views I held and the experiences I had without offering excuses or qualifications. I realise this is a risky strategy and that my apparent naivety may provoke a negative response. But my hope is that the story I tell will be sufficiently interesting and compelling to make the reader want to accompany me.

I write with insider knowledge of the workings of organised Jewish communal life, the functioning of national and international Jewish political organisations and the development of the Zionist movement. While in itself this does not guarantee insight, I believe it gives me a unique perspective from which to recall my personal, political and intellectual journey. It is the human dimension, the individual story, but not divorced from social and political reality. As such I hope it provides a better understanding of how an individual became engaged with the dynamics of an idea and a reality, Zionism and Israel, and helps get beyond the stereotypes and the slogans associated with a conflict that continues to have such a major impact on the contemporary world.

And while you may wonder how the small details of a personal story can have relevance for a conflict of such significance, it is important to remember that diaspora Jewish attitudes are a major factor policy-makers take into account when it comes to determining policy on the Israel-Palestine conflict in Washington, London, Jerusalem and elsewhere.

What I have not done is write an autobiography. I certainly include auto-biographical material and could not have described my experience of Zionism and Israel without drawing on personal facts and recollections. But I skim very lightly over those periods of my life when these matters were not provoking new thoughts. Similarly I mention other people only when their personalities, views, actions or statements seem central to my story. And while I have tried throughout to be honest about my own weaknesses and failings, I have stopped short of full disclosure since I did not want to lose sight of the central subject matter of Zionism and Israel. I hope I have got the balance right.

Antony Lerman
June 2012

ABBREVIATIONS AND ACRONYMS

(Founding date of organisations, where known, in parentheses)

ADL   Anti-Defamation League (1913), American Jewish defence organisation

AJC   American Jewish Committee (1906), advocacy organisation

BEF   British Expeditionary Force in the Second World War

BoD   Board of Deputies of British Jews (1760), official representative body of British Jews

CAABU   Council for the Advancement of Arab British Understanding (1967), London-based lobby group

CPPME Canadian Professors for Peace in the Middle East

CRIF   Conseil Représentatif des Institutions juives de France (Representative Council of Jewish Institutions in France)

CSEPS Centre for the Study of European Politics and Society, Ben Gurion University, Israel

CST   Community Security Trust (1994), private British Jewish defence organisation

ECJC   European Council of Jewish Communities, originally the European Council of Jewish Community Services (1940s)

EJC   European Jewish Congress (1986), European affiliate of the WJC

IDF   Israel Defence Forces

IDT   Israel-Diaspora Trust (1982), private discussion forum

IJA   Institute of Jewish Affairs (1942), research arm of the WJC, predecessor of JPR

IJV   Independent Jewish Voices (2007), a network of individuals representing an alternative voice for Jews in Britain

JAFI   Jewish Agency for Israel (originally Jewish Agency for Palestine, 1929)

JFJHR Jewish Forum for Justice and Human Rights (2003)

JLC   Jewish Leadership Council

JNF   Jewish National Fund (1901), founded to buy land in Palestine for Jewish settlement

JPPPI   Jewish People Policy Planning Institute (2002), think tank set up by JAFI

JPR   Institute for Jewish Policy Research (1996), independent think tank, successor organisation to the IJA
JSG   Jewish Socialists' Group (1970s), a Jewish political organisation in Britain
Machon Institute for Youth Leaders from Abroad (Jerusalem)
MCB   Muslim Council of Britain
SICSA Sassoon International Centre for the Study of Antisemitism, Hebrew University Jerusalem
Sikkuy Association for Civic Equality in Israel
UJIA   United Jewish Israel Appeal
WJC   World Jewish Congress (1936), international political body representing Jewish interests worldwide
WZO   World Zionist Organisation (1896), umbrella organisation for the Zionist movement
ZF   Zionist Federation of Great Britain (1899), umbrella body for the Zionist movement in Britain

1

FROM BOURGEOIS TO BUILDER

May they grow strong, the hands of our gifted brothers,
Who grace the dust of our land;
Don't let your spirits fall, but be joyful, with song.
Come, with one voice, shoulder to shoulder, to the aid of the people.

Chaim Nachman Bialik, 'Strengthen the hands', 1894,
anthem of the Zionist youth movement

My heart was pounding in my eight-year-old chest. I had just splashed through the shallow waters of a Surrey stream and thrown myself flat on the sloping bank. I pressed my face against the mud as I peered nervously over the edge. My sandaled feet were immersed in water, but I was so excited, I didn't give it a thought. I had a stick in my hand and was waiting for the command to clamber over the top and attack the enemy in the field beyond the fence. Two of the camp's youth leaders were nearby. I could see that they were looking at me and smiling incredulously. In a bemused tone one of them said something to the other about my 'enthusiasm'. Seconds later, as the word *Kadima!* ('Forward!') disturbed the still air of the English countryside and the sound rippled down the line of children in our tribe spread out along the bank, I was racing for the fence as the mock battle was about to begin.

Who were we fighting? This game was being played at a ten-day summer camp of the British Zionist youth movement, Habonim ('The Builders'), held in 1954 on a farm in Capel, a village in the Weald, just north of the Surrey-Sussex border. We were almost certainly re-enacting a battle between the Haganah, the underground Jewish military forces in Palestine, and the Arab armies during the 1948 war of Israel's independence. Through Israeli songs, games played using Hebrew words, stories told round the campfire and the teaching of scouting and camping lore, together with dozens of other children I learnt about Israel and Zionism, act and idea, for the first time.

I was there with my older brother Steve and neither of us had been away from home for such a long period. We were not members of the movement and it showed. Photos captured us standing on parade outside our tents in white school shirts and grey flannel shorts. Most other children were in khaki

1

shorts or cotton skirts, summer shirts, sleeveless tops or the pale blue shirts of the movement uniform. Our parents came to visit us on Open Day. I cried and wanted to go home, but they persuaded me to stay.

I didn't go to another such camp for five years. Nor did I start going regularly to the local movement group's weekly activity, which was held in a synagogue hall near our Golders Green home. Nevertheless, a seed had been planted. The decision determined the future course of my life.

*   *   *

Mum and Dad were orthodox, Ashkenazi Jews, who loved Jewish tradition. If they were not as strictly observant as they could have been, it was not out of any disrespect for the laws and teachings of the religion, but more a reflection of their wish to accommodate the modern world and of their non-doctrinal sense of Judaism's meaning. My Ukrainian-born paternal grandfather, Simcha, who arrived in England in 1901, was a member of the very traditional orthodox Federation of Synagogues, founded in the late nineteenth century to cater for Eastern European immigrants. He was a cabinet-maker with no pretensions to learning and no aptitude for making money. My maternal grandfather, Myer Miller, whose parents came to England from Poland in the late 1870s, also had little education, but, rather more successful in trade, by the 1920s he had his own small and thriving tailoring firm in Shoreditch, in London's East End.

Like all children born into observant Jewish families, my parents were first given Hebrew names, Abraham and Rachel. But Dad, one of seven children, was known as Dick since his early twenties, and Mum, who had a twin sister and a younger brother, was known as Ray. Dad's family was very poor. They lived in rented rooms in Mile End. He left school at 13. For Mum, life was considerably more comfortable. Myer and his wife Rose moved out of the East End and bought a semi-detached house on the Hendon Way, near suburban Golders Green. Ray had a relatively relaxed and modern upbringing, but maintaining Jewish tradition, getting married and bringing up a family always came first. Her formal education ended when she was 15.

Dick and Ray met before the Second World War, but Dad was soon drafted into the Royal Berkshire Regiment and packed off to the continent with the British Expeditionary Force. As 'Abraham' he might have been vulnerable had he fallen into the clutches of the Germans, so he quickly acquired the name Dick. He was an infantryman trying to keep the Germans at bay as the BEF retreated to Dunkirk. Sheltering in a ditch, he was hit by shrapnel from a German mortar exploding above him and came to in a German field hospital. He spent more than three and a half years in German prisoner-of-war camps before returning to England in a prisoner exchange towards the end of 1943.

Shrapnel permanently weakened Dad's right hand and the camp conditions left him vulnerable to bronchitis for the rest of his life. He trained as a tailor and cutter and worked for my grandfather. He and Ray married in March 1944 and Steve was born in the September. I was born in March 1946. By then we were living in our own, three-bedroom semi-detached house round the corner from my grandparents, on the Pennine estate in north-west London where all the roads were named after English hill ranges. My father worked hard. It was a good time to be in bespoke tailoring. Despite austerity, the normality and comfort he craved after his years of incarceration seemed to come remarkably quickly. Soon we were holidaying in Brighton and Bognor and then further afield in France and Belgium, where Dad was reunited with the family that visited and cared for him in his Belgian hospital before being forced east to Stalag 8b.

Mum kept a strictly kosher home. Dad joined the United Synagogue congregation in Dunstan Road where my grandfather Myer was a member. We went regularly to synagogue on *Shabbat* and observed all the festivals. I was barely four, very shy and saddled with a slight stammer when I joined my brother at the synagogue *cheder* (religion school) to learn the basics of Judaism four times a week. Although the lessons took place in a leafy suburb of London, there was still something of the Eastern European *shtetl* about the atmosphere. That world had been destroyed – not that we knew then much about what had yet to become known as the Holocaust – but you could see its genetic imprint in the faces of some of the teachers, the Hebrew primers and the occasionally severe discipline. Few concessions were made to modern teaching methods. We learnt how to read classical Hebrew to enable us to master the prayers and participate fully in the religious services. Understanding what the words meant came only later, if at all, as I was not a good student. My mind wandered. It all seemed dreary and stultifying. I longed to be playing with the children running free in the adjacent park.

Modest and gentle, my parents took their religion seriously, but they also had a fairly liberal and relaxed attitude to orthodoxy. (Mainstream orthodox practice in Britain was tolerant and accommodating, and compatible with the process of assimilation our family was undergoing.) They followed the laws and commandments as far as they could, but never preached to others. They were both active on synagogue committees. But on most Saturdays Dad had to be in his shop in Shoreditch.

Israel was a presence, but not a dominant one. Together with tens of thousands of other British Jews we kept a blue Jewish National Fund collecting tin on the mantelpiece and dropped in small change for planting forests in Israel. But I doubt that my parents had any awareness of the political ideology of Zionism. Israel gave them a sense of pride and security in a world still recovering from mass death and economic deprivation. But their Jewish lives were lived firmly within the framework of the synagogue, their nearby extended families and their many local Jewish friends. At weddings and bar mitzvahs we toasted the President of the State of Israel and then sang the *Hatikva*, which we knew then as the Jewish national anthem, but which was also the Israeli national anthem.

*   *   *

In the early 1930s, when she was a young teenager, Mum was briefly a member of Habonim, then still in its infancy (it was founded in Britain in 1929). So when it came to filling our young lives with enjoyable activities, I suspect the pleasurable memory of that experience is what induced her to send me and Steve to the ten-day Habonim summer camp in Surrey, in 1954.

Attending the camp planted in me an awareness of Israel, but it had no particular effect on my life over the following five years. I coped with being a borderline 11+ failure, with a move to what was seen at the time as a rather inferior grammar school and with my bar mitzvah, which was not without trauma. I failed the associated exam to test my knowledge of Judaism and barely scraped through at the second attempt. But around my 13th birthday, I joined the local Habonim group, following in the footsteps of my brother.

I have often wondered why my parents encouraged this. As far as I know, Israel had not become any more important for them in 1959 than it had been in 1954. And yet there is one obvious explanation. As with most Jewish boys of my age and religious upbringing, religious education came to an end with the bar mitzvah. Further Jewish knowledge could be acquired through regular participation in services and study sessions with the rabbi. But I rejected this path. Much as I disliked *cheder*, I had friends I enjoyed mixing with but now would not see as often. I'm sure that my parents wanted me to continue spending as much time as possible with other Jewish children, both doing things I would enjoy and continuing my Jewish education. Although orthodox, they did not indulge in public displays of religiosity, apart from the minimum of what was expected of them as synagogue members, so there was little chance of them sending me to a religious youth movement like B'nai Akiva. Two or three hours on a Sunday afternoon at the local Habonim group was a logical choice.

I also attended the synagogue youth club, but it was devoid of any Jewish educational or cultural content. We played table tennis, football and other sports at Habonim but in other respects it was, self-consciously, very different.

The afternoon's activities were more rigidly organised. We wore uniforms. Practically everything that we did involved the use of modern Hebrew words, so we quickly came to see the language as a living thing, for everyday use. It contrasted starkly with *cheder* Hebrew, the language of an oppressive religiosity I was beginning to abandon. The youth leaders, *madrichim* (guides) in Hebrew, were often just a few years older than us and far more than just organisers dedicated to giving us fun things to do. The most successful *madrich* had charisma, 'personality'. We were encouraged to look up to them and follow their example.

Habonim deprecated the mindlessness of the youth club and had specific educational goals. It took the outdoor, clean-living, muscular philosophy of scouting and married it to identification with Israel. It was not doctrinally anti-religious, but what could be further from the musty *cheder* than hiking in the countryside and lustily singing modern Hebrew songs? This linked us to an Israel typified by images of young, bronzed Jews, working on their ancestral land, but committed to rebuild Israel as a modern state, the home of the 'new Jew'.

The smattering of military culture present at times was a far cry from the regimentation and cadet uniforms of the Jewish Lads' Brigade. The Jewish soldier in Israel epitomised the 'new Jew', an image very far removed from anything we had encountered in the Jewish diaspora. He carried the torch of Jews who took up arms against the Nazis. And the ideal Jewish soldier was the Palmachnik, a member of the Palmach, the elite fighting force of the Haganah. In Habonim the Palmach symbolised the left-wing, democratic nature of Israel's citizen army, because Palmachniks lived and trained on kibbutzim. The Palmach had a major influence on Israeli politics and culture, and shaped the way Israelis saw themselves in the early years of the state.

The rousing anthem of the Palmach ('Misaviv yehom hasa'ar', 'All around us the storm rages') was among the many Israeli songs we were taught as part of a programme that immersed us in aspects of Israeli culture. Many were about Israeli or Jewish heroism, but also the biblical connection between Jews and the Land of Israel, nature and pioneering. Especially stirring was the anthem of the youth movement, the poem 'Techezakna' ('Strengthen the hands') written in 1894 by Chaim Nachman Bialik (1873–1934), the most influential of the modern Hebrew poets and considered the poet laureate of Jewish nationalism.

The movement wasn't as dour and mirthless as it may sound. In contrast to the ideological seriousness there was the tradition of the 'zig', the humorous, pun-laden sketch, part cabaret, part precursor to *Beyond the Fringe*, which lampooned aspects of the movement itself, or topical events. It was a fixture of any organised movement party, celebration or final night of camp. The youth leaders would endeavour to involve as many people as possible in writing and putting on zigs, but talent always rose to the top and a few people dominated this comedy scene, although I was not one of them. Ability to perform and raise a laugh was highly prized.

The youth movement experience was most fully realised at weekend and summer camps. The one I attended in August 1959 was very similar to the camp I went to in 1954, only rather more ambitious. We hiked across country in small groups for two days, carrying bivvy tents. On the second night we had to mount a mock attack. The 'bravery' and enthusiasm of the eight-year-old had been replaced by the nervousness of a 13-year-old and I chose to remain behind to look after the camp rather than trek off into the frightening night.

The Habonim activities were fun, new and different and offered an appealing mixture of group camaraderie, independence and sharing. This contrasted with the individual effort and endeavour demanded by a much harsher regime at Orange Hill County Grammar School for Boys, where I was struggling to keep up. At Habonim I had the opportunity to meet and mix with girls and, especially at camps, to pair off in relatively supervised circumstances. The process of absorbing Israeli culture, becoming aware of something called Zionism and being introduced to socialist political ideology was all very gradual. Even so, as a fairly shy child and something of a homeboy, I drifted away for a while. The weekly meeting of my group changed to a Saturday evening and I occasionally chose to stay at home. I had other interests: table tennis, making models, slot-car racing, constructing transistor radios. But I also had a rebellious streak and did all I could to avoid attending synagogue. Habonim gave me a safe outlet for that rebelliousness and for the fulfilment of the new range of emotional needs thrown up by puberty. So I began attending regularly again, developed close friendships and my first serious relationship with a girl. By the time I was 16, Habonim was the centre of my social life.

I only began to develop signs of intellectual curiosity when I was 15. Good teachers awakened my interest in history and English. I started to listen to classical music, with the help of my English master who lent me records of Beethoven's 5th and 3rd symphonies. Older friends introduced me to modern poetry, to the novels of Jack Kerouac and the jazz of Thelonius Monk. I started writing poems, began making regular weekly trips to Charing Cross Road to buy novels and political texts, and I developed left-wing opinions.

The movement promoted agricultural work as the most important task for Jews wanting to build the new state and we were introduced to it at the summer camp for 16-year-olds. This was the age when you might be asked, as I was, to become a *madrich*. And at 17 you could attend the one-year youth training course (*Hachsharat Noar*) covering basic agriculture, modern

Hebrew, Jewish history and Zionism at the movement's David Eder Farm, near Horsham, Sussex.

In the mid 1960s Habonim had about 20 full-time employees. Apart from the *Mazkir* (the national secretary) and youth leaders running the six major centres, staff organised the camps, controlled the finances, managed the farm and directed the *Hachsharat Noar* course. But in addition, there were four or five emissaries (*shlichim* in Hebrew) from kibbutzim in Israel who spent between one and three years working as advisers to the movement. They were usually former members of the movement who knew Habonim well. But increasingly, young *sabras*, Israeli Jews born in Israel, who lived on kibbutzim were sent to the UK to bring to the movement and its activities an injection of authentic contemporary Israeli culture, idealism and youthful sensibility. With over 2,000 members, meetings taking place all over the country at least once a week (and in the larger centres practically every evening), about ten national camps that ran in the summer and two in the winter, as well as various weekend camps throughout the country, Habonim was a sizeable and complex organisation. And it was also international, with independent branches in South Africa, Australia, France, Switzerland and elsewhere.

Running the affairs of the movement as a whole was the *mazkirut*, the national secretariat, which comprised most of the full-time youth leaders and organisers, and the emissaries. It was the *mazkirut* that appointed the *mazkir* from among the ranks of the full-time workers. He – in those days, it was always a 'he' – had the heavy responsibility for running the movement, usually for two years.

By my 16th birthday I had absorbed enough of the movement's ideology to feel that I had a clear grasp of what I believed about Zionism, Israel and socialism. I accepted that Jews had a historic right to return to their ancient homeland, the Land of Israel, and create their own state. But that state had to be a socialist society with the kibbutz – an agricultural collective based on complete equality, the abolition of private property, communal rearing of children and direct democracy – as its highest expression. This socialist Zionism, or labour Zionism as it was also called, was a form of liberal Jewish nationalism, and I had no difficulty in reconciling it with the internationalism of the wider socialist movement because there could be no '*inter*-nationalism' without peoples first realising their right to national self-determination. Like many others in the movement, as a socialist I supported the Labour Party, although some members inclined towards Marxism. I also supported the aims of the Campaign for Nuclear Disarmament, another cause embraced by many in the movement, and remember joining the final day of the 1963 Aldermaston March, marching under a Habonim banner.

I saw Palestine in classic Herzlian terms as 'a land without a people for a people without a land'. Arab opposition to the Jewish state was entirely illegitimate. A Palestinian was a Jew who had immigrated to Palestine in the years before the establishment of the state. We wore the Arab *keffiyah* (traditional headdress) like a scarf, as a sign of our youthful pioneering loyalty to the state. Israel was a country being built from scratch by young, strong and dedicated Jewish idealists, uninterested in material possessions and unencumbered by outdated views on sex and personal relationships. They were draining swamps and making the desert bloom. Hundreds of thousands of death camp survivors and Jews expelled from Arab countries after 1948 had been ingathered to make the new nation. It was fragile and under threat from the Arab states, which refused to make peace with the Jewish state. We regarded the aims of the Jewish terrorist underground of pre-state days – the Irgun Tsvai Leumi or Etzel (the National Military Organisation in the Land of Israel) and the Lohamei Herut Israel or Lehi (Fighters for the Freedom of Israel) – as legitimate: only their methods went too far, so we mildly condemned them. I accepted the narrative that the Arabs left Palestine voluntarily at the behest of the combined Arab armies who promised them that they would return after the Jews had been defeated and driven into the sea. Having failed in that aim, incursions were constantly being made into Israel by murderous Arab bands called *fellaheen*.

The future of the Jewish people lay in mass *aliya* (immigration); diaspora Jewish life was doomed. While only a small proportion of Israel's population lived on kibbutzim, we believed in encouraging as many Jews as possible who wanted to live in Israel to choose the socialist Zionist option. To us, British Jewish leaders who were staunch supporters of Israel but had no intention of emigrating were hypocritical 'armchair Zionists'.

Along with Zionism, the movement impressed on us certain values: high standards of personal morality; fulfilling commitments; sharing chores; not saying one thing and doing another; avoiding favouritism and treating everyone equally. Equality between the sexes was assumed, but, like the other values, imperfectly pursued.

While some of my friends outside of the movement could not understand its appeal and made fun of the scouting and Israeli dancing, I never had the sense that I was involved in something of which I should have been in any way ashamed. On the contrary, we tended to see ourselves as the elite, intelligent leadership of Jewish youth. This confidence extended to how we saw ourselves in relation to the general public. We walked under a socialist Zionist banner on the Aldermaston marches, showing how comfortable we felt openly displaying our Zionist loyalties.

The only hint of controversy about Zionism that I was aware of was *between Jews*. Occasionally I played table tennis matches for the synagogue youth club against East End Jewish youth clubs associated with Reform Judaism. The Reform movement originally opposed Zionism and in Britain in the 1950s and early 1960s was still in the process of coming to terms with Zionism's success. The clubs largely ignored Israel and did not encourage people to go to live there.

There was controversy too among the various Zionist youth groups. As politically progressive mould-breakers representing the rebellion of youth, we looked askance at the besuited, straight-laced young Zionists of the Federation of Zionist Youth. We were slightly in awe of those whose socialism seemed of a purer, unvarnished genus: the Marxist Zionists of Hashomer Hatzair (The Young Guard). And although there were some observant Jews in Habonim, scepticism about religion was commonplace, and so we saw ourselves as more enlightened than the B'nai Akiva, the main religious Zionist group. The one group that practically all the other movements reviled was the revisionist, right-wing Betar, the followers of Zeev Jabotinsky (1880–1940), which believed Jews had an inalienable right to the land both sides of the Jordan. In our eyes they disfigured the attractive, liberal and progressive face of Zionism and were an aberration.

For all the increasing ideological seriousness that I encountered as I approached 18, there was nothing to prevent me from going elsewhere. No *madrich* gained respect through either force or bullying, or by barking orders. Character, personality, talent, charisma, athleticism, proficiency on the guitar, good looks, confidence, persuasiveness, quiet intelligence – these were some of the attributes of good youth leaders that helped bring people back week after week. But while leadership was important, it was matched by an irreverent attitude to authority.

In my last two years at school, I studied just about hard enough to secure offers to read for a degree in sociology at the London School of Economics, Manchester University and the recently opened Essex University. I succeeded in getting the A-level grades I needed to be able to pick which of the three I wanted to attend, but my mind was focused on a more immediate and daring scheme. Driven by the desire to see Israel for myself, enthralled by the aura that surrounded movement members who had been to Israel for an extended period – a rarity at the time – and possessed of a rebellious and rather stubborn wish to exert my independence I decided that I wanted to participate in the one-year course run by the Institute for Youth Leaders from Abroad in Jerusalem. If the movement's executive agreed that you should go, all expenses were paid. Graduates of the course became key personnel in the movement when they returned. They weren't yet Israelis, but in many ways they were the closest we came to encountering both the country and the people.

By now, my parents were beginning to question whether encouraging involvement in Habonim was such a good idea. My brother wanted to go on this course in 1963, but they had refused. I wouldn't take no for an answer.

2

SUNRISE OVER THE CARMEL

The essence of Labour Zionism ... lay in the promise of Jewish work: the idea that young Jews from the diaspora would be rescued from their effete, assimilated lives and transported to remote collective settlements in rural Palestine – there to create (and, as the ideology had it, recreate) a living Jewish peasantry, neither exploited nor exploiting.

Tony Judt, 2011

In August 1964 I left Victoria Railway Station on the boat train bound for Marseilles and a ship to Haifa. I had never been away from home for more than two weeks at a time. Known simply as the Machon (Institute), the course I was soon to start aimed to equip us with the advanced knowledge and skills needed to be more effective movement leaders when we returned home. Nine of us from British Habonim were to spend six months studying in Jerusalem and five months living and working on two kibbutzim: the first had no English-speaking settlers; living on the second were members of British Habonim who settled there from 1948. I had little sense of what was to come but relished the thought of being independent and knowing that I would soon be seeing this country which loomed so large in my life. I just wanted to get going.

We sailed across the Channel, took the train to Paris, changed for the night train to Marseilles from the Gare de Lyon, and then boarded the ship taking us to the northern port of Haifa in Israel. We could have flown, but travel by train and ship was cheaper and, more crucially, was seen to have a two-fold ideological benefit. First, travelling together gave us the opportunity to put into practice our socialist beliefs. We were expected to pool all of our spending money – we weren't allowed to bring more than £50 each for the entire year – and create what was called in Hebrew a *kupa* (fund). One of us was elected as the treasurer (*gizbar*) responsible for looking after the money and doling it out as and when we agreed we could spend it – almost exclusively on cigarettes and snacks.

Second, for a Zionist, going to live in Israel was not simply a matter of emigrating. The Hebrew word for it, *aliya*, means 'going up', the term used in the Bible for journeying to the Promised Land, and it symbolised an act of

11

personal ideological fulfilment. *Olim* (immigrants) were going to a 'higher' place where the regeneration of the Jewish people was in progress. Although we weren't emigrating, it was felt that flying direct would not give us an opportunity to appreciate the meaning and symbolism of the act of *aliya* that we might one day undertake. Excitement mounted as we drew closer to Haifa and prepared ourselves for the traditional activity of staying up on the last night to see the sun rise over the Carmel, the hill upon which the city was built.

As we disembarked, all was bustling, relatively good-natured chaos, or so it looked to me through bleary eyes and the clammy heat. We were met by Geoff Goodman, a member of Kibbutz Amiad in the northern Galil (Galilee), where we would be living during the second half of our stay. A wiry, blunt-speaking *oleh* (immigrant) from Leeds, he was from the English Habonim members who joined the kibbutz in its early days. With two weeks until the course began in Jerusalem, he took us by Egged bus to Amiad to acclimatise to the country. Standing and fighting sleep, I remember the clouds of dust and grove after grove of orange trees as we clattered and bounced along at perplexing speed. After a couple of hours, thirsty, exhausted and thoroughly shaken, we arrived.

Amiad ('my people for ever') was one of four kibbutzim, all in the north of Israel, which members of British Habonim had either joined or helped found. One of the challenges facing these collective settlements was to have enough members to create viable and sustainable societies. To achieve this it was important that children born on the kibbutz chose to remain after army service and that the place was attractive to newcomers. With a membership of around 100 adults Amiad was seen as struggling to achieve equilibrium and much hope for its future was invested in movement members of our generation who had committed themselves to live there and had already begun to arrive in significant numbers. We nine machonniks were still considered too young to commit ourselves to settle at Amiad, although one or two of our number had already made up their minds to do so. One of Geoff's key tasks was therefore to nurture the relationship between us and the kibbutz and to create a bond that would pull us back there when the time came for us to leave the UK to settle in Israel for good.

Each of us was assigned to a family with whom we would socialise at tea-time – after the siesta and before eating dinner in the communal dining hall – and who we were encouraged to see as surrogate 'parents'. Getting to know them and their families was intended to help strengthen our relationship with the kibbutz. But we were not presented with life at Amiad as some kind of easy-going, laid-back paradise. The kibbutz members took delight in testing our resolve. They wanted us to survive the encounter with *actual* manual labour, but also displayed a natural scepticism, as if they had had their hopes raised before only to experience disappointment later on.

After arriving at the kibbutz we were given a day or so to rest up. Then, for the few days remaining, we were set to work. We boys were sent to the most physically demanding place of all: the banana plantation by the shores of the Kinneret (Sea of Galilee), 700 feet below sea level, where the temperature sometimes reached the low 40 degrees Celsius. Because of the heat and the 20-minute drive from the kibbutz to the plantation, we were woken around 4 or 5 am, given sweet black tea with bread and jam and then whisked off in the back of a Dodge pick-up down into the valley, taking each hairpin bend at stomach-churning speed.

We were assigned the most menial tasks: carrying the freshly cut bunches of bananas from the furrows to the stacker on the trailer in the nearby track; distributing seven-foot sticks throughout the plantations for propping up the heavy bunches. We worked steadily while the weather was still relatively cool. After a few hours we were taken to the corrugated iron shack in the middle of the plantation, which served as the communal eating hall, where we devoured a monster breakfast. It was then back to work for a few more hours before returning to the kibbutz for a late lunch, hands stained from the sticky juice of the cut stalks.

Towards the end of the first week I came down with gastric flu, but I still set off, albeit in a greatly weakened state, to spend a few days with my mother's cousins, Ray and Yael Geffen, who left England for a kibbutz in the 1940s as members of the Marxist-Zionist youth movement Hashomer Hatzair. They left their kibbutz and were living in Kiryat Tivon, near Haifa, with two children. Ray taught at the nearby teacher-training college Oranim, which served the kibbutz movement. It seemed strange to be back with family so soon, but drained of energy, pounds lighter and still unable to hold down a full meal, and altogether somewhat overwhelmed by the experience of making my way across a country whose language I was unable to speak, I was grateful for their warm hospitality.

Hashomer Hatzair was the most austere and ideologically rigid of the Zionist youth movements. It only abandoned support for Stalin, who died in 1953, shortly before I met my cousins. They had been deeply attached to kibbutz ideology, but by the time I met them their enthusiasm for it had gone. They were delighted that a member of their extended family had come for a long stay in Israel and intended to return to live, but they did not hesitate to let me know how critical they had become of the kibbutz. Whenever I spoke about my ideological aspirations they humoured me, but without going as far as to discourage me entirely. The experience of being challenged by them was intimidating and unsettling, but they meant well. They must have felt that more realism on my part would result in me making a 'success' of *aliya*. Life had been very difficult for them on the kibbutz and adjusting to living in town after such an experience was also not easy. But I could see that more was at stake and was nonplussed when Yael lamented that her Hebrew would never be good enough to allow her to fully understand Hebrew novels or appreciate Hebrew theatre. I was already aware that integrating into Israeli society would be a challenge. The Israeli-born young people we had met on the kibbutz insisted on treating us as English, while we thought of ourselves as primarily Jewish with such a close affinity to Israel as to be but a small step away from being Israeli. But I had no idea that educated people, who had already spent close to 20 years in the country, and whose Hebrew must have been of a very high standard, could still see less than perfect language skills as a major barrier to being fully comfortable with Israeli culture.

I knew that many Zionists keen to live in Israel were either uninterested in living on a kibbutz or were not in favour of the kibbutz's collectivist ideals. However, there was something different about the views of people who had experienced kibbutz life, ultimately rejected it and yet remained Zionists and stayed in Israel. When I left them to make my way to Jerusalem for the start of the youth leadership course, I was confused, but youthful naivety and conviction helped push the Geffens' unsettling words to the back of my mind.

*   *   *

The Machon L'Madrichei Chutz L'Aretz, the Institute for Youth Leaders from Abroad, was set up by the Jewish Agency for Palestine in 1946. We were the 35th course and there were 104 of us – from Britain, France, Switzerland, Holland, Canada, the US, Morocco (participants who were only able to join the course by telling the Moroccan authorities that they were leaving to spend a year in France) and South Africa.

Ideologically we represented a wide spectrum of Zionist youth groups from the apolitical Young Judea in the US to the hard-line Marxists of Hashomer Hatzair in South Africa. It was a reflection of the dominance of labour Zionism that the few members of the right-wing Zionist revisionist group Betar were seen as separate from the rest of us. Religious Zionist youth groups, for whom regular services and strictly kosher food were essential, had their own institute. Had we been studying and living together, there would certainly have been explosive ideological confrontations as the very left-wing Zionists were aggressively anti-religion. Even among left and liberal groups there were marked ideological differences, exacerbated by national loyalties.

We lived and were taught in Katamon, a quiet, run-down neighbourhood with large houses mostly given over to apartments and multi-occupancy. The building where the boys slept – a former brothel, we were told – was some five minutes' walk from the Machon in Hizkiyahu Hamelech Street where classes were taught and the girls lived. For breakfast there was sweetened Wissotsky tea, bread, margarine, jam, a kind of semolina porridge called *deisa* and, occasionally, a cereal similar to Sugar Puffs. If we were late we would pick up a doughnut and a glass of sweet *gazoz* (a carbonated drink flavoured with a thick syrup) from a tiny kiosk on the way.

We studied six days a week. Every morning for a couple of hours we learnt to speak and read modern Hebrew by the *ulpan* method: the class was conducted entirely in Hebrew from the first day and within a few months I was fairly fluent. The rest of the teaching day was devoted to Jewish and Zionist history, the geography of the land of Israel, Israeli songs and folk dancing, and youth leadership skills.

When we ventured out beyond Katamon we encountered a divided, dusty, self-contained, very provincial city. It was a sleepy, quiet, ramshackle place. The Eastern ceasefire line ran along the walls of the Old City. We were taken to lookout posts on the Israeli side so that we could peer at Jordanian soldiers behind sandbags 100 metres away. But the situation had become so institutionalised it seemed everyone simply took the division of the city for granted.

Getting to know the main sites of significance for Jewish and Zionist history, which linked the ancient Israelite state and the modern Israeli state, was a key part of the course. Every month or so we would be taken on a three- or four-day trip to a different part of the country. The highlight of these tours was the early morning climb up Masada, the fortress-like hill by the Dead Sea where, in 73 CE, the Jewish Zealots killed themselves rather than be taken alive by the Romans. The place had become a symbol of the kind of Jewish resistance, determination and heroism that, we were taught, characterized the struggle to create the State of Israel. This is where Israel Defence Forces conscripts were brought for their passing-out parades, held as the sun rose over the Judean Hills.

We did not all take the studying very seriously. When exam time came round, I remember sitting with notes perched on my lap out of sight of the invigilating lecturer, and I wasn't alone. Nevertheless, a young historian, Gideon (Giddy) Shimoni, who had been the *Mazkir* of South African Habonim before emigrating to Israel and taking up a lectureship at the Hebrew University in Jerusalem, taught us Jewish and Zionist history and was an outstanding educationalist; caring, sensitive and humane. The director of the Machon, David Brodsky, who also did some teaching, was a commanding presence. Tall, with an upright bearing and white hair, he must have been in late middle-age, though there was something ageless and serene about him. Of the Machon students he reportedly said: 'Look at the difference in them from when they arrived and look at them now when they are leaving – just a year in Israel at the Machon is sufficient to change a group of sweet and mixed-up children into a group of determined youth.'

After a few months a group of senior Israeli high school students came one evening for a discussion in Hebrew. In the end the conversation was conducted in English, their English being much better than our Hebrew. It was an awkward encounter. Although they seemed very young and gauche, they were soon to be drafted into the IDF. At some point talk turned to Zionism, *tsionut* in Hebrew. I expected this to be an ideological conviction we had in common. Instead, most of them expressed disdain for the term, which left me thoroughly confused. How could they be so dismissive about the ideology that inspired the establishment of their state, that had brought most of us to Israel and that we were to teach to others when we returned home? How was that compatible with the cream of educated Israeli youth using the word as an epithet to mean 'rubbish'?

Some years later I learnt that by the mid 1960s in Israel, the word 'Zionism' had lost its appeal for young people. Uri Avnery, then the *enfant terrible* of Israeli society, described it in his 2009 book *The Other Side of the Coin* as 'a term commonly used in Israel for empty political outpourings'. This disavowal of Zionism by highly educated young Ashkenazi Israelis was an expression of rebelliousness towards their parents' generation: Zionism had been forced down their throats for so long and had lost its meaning. They were all proud to serve their country and were fiercely confident in their Israeli identity, but this was something that came naturally to them because they were born there. That we were using the word *tsionut* as if it had no connotations of the boring diatribes of an older generation placed us with their parents rather than with them.

I had come to Israel thinking that being Jewish and having a commitment to Zionism and *aliya* would be the basis of a natural affinity with young Israelis. But they had been influenced by the country's strong resentment of the last years of the Mandate and were suspicious of our British identity. We knew enough about that history to share the criticisms of the British, making it even harder to come to terms with the fact that we – putative socialist Zionist pioneers – were also the objects of that resentment.

*   *   *

The nine of us from British Habonim would meet occasionally to discuss questions of socialist principle and practice that needed to be settled even when the most minor demand was placed on the communal fund, the *kupa*. For example, quite a few of us smoked, but we couldn't afford even the cheaper of the standard brands of Israeli cigarettes. So it was a relief when Geoff brought us cigarettes from Amiad, even though they resembled dried camel dung. They were unfiltered, as small as Woodbines (if not smaller), and if you kept them too long, the tobacco dried out and slipped to the bottom of the pack.

There was a very strong emphasis placed on the importance of maintaining the cohesion of each national youth movement group and developing a sense of overall group identity for everyone from different countries who belonged to the same movement (or to a sister movement). The French dominated our multinational youth movement group, leaving us Brits (the boys, at any rate) feeling somewhat inadequate. It wasn't only because of their boisterous anti-Americanism, it was also their Gallic style. They smoked pungent Gauloises, listened to the politically charged music of Jacques Brel and appeared to be far more comfortable with Israelis and their prickly sensibility than we were.

By way of introducing us to innovative educational techniques, an extremely elaborate, dramatic role-playing event was staged during the course. The main building of the Machon and its immediate surroundings were transformed into the Warsaw Ghetto for a day. Some of the course participants played roles as leaders of the Jewish resistance and Nazi soldiers and officers. The rest of us were the remnants of the Jewish fighters. The central act of the drama was the moment, early in 1943, when the Jewish leaders had to decide whether to continue fighting despite hopeless odds, or to try to escape with as many survivors as possible.

We knew in advance about this event, but when we heard artillery and gunfire and saw uniformed Nazi soldiers walking the normally quiet streets outside the main building late in the afternoon, the effect was shocking and chilling. At dusk we were divided into small groups and led up mock alleyways, through holes in walls, dodging German soldiers and the sound of barking dogs, to the meeting where the fateful decision was to be taken. Once there, we huddled together in candlelight while the leaders of the various Zionist and non-Zionist factions argued about the action that should be taken to resist the impending destruction. Mordechai Anilewicz, a member of Hashomer Hatzair, commander of the Żydowska Organizacja Bojowa, the Jewish Combat Organisation, and leader of the ghetto uprising, prevailed. Pioneering Zionist youth would not allow Jews to go like sheep to the slaughter.

By the time the Jerusalem period of the course ended I was proficient in Hebrew, had experienced the searing late summer heat and the bitter winter cold of Jerusalem and become familiar with the intensely bureaucratic nature of Israeli society. I knew about *protektsia* – the influence and connections required to get things done or achieve personal advancement – but had none (nor did I really need it then), the high taxes and the two-year wait to obtain a phone line – and there was no television service. While we were there the Beatles were banned from playing a concert for fear that the music would corrupt the nation's youth. I hadn't been to Communist Eastern Europe, but when I did go some years later, I realised that the little Israeli street kiosks or shacks with their tiny windows, selling *gazoz*, pretzels, doughnuts, cigarettes, matches, lottery tickets and cheap gadgets, were very similar to those in Poland or Russia.

*   *   *

At the beginning of February 1965, our international group of Habonim youth movement members, together with some unaffiliated course participants, left Jerusalem to spend two-and-a-half months at Kibbutz Yifat in the lush Jezreel Valley, or the Emek as it was known, close to the town of Migdal Haemek in northern Israel. Established in 1954, after Stalin's death, when members of the nearby Kibbutz Ramat David left to form their own collective settlement (following the political split over Marxist socialism in the largest kibbutz movement, Kibbutz Hameuchad), Yifat had 600 members and, as with most kibbutzim, was largely agricultural. It was not a particularly welcoming place. We slept in very basic dormitories, worked mostly in the citrus groves and orchards picking fruit or planting trees, but also fulfilled communal dining room duties and other menial tasks. We were each assigned to a family for afternoon tea. Early-morning tree-planting was painful as the spades we used had metal handles and were almost impossible to hold because they were so cold. I found the work hard, dull and mindless. The camaraderie of working together in a large group provided some light relief. But time dragged. At Yifat we were like cannon fodder, treated warily and tolerated, as if the kibbutz was doing us a favour. Yet we thought our presence was a gift to them.

Yifat felt very austere, aloof and impenetrable, as if it had experienced a major trauma and was still recovering. Yet it also had the air of being part of an elite sector of Israeli society that jealously guarded its integrity. It was located very close to a military airfield and one or two of the young men, children of the original kibbutz members, were themselves pilots. One morning we were tree-planting together as fighter jets were landing and taking off from the airfield. The young Israelis stopped briefly to clap and cheer their comrades.

My feelings about the 'otherness' of the kibbutz were confirmed in a rather uncomfortable way one afternoon when I went to visit the kibbutz family to which I had been assigned. The father and mother were highly intelligent, gentle and reserved, though they tried to make me feel at home. One of their sons was a fighter pilot I had worked with planting trees. He was tall, powerfully built with closely cropped hair. When on leave, as he was that afternoon, he would return to the kibbutz and spend some of the time with his parents. I was talking to them and enthusing about the need for a closer relationship between our group and the children on the kibbutz when I realised that they both looked rather awkward and anxious. The son, who had kept himself apart until then, suddenly intervened in the conversation and began lambasting boys in our group for 'corrupting' daughters of the kibbutz. I knew that relationships had been struck up between the French boys and some of the girls, but only now did I understand that they had been having sex. I was left confused and silent. This did not seem to be about sexual exploitation, but rather a fear of the unclean alien diluting the gene pool, polluting the purity of the kibbutz. The son represented the views of some who would rather not have had us there at all.

Talking with the French later, they made no attempt to deny that they had had sex with kibbutz girls. In fact they were entirely frank about it. Not that they seemed to be boasting about it as some form of sexual conquest. Their justification was a 'principled' one, even 'ideological'. To them, these were perfectly natural relationships that had led to sex. It was 'bourgeois' to deny such urges and far better to give way than sublimate them in masturbation. From then on, contact between us and the kibbutz youth was heavily restricted.

*   *   *

It was a short journey from the Emek to the Galil, from Yifat to Amiad, but the contrast was stark. Flat, fertile and dotted with numerous kibbutzim and moshavim (cooperative villages), the Emek was like a showcase for the success of Zionism. The north-eastern Galil was hilly, the land studded with rocks and boulders and with fewer Jewish settlements. East of Amiad, across the Jordan rift valley, were the Syrian Golan Heights. To the west of the kibbutz was a pine forest and behind that more hills stretching up towards the biblical city of Tsfat, a centre of kabbalah, Jewish mysticism. To the north was the small town of Rosh Pina. And if you drove south you would first see and eventually arrive at the Kinneret. Amiad was in an isolated spot, near the ruins of Jubb Yusuf, rumoured to be Joseph's Well, where there were the remains of a *khan*, an inn.

The original settlers were a group of Palmach members who established the kibbutz in 1947 on a hill two kilometres south of modern Amiad, naming their settlement Jubb Yosef after the nearby ruins. Two years later they moved to the current site, renaming the kibbutz Hahoshlim ('the hardened'), but then changed it to Amiad. Dutch and English Jews from Habonim joined the original settlers in the late 1940s. A further influx of Habonim members of our generation had begun to arrive. After spending our very first week in Israel at Amiad, returning there was almost like coming home.

Where Yifat was large and impersonal, Amiad was small and intimate. Although the surrounding countryside looked barren and unforgiving, the kibbutz itself had well-tended and watered lawns and gardens, many shady trees and mostly single-storey buildings. The newly-built dwellings, where most of the members lived, were small but homely, with neat front gardens and verandas – like mini-bungalows joined together as a terrace. Children slept together in children's houses, so most of the kibbutz family homes had no more than a living room, bedroom, kitchenette, shower and toilet. Everyone was supposed to eat in the communal dining hall (one of the few large buildings on the kibbutz). The main meal was at lunchtime. Dinner, except on Friday nights, was usually salads. Some ate at home in the evening, a practice that was becoming more common but was frowned upon by ideological traditionalists. As dinner ended, a key period in the daily life of the kibbutz began: making arrangements for the next day's work. Although most members had regular work responsibilities, since the kibbutz was essentially an agricultural collective, certain branches had changing demands for labour. The transient population – people like ourselves and volunteers who came to work for short periods in increasing numbers from many countries – was assigned wherever it was needed, though most of us worked in the same branch for most of the time. The work-scheduling process was like a noisy marketplace. The mostly male heads of the branches would negotiate with each other, cajoling, arguing, joking, gesticulating and laughing, until the deals were done.

Amiad was not as ideologically purist as some kibbutzim, but still uncompromising on the fundamentals of socialist Zionist ideology. All property was held in common. Members were allowed to own private possessions – books, records, pictures, photographs, and so on – but practically everything else was provided by the kibbutz. You might be allowed to keep major gifts from family and friends, but only with the approval of the kibbutz members and even then, there was a kind of understanding that if such gifts were no longer needed they would be returned to the common pool for general use. Everyone received the same personal allowance, but private bank accounts were not allowed. If someone received an inheritance or windfall, the principle was clear: the money was given to the kibbutz for everyone's benefit.

For a brief period after birth, babies lived with their parents, but within weeks they were moved to the children's house, where they slept three or four to a room. Mothers would go to feed their babies during the day or night. They took them home at tea-time before delivering them back to the children's house after dinner. Under this system adults were almost always available to work for the collective; men and women did not have to adopt the roles forced on them by bourgeois society. I thought this was the height of progressive socialism. Children developed very close bonds with each other and had less dependent relationships with their parents. But I soon learnt that some of the parents, particularly mothers, rejected this positive picture, hated the children's house system and wanted them to live at home.

Manual labour in the fields and plantations, in the cowsheds and chicken runs, was prized over any other form of human endeavour. The kibbutz had its teachers, accountants, bookkeepers, storemen, nursery assistants and a full-time general secretary (*mazkir*, really an executive chairman), but no one was held in higher esteem than the ploughman, tractor driver, herdsman, banana grower or truck driver. If you wanted to study at college or university, the needs of the kibbutz came first. History, literature, art and philosophy were appreciated as desirable for a civilised society, but not a priority for people building a socialist community. Nevertheless, there were always exceptions. These were usually members who had served their time in agriculture and, like everyone else, had to fulfil certain work responsibilities common to everyone.

The division of labour between men and women was stark. Some women, especially the early settlers, worked in agriculture, but most worked in traditional female occupations, as cooks, nursery nurses, teachers and in the laundry. Some tended the gardens, work that was seen as lighter and more suited to women. This inequality was justified largely on the grounds that 'it was what the women wanted to do'.

One ever-present responsibility, shared widely in Israeli society, was army service: conscription at 18 for two years' training and service, and then a period of *miluim* (reserve duty) each year of up to a month, with the possibility of additional call-up in the event of a national emergency or war. The ethos of the citizen army was still very strong and kibbutz members were disproportionately represented in the officer class and elite units.

Mo Wolkind, Franklin Hessayon and I had worked in the banana plantation during our first visit and went back there. It was located on an extensive track of land on both sides of the north-south road on the western shore of the Kinneret, in an area called Tabha. We worked under the supervision of the kibbutz members running the plantation, but the place would have ground to a halt without the half a dozen or so Kurdish-Jewish hired workers from Tiveria (Tiberias) who did practically all the harvesting and the pruning. They were a fierce-looking bunch, but worked like dogs (on piece rates), treated us with a rough and joshing kindness and were dedicated to their families and cultural traditions.

One man who was certainly not an immigrant and without whom the plantation would have ceased to function was the caretaker, Mahmood, a local Arab who lived on the plantation in a hut with his wife and children. He was tall, loose-limbed, quietly-spoken and always looked concerned and wary. Perhaps this was because of the weight of responsibility for a large area which anyone could access at any time. Or perhaps it was a mark of the uneasy relationship between Arab and Jew. My contact with Mahmood was minimal.

The plantation's partly transient workforce included a few young sabras. They were from a Nahal unit made up of army conscripts from towns and cities who were members of Israeli socialist Zionist youth movements planning to settle on a kibbutz after they finished their training. In preparation for that step they spent part of their army service on a kibbutz. They were boisterous, aggressively masculine and cocky; they found our 'Englishness' a source of great amusement and our discomfort with the conditions a cause for constant ribbing. Often sarcastic about our ideological commitment to Israel and Zionism, they were nonetheless deeply committed to Israel, like the high school students we met with in Jerusalem. As native-born Israelis, their patriotism was natural and visceral and needed no intellectualising.

To integrate into kibbutz society, it helped to be working in one of the most physically demanding agricultural branches. We endured the intense Tabha heat, with temperatures often beyond 40 °C. We were among the earliest risers and the last ones to finish. Working outside the kibbutz we encountered that little bit more of Israel's raw and rather rugged society. The Kurdish-Jewish hired workers gave us a perspective on Israel's immigrant population that no books or lectures could provide. The occasional swim in the Kinneret at the end of the day, by the plantation's pumping station, with a few volunteers, sabras and kibbutz members also all helped.

We had been taught that kibbutz was an egalitarian society, with no difference between the head of an agricultural branch and a labourer. But it did not take long to see that there was a complex hierarchy based on leadership qualities, managerial talent and the role a member played in building the kibbutz under the tough early conditions. It wasn't difficult to identify who the leading figures were and how they competed with each other for power and influence.

For most of the time, I was too busy with work and play, with the absorptions of the moment, to be worrying about my long-term eventual absorption into the country. But as the year passed, I began to experience doubts and my need grew for reassurance that kibbutz was really for me. I felt increasingly comfortable in Israel, but what troubled me, both at Amiad and Yifat before, was the boredom. Too many long hours of repetitive, mindless labour. I was desperate for the time to pass, for the working day to come to an end. I accepted the theory of the moral value of manual labour, how it transformed the bourgeois, diaspora Jewish self and contributed to the building of the Jewish homeland by developing land that was hitherto barren. But I couldn't ignore the feeling that I found nothing intrinsically valuable in it. As much as I told myself that if it worked for the pioneers who had gone before me, it should work for me, in practice, it just didn't.

At first, and for many years after, I saw this as a personal failing. I certainly wasn't ready to entertain the idea that there was something wrong with the theory, not on the basis of only two and a half months living on a kibbutz. And yet even then I was aware of a disconnect between what I had learnt about Israel and kibbutz and what I was encountering. There were clear signs of growing Israeli consumerism. I had travelled the length and breadth of the country and although the kibbutz was still held in relatively high esteem, its contribution to the development of Israeli society and the economy was necessarily limited. The experience of my cousins in Kiryat Tivon and the fact that the vast majority of Israelis were not queuing up to become kibbutz members added to my doubts that Israel could eventually become one vast kibbutz-based society – a notion that I entertained in my more ideologically utopian moments.

For kibbutz to be a fully socialist, communal society, it had to rely on the work capacity of its members. But many kibbutzim found it impossible to do this and over the years some had developed the practice of employing hired labour – Arab and Jewish – on a more or less permanent basis. So, how could you be truly socialist if you exploited the labour of others to maintain your socialist lifestyle? And yet, at Amiad, in the banana plantation, there would have been no bananas without hired labour. When I questioned members of the kibbutz about this, I was told that while most agreed in theory that hired labour was wrong, given the realities of developing productive agriculture, it was impossible to do without it. But if the kibbutz didn't employ these people, or sacked them, wouldn't the 'sin' against socialism be even worse? Wasn't solidarity with other workers a fundamental principle of the labour movement? It was all very well to build yourself a little socialist island, but if that was at the expense of socialism elsewhere in society, could that be right?

* * *

Compared with the outward journey, the slow boat trip back to Marseilles and London was an introspective experience. We were more subdued and kept more to ourselves. I knew that Israel had changed me and as the train pulled in to Victoria Station in late July, I was aware that I had a clear responsibility to use my new knowledge and experience in the service of the youth movement. I had so much wanted to be free of the constraints of home and parental control and this is certainly what the Machon, kibbutz and Israel gave me. And yet I had submitted to the all-embracing structure of the youth movement and everything it offered. The year's path was laid out for me. All the big decisions in my life were made for me. The small, unpredictable day-to-day decisions were manageable. What awaited me back in England was far more open-ended.

3

SOCIALIST ZIONIST

One joins the movement in a valueless world,
Choosing it, till, both hurler and hurled,
One moves as well, always toward, toward.
                                    Thom Gunn, 1957

At the end of September 1965, with nothing more than a full suitcase, I was driven north to Manchester by friends in an old Hillman Minx to begin my degree course in sociology at the university. They dropped me at my digs somewhere off Cheetham Hill. It was raining.

New students were obliged to live in university-approved accommodation, or with family. I had a tiny room with no desk in a small terraced house, owned by a kindly Jewish middle-aged couple. The cost of the digs included breakfast and a large, unpalatable dinner. I had to be home every day by 6 pm for my 'tea'. I would then escape to my room, but its dismal aspect, the nylon sheets and the whiff of overcooked stew rising from the kitchen were deeply dispiriting. In contrast, my youth movement friends lived together in a roomy flat above the recently refurbished, large Habonim youth centre not too far away in Upper Park Road. It was there that I spent most of my free time: running activities as a youth leader and socialising.

Apart from the emissaries sent to work for two years in British Habonim, it was a rarity for a youth leader to have had such a close and lengthy encounter with the country that gave the movement its *raison d'être*. We represented the authenticity of Israeli and kibbutz life and were expected to inject that into youth movement activities. These expectations were often high and not easy to fulfil. On the other hand, life in the movement had gone on without us.

The university was something of a shock. It was large, impersonal and unfriendly. Within a month, I could stand the digs no longer and I moved into the flat above the youth centre with my friends. Life improved enormously, but the university courses were either boring or too difficult. By February 1966, I was so unhappy with the course, confused as to why I was in Manchester at all and regretting that I had not gone to the LSE that I decided to leave. Part of my unhappiness and unease was the result of never

25

having fully adjusted to returning from Israel. Although the country was part of me in a way that it had never been before, it's not that I wanted to go back there immediately. But I had been left with so many partially assimilated experiences and unanswered questions and now faced a new set of personal and public challenges that seemed utterly disconnected from them. Nevertheless, I could not but feel something of a failure for leaving. I had let down those responsible for the youth movement activities in Manchester. I had raised doubts about whether sending me on the Machon in the first place had been a good 'investment' for the movement. And I felt that I had disappointed my parents, even though they were very understanding. I returned to London to live with them and set my sights on a more modest horizon. In September 1966 I took up a place at what was then Regent Street Polytechnic (now Westminster University) to study sociology. In these more congenial, stable circumstances, I found some respite from the confusions I faced in Manchester. I mostly enjoyed and coped well with the courses in social theory, moral philosophy and ethics, statistics and economics at the Poly and made friends with a few of my fellow students.

* * *

From studying political and social theory and learning about political and social movements, I became more interested in how Habonim became what it was and in its place in the wider political and ideological landscape. But I was barely conscious of the movement's early history and had a very idealised view of its past. The movement had lost some of its momentum since the first years after the establishment of the State of Israel in 1948, but I believed that it could be reinvigorated and that its unique ideals were still worth fighting for. From time to time, the past was invoked in bouts of self-congratulation. I thought this was an ambiguous exercise. Given that past leaders were now adults who, by definition, had passed on the torch and no longer possessed the capacity for revolutionary change that we, as youth, were blessed with, why should we draw attention to them?

This blindingly certain, youthful arrogance is captured in an eight-part essay I wrote in the first half of 1967, when I was 21, which was intended for publication in the youth movement magazine. In the first part of what reads now like a personal political manifesto I wrote: 'The Youth Movement with a real aim and ultimate purpose is still the only practical body of revolt left in the world.' I headed the last section with these lines from 'On the Move' by the Anglo-American poet Thom Gunn:

> One joins the movement in a valueless world,
> Choosing it, till, both hurler and hurled,
> One moves as well, always toward, toward.

In the essay I tried to provide a rationale for the importance and relevance of the socialist Zionist youth movement, which I argued was losing its way. Although I had already spent the best part of a year in Israel, and was intending to go and live there, in this entire 10,000-word essay, the word 'Israel' appeared only once and the word 'Zionist' three times. For me, and I'm sure for many others in the movement too, at that time our socialism was of more immediate importance to us than our Zionism. I pleaded for a return to the ideological purity and committed engagement of the youth movement's past. I argued for more self-criticism and more incisive social criticism. 'Even we social revolutionaries are very poor imitations of our predecessors', I wrote. 'Somehow we are suppressing our own will to think and discuss, to express and create. Instead we are giving way to certain materialistic indulgencies that are really incompatible with what we believe in.'

I ended the essay quoting Thom Gunn again, appropriating three lines from 'On the Move' that celebrate youthful existential aimlessness:

> At worst, one is in motion; and at best,
> Reaching no absolute, in which to rest,
> One is always nearer by not keeping still.

I turned these words into an ideological rallying cry. More than 40 years later, I can see that I should have left Gunn's words to speak for themselves. However, I can also see why the poem's acknowledgement of the necessity of moving on, the inadequacy of 'home', struck a chord. I was a second-generation, assimilated, English-born Jew, living comfortably in suburban London, and yet I was preparing to give all that up to live in, and if necessary fight for, a country on another continent with a different culture and a far lower standard of living.

For those of us who took the political ideology of Zionism seriously, there was no shortage of texts for us to study. While I don't remember reading the works of Zionist thinkers in any systematic fashion, I did read enough to be well aware of the main developments in the Zionist idea, from the inchoate longing for the homeland of the largely non-political Hovevei Zion (the Lovers of Zion) immigrants of the 1880s to the hard-headed, state-demanding political Zionism of David Ben-Gurion in the 1920s and 1930s. Out of all the Zionist thinkers, three stood out – unsurprisingly, given that the ideology of the movement was based largely on their ideas: Ber Borochov, A.D. Gordon and Berl Katznelson.

Borochov (1881–1917) was born in Russia and was a central leader and ideologist of Poalei-Zion (Workers of Zion), the Zionist Marxist Workers Party. The attempt to reconcile Marxism and Zionism was his unique contribution to Zionist ideology. But Borochov did not justify the choice of Palestine as the place to build a normal Jewish people on religious, biblical or historical grounds. He simply saw it as inevitable that Palestine was the place where territorial autonomy would be obtained. And Borochov believed that the socialism to be built there would also be for the benefit of the Arab population as they had common class interests with Jewish workers.

The element of Borochov's idea that captured my imagination was his description of the Jewish people as an inverted pyramid. A 'normal' people had a mass working class that formed the basis of the pyramid, with a small capitalist class at its apex. For the Jewish people, the capitalist class was proportionally much larger, the working class much smaller. Before the revolution could come, this imbalance had to be corrected and it could only be done when Jews were gathered in a country of their own.

Although hardly anybody now even remembers his name, Borochov had a huge influence on political Zionism. Ben-Gurion, Israel's first prime minister, was a member of Poalei-Zion and a convinced Borochovist in the 1920s. But Borochov never went to Palestine and although he believed that Jews should be closer to nature, the idea that socialism could be created in communities separated from the rest of society would mean that Jews were not participating in the class struggle.

If my selective interpretation of Borochov's ideas enabled me to reconcile my late 1960s British and internationalist socialism with Zionism, the thinking of Aharon David Gordon (1856–1922) – almost always referred to using only the Hebrew initials of his first and middle names: 'Alef Daled' – provided the rationale for middle-class university students and people training in law or accountancy, for example, to give all that up and become farmers. Gordon was from the Ukraine and took his family to Palestine in 1904 when he was already middle-aged. Doing ill-paid and exhausting manual work, he finally found his way to Kibbutz Degania in the Galil, where he lived in a ramshackle hut. A self-educated intellectual from a wealthy orthodox Jewish family, he spent his non-labouring hours developing his philosophy of work as a value in itself. The only way Jews would cease to be an abnormal, parasitic people, cut off from nature for 2,000 years, would be by returning to the land in the Jewish homeland. Gordon founded the non-Marxist Ha-Poel Ha-Tzair (Young Worker) labour Zionist movement and his pragmatic Zionism was central to the outlook of Mapai, the Israeli Labour Party.

But putting the dignity of labour above all else was questioned both by parents and some members. Wouldn't Israel benefit more from young people working in their professions, whether on kibbutzim or in towns and cities?

There was undoubtedly something quasi-religious about Gordon's ideas. Manual labour, the land, the soil and the collective were tangible features of the material world, yet in Gordon's thought they became transcendent notions with the power to purify the Jewish soul. Despite the fact that I had returned from Israel with considerable doubts about whether I could bear the boredom of manual labour, I still found sustenance in Gordon's theories.

The third thinker was Berl Katznelson (1887–1944), born in Bobruisk, White Russia. Known to everyone as Berl, he was one of the most influential of Zionist leaders and one of the three foremost leaders of the Yishuv (the Hebrew term used to describe the pre-state resident Jewish communities and the settlers who came to Palestine after the emergence of modern Zionism) during the inter-war years (the others were David Ben-Gurion and Yitzhak Tabenkin). He established many of the institutions of the labour Zionist movement that decisively shaped the character of the emerging state. His importance for us lay in the central role he played in crystallising the kibbutz movement and in inspiring young people, with whom he had a very close rapport, to follow the path of socialist Zionist pioneering. I learnt later that it was Berl who was largely responsible for turning the Habonim movement into a vehicle for 'education and training for a life of work on the land', the classic definition of the work of Hehalutz (the Pioneer), the association established in 1918, which became the umbrella organisation of the pioneering Zionist youth movements. His personal representative, Lassia Galili, came to England in 1935 and over the following two years helped engineer the effective takeover of the youth movement by the more ideologically-motivated senior members who were socialist Zionists.

Born out of the idea of educating young Jews about Zionism through Jewish scouting, Habonim was thereby transformed into a socialist Zionist youth movement, which had more in common with the left-wing versions of the German Wandervogel, the nationalist, romantic, back-to-nature youth movement of the early twentieth century, than with Baden Powell's Boy Scouts. By the beginning of the Second World War, it had adopted as its principal aim the sending of young Jews to settle on kibbutzim in the emerging Jewish state. Some key figures of the Jewish labour movement in Palestine – Teddy Kollek, the future mayor of Jerusalem, Galili, who became head of education in the Israel Defence Forces, and the inspirational Berl – were responsible for this change.

* * *

In early summer 1967 I was swept up in the mounting Middle East crisis, stunned and then utterly absorbed by the Six-Day War and its outcome. Very many Jews, including significant numbers who previously had no links with or close feelings for Israel, felt the same. I feared for Israel's future, rejoiced in its overwhelming victory and wanted to join the many thousands of people who were volunteering to go out to Israel and support the country's infrastructure, while so many Israeli citizens who had been called up to fight remained in uniform. But because of my involvement in the youth movement, unlike the vast majority who either wanted to go or who went, the possible fulfilment of my wish became a matter for collective decision-making. Of course, in wanting to volunteer, I was not alone among senior members who held positions of responsibility in the organisation. There were many people, either working full time for the movement or undergoing agricultural training at the movement's farm in Sussex, who were soon to emigrate to Israel and therefore given priority as volunteers.

Although I was disappointed that I could not go, I soon decided that I should discontinue my studies and offer to work full-time for the movement. Because of success in the Six-Day War, the popularity of Israel and admiration for its exploits were very high. Not only was there no stigma attached to feeling close to Israel and proclaiming it publicly, there was almost a sense that every Jew's personal status was enhanced as a result of the widespread praise for Israel's victory. My decision to put my ambitions in relation to Israel and kibbutz first was therefore a fair reflection of my innermost desires.

But even at the time I knew that my decisions arose from more complex motives. I was never fully engaged in my studies and I felt comfortable in the world of the youth movement. And as I began to acknowledge that the path I had now chosen would almost inevitably lead me back to Kibbutz Amiad, I convinced myself, two years after returning from Israel with doubts about it, that there was, after all, an authenticity and value in manual labour more worthwhile than my studies and what they might lead to. With no serious hesitation I placed my future in the hands of the movement's national secretariat.

Events had taken place that were about to change Israel, the nature of Zionism, the Palestinians, the entire Middle East conflict and the balance of forces in the region. And yet in Habonim we were behaving as if the minutiae of decision-making about the fate of each individual was of supreme ideological relevance for the future of the State of Israel. In my case this meant that my future role in the movement was briefly the subject of an argument about the ideologically correct path the individual should take to reach the ultimate goal of kibbutz membership. I assumed that I would be appointed as a full-time youth worker somewhere. But there were those in the movement who said I should be sent to the Eder Farm, where intending emigrants were normally obliged to receive agricultural training for at least six months and live an entirely communal life prior to leaving for Israel. In part, this discussion about my future had little to do with me personally. It was simply a matter of reconciling movement ideology with the practical demands of running a large national youth organisation, which now faced a shortage of full-time workers. But in part, the discussion was also personalised, because there were some in the movement's leadership who, not unjustifiably, saw me as immature, unreliable and unable to practice what I preached. They believed that a spell on the farm would either transform me into someone whose beliefs and actions were as one, or that it would expose me as someone unfit for a senior full-time role in the movement.

Known as the *hachshara* ('training'), the Eder Farm was one of many such centres, the first of which were established in Eastern Europe in the 1920s. Before and just after the war, there were quite a few in Britain, but by 1967, the Eder Farm was the only one left. It might well have been the only one left in the Western world. Situated in a remote part of the East Sussex countryside between Horsham and Worthing, the farm was approachable only by private vehicle or on foot. An article in the *Brighton and Hove Argus* in 1958 called it 'The Sussex Kibbutz'.

The *hachshara* was a significant focal point for the movement. Important meetings and seminars were held there. Habonim members living on the farm, who had all committed themselves to life on kibbutz, were seen as a kind of ideological vanguard. This was where people were actually living out the ideals in which we all professed to believe. By the late 1960s, however, the Eder Farm was a troubled place. Its income was far too meagre to pay for the upkeep of the farm and the people living there. Conditions were very basic. Doubts were being expressed about its relevance since kibbutz agriculture was increasingly mechanised. There were rarely enough people to make it a viable community. This led to tense relationships, demoralisation and loneliness. Nonetheless, there was a certain ambiguity in our concern for the conditions on the farm and the state of mind of the people living there. Asceticism was at the heart of the *hachshara* ethos, a glorification of the frugality and simplicity of the lifestyle, almost to the point of revelling in the cruelty of the experience. It was for a higher purpose. The wishes of the individual were sacrificed to the needs of the collective. But by that time, even the most left-wing kibbutzim had largely abandoned this kind of harsh regime.

It was partly a sign of the declining significance of *hachshara* and partly a reflection of the pressing manpower needs of the movement that, in the end, I was sent to the Glasgow branch to be its full-time youth leader, running a youth centre that catered for the needs of around 150–200 children and young people. I travelled north in late summer 1967 with all thoughts of going to Israel as a volunteer now behind me.

* * *

Glasgow Habonim members were known for their intelligence, self-confidence, seriousness of purpose, dry humour, warmth (mixed with a degree of initial wariness towards outsiders) and strength of character. A formidable parents committee and the senior members demanded a lot of their full-time youth leader. I was following in the footsteps of a charismatic and creative predecessor, Barry Coleman, an inspirational Mancunian, during whose tenure a tragic coach accident occurred on a movement outing. The vehicle caught fire and it left many young people terribly scarred, both physically, from serious burns, and mentally.

The youth centre, or *Bayit* (which simply means 'house') as it was known, was in Langside on the south side of the city where much of the Jewish population had initially clustered. I lived in a two-room flat above the youth centre and subsisted on a diet of fried eggs, white bread, kosher food from Morrisons, the Jewish deli across the road, and cream cakes from the bakery a few doors away. I used to sleep late and then seemed to spend much of the day smoking and talking with various senior movement members who dropped by.

My predecessor was a hard act to follow. The trauma of the coach accident hung like a dark cloud over the *Bayit* and I had neither the emotional maturity nor the psychological understanding to provide the support that many hoped to get by coming there. I became deeply involved in the lives of the youth movement members in Glasgow, but there was always a part of me that was never fully there; I was at the heart of intense debates about the future direction of the movement. At times I could understand the attraction of the less ideologically-driven Zionist youth movements, for which the act of *aliya* was not loaded with such symbolism and was not dependent on the decision-making processes of other people.

Among the questions raised in the discussions about the ideological and political future of the movement were: What were the implications of the Six-Day War for the future of socialist Zionist pioneering? Was living on kibbutz really the highest expression of Zionism or should other forms of *aliya* now be accepted alongside kibbutz, such as founding a collective in a development town or a major city? A new generation of movement members was seriously considering settling a new kibbutz. Was this the right direction for the movement to take? And more personally, should I join them?

At the end of the 1960s, the challenges facing Habonim were more daunting than anything that it had faced for 20 years. Rebellious youth were now centre stage in Western societies, expressing some ideas that were very different from those we held to in Habonim and some that were very similar. New versions of radical socialism were increasingly popular. Our form of rebellion seemed dated and narrow by comparison. What did we have to say about the Vietnam War or the repressive state? Social, political and ideological changes were happening in Israel too, with which we could barely keep up.

Discussions about the future led to me becoming *Mazkir* of the movement in the summer of 1968. I had harboured such ambitions, although this was not a post you were supposed to covet, rather something you would reluctantly accept for the good of the movement. At 22 I found myself heading an organisation with over 20 employees, five emissaries from Israel, five youth centres, a large house in north-west London where many London full-time workers lived and a farm.

I was very fond of many of the people I met in Glasgow, among whom was Naomi Slater, who became my first wife, but I felt that I was leaving under a cloud and that I had not been terribly successful. This only reinforced my conviction that I was now about to do something more suited to my talents. Providing ideological leadership, organising and mobilising members of the movement, playing a leadership role in efforts to get the various Zionist youth groups to work together and trying to influence the wider Zionist movement to take *aliya* more seriously – these are some of the things I wanted to achieve. If I had any model for what I wanted to do or who I wanted to be, it was not so much the example of people who held the job before me, but rather the image of the revolutionary organiser – not just any revolutionary, but Leon Trotsky. I was no Trotskyite politically, but had been stirred by Isaac Deutscher's three-volume biography of Trotsky as well as other writings on revolutions and revolutionaries. And it was the practical ability to galvanise and organise groups of people, unite them around an ideological manifesto, build a movement brick by brick and chair committee meetings to achieve specific goals that I wanted to believe I had. This was the kind of leader I wanted to be.

In the year I became *Mazkir* of the movement, Jews were still experiencing the euphoria generated by Israel's success in the Six-Day War. And in common with the rest of the Zionist movement, senior members of Habonim were preoccupied with the question of what should be done about the territories now occupied by Israel. By 1968, most members who planned to settle on Amiad had either gone to Israel or had left the movement. A new group had formed but had not yet decided on which kibbutz they should settle. After the Six-Day War, the debate changed radically: the possibility of settling beyond the Green Line emerged as an option. I no longer recall who precisely made this proposal. It was certainly not considered illegitimate to discuss it. On the contrary, the Israeli emissaries who were sent to act as 'educators' and 'organisers' encouraged consideration of the idea. The proposal appealed to me as it satisfied the desire of many people who wanted to start something new rather than join an enterprise founded and dominated by others. Some of us were convinced that this was the *new* pioneering, a manifestation of the spirit of the socialist Zionist thinkers and pioneers of pre-state days. But there soon developed very strong opposition to the idea on the part of some of the new generation who had already signalled that they wanted to form their own group, but were ideologically opposed to settling beyond the Green Line. These were largely, though not exclusively, university students also involved in the radical student movement of the late 1960s. A fierce debate ensued.

Even though I was heading the movement, I remember being bewildered by the discussion and did not feel that I could give a lead. This was also a personal issue since I was considering whether to remain with the remnants of those going to Amiad or to join the group formed by the next generation, wherever they planned to go. And I had already expressed support for the idea of settling beyond the Green Line. My thinking was partly influenced by the most senior of our emissaries, Romanian-born Zalman Gaster, a quietly spoken, rather shy, former Palmachnik, but with a steely resolve and a fierce intelligence. He encouraged talk of settling in the occupied territories, although partly on the grounds of military necessity. Zalman was bitterly opposed to the new left and when members of the movement planned to join the 17 March Grosvenor Square demonstration against the Vietnam War, he threatened to demonstrate against them.

The issue of where to settle was eventually resolved. Some decided to join a new kibbutz being created beyond the Green Line on the Golan Heights. Others could not accept this. Most of the latter eventually left the movement and did not emigrate to Israel. For a time I became a member of the Golan group. But in late 1969 or early 1970, before leaving for Israel, I rejoined the Amiad remnants because I felt socially closer to them.

For most of us, the Palestinian national movement had not yet impinged on our consciousness and we showed no sympathy for Palestinian rights. I seem to recall that some who objected to settling beyond the Green Line did so because they believed in the principle of not settling on land taken by force. But while writing this book, former new left Habonim members told me that they left the group planning to join a new kibbutz because they opposed settling on occupied Palestinian land and believed that it should be returned to its inhabitants. Those who chose to join a Golan settlement certainly believed that not *all* the land taken in 1967 would be given back to the Arabs.

We saw ourselves as guardians of moderate and liberal socialist Zionism, so how is it that the vast majority of us slipped so easily into a way of thinking that legitimised the occupation? We now know that it was Israel's Labour government at the time that encouraged and financed settlement beyond the Green Line, as did all subsequent governments. There was no mass socialist Zionist opposition to this movement, but rather a telling de facto alliance between the messianic Zionism of post-1967 and the secular Zionism that provided the ideological and practical justification for the State of Israel.

The argument over settling beyond the Green Line was emblematic of the difficulties I faced during the two years I was *Mazkir* of the movement. Everything seemed to become less clear-cut, both ideologically and personally. So it is perhaps no surprise that I cannot recall the embryonic pro-Palestinian views of the new left members. On a brief trip to Israel in 1969 a South African-born Israeli friend shocked me with her critical views about the Zionist project and Israel's treatment of its Arab citizens. I simply had no way of assimilating the arguments she advanced. Other views were then circulating, which challenged the Zionist story, especially concerning the fate of the Arab refugees. I recall a set of two-page briefings with maps, designed to counter what we were told was 'Arab propaganda' claiming that Israel expelled the Arabs from areas it conquered in 1948. I was shaken by the very fact that it now appeared to be necessary to mount this defence. Surely there could be no doubt that the Arab version was wrong, or could there?

It was under my watch that we took the hugely symbolic step of closing the *hachshara*. For all its faults, it had been a living example of the ideals to which the movement aspired. In many respects it represented communal living more complete than kibbutz itself. And yet kibbutz was certainly not going to change in order to accommodate the increasingly outdated ideological purity of a handful of British immigrants.

As the date of my own departure for Israel neared, I began to think more about my personal future. I still believed that kibbutz would be my ultimate destination, but began to consider the possibility of going first to Jerusalem to study history at the Hebrew University. When this idea became public knowledge in spring 1970, there was considerable disquiet in the movement. Having been a consistent advocate of maintaining the 'kibbutz-first' ideology, this seemed contradictory to say the least. But I was increasingly conscious of having no qualifications and an untrained mind. Why not put my academic aspirations first and delay moving to kibbutz for a few years? I applied to the university and was accepted. Naomi and I were married in July 1970 and we left for Israel at the end of August.

4

'IT IS NO DREAM'

'V'shavu banim l'gvulam!'
(Your children shall return to their country!)

Immigrant's Document No. 47872, 13 August 1970

In 1964, I travelled to Israel with eight other 18-year-olds, one small trunk and £50, spending two days on a train and five days on a ship to get there. I knew virtually no Hebrew. For most of the year practically everything I did was planned and organised by others. On 31 August 1970, Naomi and I flew direct from Heathrow to Lod Airport near Tel Aviv. I entered Israel as an Israeli citizen, identity no. 0-1335204-2. Naomi was already a citizen. Her parents made two attempts at living in Israel while she was a child and only came back to Glasgow the second time when she was in her early teens. I had chosen to enter the country as a citizen and not as a temporary resident as a sign of my ideological commitment and also because it gave us tax privileges. We made our way to Jerusalem where we arrived late at night at a student hostel, which was to be our temporary accommodation for the first month. The room contained little more than two single beds, a table, a couple of chairs and some bed linen.

I felt slightly strange and uncomfortable about suddenly finding myself living in a city in Israel when I had spent the better part of five years believing that once I emigrated I would never live anywhere else but on a kibbutz. But other former movement friends who had flirted with kibbutz life were now also living in Jerusalem. Having them there to help us integrate and cope with Israeli bureaucracy helped make the experience of immigration more manageable.

We spoke fluent Hebrew and I knew Jerusalem well, which gave us a head start, but this was a different city from 1964. It was no longer such a sleepy backwater. The removal of the physical barrier between East and West Jerusalem after the Six-Day War had turned the place into a chaotic, bustling, expanding city where tourist buses funnelled hordes of sightseers into the Old City. Rusty old Jordanian Mercedes taxis, their roof racks laden with chickens, sacks and suitcases, made their way west; Israeli soldiers, rifles hanging loosely from their shoulders, milled around as they waited for lifts home or to their military bases. The occupation was three years old but it still felt fresh and novel.

Not that we saw much of East Jerusalem. As new immigrants we were allocated an apartment provided by the housing authority, Amidar, on the eighth floor of a new-ish block in the scruffy south-west Jerusalem suburb of Kiryat Menachem. After a month we moved in. It had three rooms and a kitchen, and was furnished with four iron bedsteads and straw mattresses, two small chairs and a small table. There was no cooker, fridge, boiler or heating. But at least it was home, even if it was some distance both physically and socially from up-market areas like Rehavia or even leafy Bet Hakerem.

I had a small stipend from the university but we urgently needed to find work. Mine had to be fitted around a month-long, compulsory Hebrew-language course at the university. After a brief and dismal stint as a teller at the tiny branch of a bank in the King David Hotel, a job at which I was utterly hopeless, my limited degree of *protektsia* landed me part-time English-teaching for reasonable pay at a school for emissaries being sent by the Jewish Agency for Israel to diaspora Jewish communities. Meanwhile, Naomi found a full-time job as a teller in the branch of an English bank on the edge of Machaneh Yehuda, a colourful and raucous street market. There was still a two-year wait for a phone line so we were reliant on the antiquated, token-based public phone system to keep in touch with friends.

By the time term began, I had passed my academic Hebrew examination, felt comfortable with my English teaching and was enjoying renewing old friendships. I walked a great deal and became fond of the narrow, dusty alleyways, the ancient-looking typography on the *yeshiva* and *Bet Midrash* signs, the sweet smell of freshly baked raisin *challah* bread on Friday afternoons. Despite the changes, there was still something reassuringly provincial about Jerusalem, as if time had passed it by. Men from the strictly orthodox sects – Haredim, Hasidim, Neturei Karta – scurried about, incongruously in a hurry to get somewhere. Everything shut down for *Shabbat* from late Friday afternoon to late Saturday afternoon. We complained to each other, but it seemed part of the city's colour and culture.

Until I arrived to settle in Israel as a citizen, if I thought about the politics of the country it was mostly in connection with the role of the kibbutz in Israeli society or, at most, the importance of socialist Zionism for the country's development. I even saw the question of the territories occupied in 1967 only through the narrow-angle lens of what it meant for pioneering agricultural settlement. But it was impossible to live in Jerusalem and ignore either the domestic or international political situation. One of my sharpest memories is of riding a crowded city bus one evening in late September and hearing over the radio that Colonel Nasser, Egypt's leader, had died. Animated conversations broke out as passengers considered the implications of this momentous announcement.

The incident made me think about my attitude to Israeli politics. Was I only interested in kibbutz-related political idealism or did I want to extend that to involvement with left-wing politics in the city? Staying out of politics cast doubt on the strength of my ideological convictions, so I resolved to join Mapai, the main left-wing party that had governed the country in coalition since 1948.

I sought out the Mapai office in the centre of town, on Jaffa Road. It was an old, rather impressive villa with a large courtyard. When I explained what I was there for, the secretary at the desk looked at me incredulously. Eventually, she shunted me off to see someone responsible for the youth section. A large man in his early thirties sat behind a small desk. He asked me no questions, just launched directly into a political lecture, much of which I did not understand because I was unfamiliar with the Hebrew vocabulary of politics. When he finished I told him a little about my background and asked whether there was anything I could do, how I could get involved. In a sharp and impatient tone, he was dismissive of my involvement with the kibbutz movement and said I should forget about contributing to policy discussions. That could only come after years of party work, like stuffing envelopes and distributing leaflets. I don't know exactly what I expected but this was not it. I got up, made my excuses and left.

The bus often seemed to be the place where I experienced social and political tensions. On one occasion a Haredi man remonstrated loudly with an Arab woman who sat down next to him. Eventually he got up, ranting and raving and stormed off the bus. An even more disturbing incident followed an argument that developed between a young bus driver and some passengers who had just boarded. Without warning, the driver veered off his route and headed rather too fast in an unfamiliar direction. He eventually pulled up outside the Jerusalem municipality in the Russian compound in the centre of the city and we sat there, unable to get off. There was apprehensive but resigned muttering all around. Eventually I heard one woman say knowingly to another: 'Zeh-hu. Hu Aravi mi Bet Sefafa' – 'That's it. He's an Arab from [the village of] Bet Sefafa.' This was the first time I had encountered any open anti-Arab prejudice.

By the autumn my courses, which were taught at the Givat Ram campus in West Jerusalem, had started and I was struggling. The syllabus was rather rigid. Studying democracy in the Roman polis was compulsory. It was taught in Hebrew and contained words that were all new to me. I decided to change direction and re-registered as an English major, but more than a month had passed and it proved difficult catching up. I soon realised that I had been too hasty. The courses did not engage me and I felt foolish for abandoning history, the subject I had dreamed of coming back to for so long.

An earth tremor that hit Jerusalem in November was followed by our own seismic event in the form of the news that Naomi was pregnant. The implications were too complicated to think about at first, but we were happy to be having a baby. As the weeks passed, however, our new circumstances and the exigencies of studying and working seemed to leave us more isolated. The cold Jerusalem winter closed in and did nothing for our spirits. The apartment had no central heating and it was difficult to keep warm with the heaters we had. I was managing to sustain my university work and teaching, but mounting feelings of insecurity led me to start thinking about a way out of our predicament.

I had not abandoned the idea of eventually going to live at Amiad, so one option was to leave Jerusalem for the kibbutz in the hope of eventually being allowed to study a subject of my choice. There, the social support was all-embracing, Naomi would need have no concerns about ante-natal or post-natal care and we would have no financial problems. We went for a weekend visit – our second since we arrived in Israel – and were made very welcome. Our friends reassured us that if we came to live there, everything would be done to help us settle in. We never contemplated returning to England. I managed to convince myself that this was for the best, but at moments it felt like failure. The kibbutz gave me no assurances about studying. Despite all the good reasons for making the move, I worried that I was cutting and running, unable to persevere. I did not want to leave my Jerusalem friends and was ashamed at what they would think.

In the early spring of 1971 we returned the keys of our apartment to Amidar, I formally left the university and the kibbutz sent down a van and driver to pick up our belongings. We were going to a place I thought I knew well and Naomi was now familiar with too. Amiad felt safe. And yet a feeling of disappointment stayed with me.

*　*　*

The kibbutz was situated at the foot of a hill on the western side of the road running north from Tiveria to the town of Kiryat Shemona, about four kilometres from the Jordan river. A large and impressive community centre had been built in the middle of the settlement, next to the swimming pool, with money donated by a wealthy, sympathetic benefactor from the UK. The factory, a small operation when I came in 1965, had expanded significantly. It produced plastic mouldings, mostly for irrigation equipment. And the volunteer population of the kibbutz had grown, making a marked difference to the social life. Otherwise, apart from an impression of increased relative affluence, the place looked much the same.

Our initial hopes for how our lives would change by moving to the kibbutz were all realised: friends close by, security, support for Naomi during pregnancy. I returned to work in the banana plantation. Naomi was assigned to one of the children's houses. All of the collective living arrangements were as they had been in 1965. We were given a simple apartment with a veranda, one room and a shower-toilet. Work clothes were provided. The kibbutz cigarettes, the dry tobacco still liable to end up at the bottom of the pack, were free. We worked Sunday to Friday and every three weeks also had to work on *Shabbat*, the designated day off. We stored these rest days and could, theoretically, use them later. The number of *Shabbat* days owed to you was a mark of your dedication to the work ethic. Every week there was an *asefa*, a meeting of all the members of the kibbutz that non-members could attend, chaired by the *mazkir*, the general secretary. Issues affecting the kibbutz were discussed and decisions taken. In closed session, with only members present, this was the body that decided on kibbutz membership. Prospective members like ourselves were expected to attend open meetings.

Despite the less than satisfactory circumstances, coming to the kibbutz was a very significant moment. I was no longer a raw, 18-year-old first-timer. I could cast doubts aside and throw myself into the life of the kibbutz, live my ideological dream. (I still valued Herzl's famous saying: 'If you will it, it is no dream.') This was now home, for me, Naomi and for the child we were expecting. And it was easy to enter into the routine.

Any village-like society takes a close interest in newcomers. Whatever you did – as active participant in kibbutz life or not – it was noticed. The kibbutz was like a huge goldfish bowl. As a prospective member you were scrutinised from the start, judged as a worker, a contributor to society, someone who should be living up to the ideals and keeping to the rules. But scrutiny was more intense at Amiad because membership remained small and a high proportion of prospective members who had come from British Habonim had left after one or two years. This engendered disappointment, dashing hopes of reaching a more viable critical mass. But it also generated resentment. The kibbutz believed that it went out of its way to welcome the British newcomers and help them integrate. And then, in short order, they upped and left.

And there was another problem. The whole process of *aliya*, and specifically *aliya* to a kibbutz, was still regarded like a journey to the peak of a mountain. Leaving the kibbutz meant that you hadn't properly completed that ascent and were somehow inadequate. Leaving kibbutz *and* Israel was a double misdemeanour. You were stigmatised by being called a *yored*, which means 'someone who goes down', to emphasise the contrast with an *oleh*, 'someone who goes up'. You weren't just 'going down', you had failed, were morally deficient and lacking in backbone, betraying the Jewish people as it renewed itself in its historic homeland.

In six years, little had changed on the banana plantation that stretched back from the shore of the Kinneret. But familiarity was both a blessing and a curse. Being a prospective member and not just a temporary volunteer, I was soon levered into a position of responsibility. I still had to reacquaint myself with everything that I had done before – picking, pruning, loading – and learn much more, especially about irrigation. So much so that I was put in charge of maintaining the irrigation systems for the entire plantation. Grand as that may sound, I was little more than a novice plumber.

I spent most of the time doing this work on my own, walking up and down the furrows checking sprinklers, largely shaded from the heat by the wide banana plant leaves. I should have grown healthy from all the walking, but I smoked heavily, was more than partial to ripe bananas when I came across them and relished the huge breakfasts of eggs, French toast, jam, sweet tea and *botz* coffee. This was useful work and I should have been satisfied having some independent responsibility. But the old doubts about manual labour came creeping back to me as the weeks passed. The hours dragged and I took increasingly long breaks. Occasionally I took a book with me and sat reading under the broad leaves until my conscience got the better of me.

There were times when all hands were needed for picking or planting, or when we would supervise small teams of volunteers doing the mind-numbingly boring work of distributing *senadot*, the wooden poles used to prop up the heavy bunches of bananas hanging from mature plants. There was camaraderie in those moments, which made the experience more tolerable. Occasionally, on the way back to the kibbutz in the afternoon my burly American friend Spencer and I would stop off at the Loaves and Fishes at Kfar Nahum – better known as Capernaum – close to the Kinneret and drink black beer and smoke good cigarettes.

We hadn't been on the kibbutz more than five months when our son Ilan was born by caesarean section in the hospital in Tsfat up in the hills to the west. The last weeks had been difficult for Naomi as we hoped that the baby would be born naturally. But he looked so angelic, without a blemish on his round face, swaddled in a blue cotton sheet and blanket as they brought him out of the theatre, from which I had been excluded, to show him to me. Having the support network of the kibbutz made this process much easier than it would have been had we stayed in Jerusalem. So in that sense, our move to the kibbutz seemed to have been the right decision.

But the initial relief did not last. I tried to immerse myself in the work culture but the old feelings of intense boredom had returned and remained. A part of me still wanted to be seen as someone who could become fully integrated into the kibbutz as it was, as it saw itself. But I was developing a critique of kibbutz life, which meshed with what some others of my generation were thinking and was influenced by the countercultural ideas of the late 1960s that had barely touched me over the previous four or five years.

I listened to Cat Stevens, the Beatles' *Sergeant Pepper*, Crosby, Stills, Nash and Young, George Harrison's *All Things Must Pass*, Procul Harum, Santana, and became obsessed about finding deep meaning in their lyrics. Where the musical atmospherics left me tantalised, touched and yet confused, when I read Richard Neville's *Play Power*, Germaine Greer's *The Female Eunuch* and Timothy Leary's *The Politics of Ecstasy*, I discovered a new world of ideas through which I thought I was able to make sense of my doubts about kibbutz life. I'm sure that part of the attraction of finding fault with kibbutz ideology and structure was that it enabled me to externalise my feelings of boredom and the guilt they provoked, and channel these into producing a persuasive critique. Although I had a strong sense that I just couldn't cut it, the fact that others were also expressing dissatisfaction gave me some reassurance that there was something real, tangible and objective in my reasoning.

My state of mind was not helped when I found myself falling foul of the rules and regulations of the kibbutz more often than was tolerable for people who offered themselves as candidates for membership. After Ilan was born, my parents came out to Israel to see their first grandchild. As a gift, they brought with them a lightweight, folding baby-buggy, something still relatively new at the time and certainly unfamiliar on the kibbutz. Bulky, traditional pushchairs were available to all. Yet we soon learned, in a roundabout way, that accepting this modest gift for our personal use contravened the kibbutz's rules on owning property. We should either have declined the gift or offered it to the kibbutz for communal use. But once it was made clear to us that we had done something wrong, as newcomers we were allowed to keep the buggy, it being understood that we would not make the same mistake again.

I experienced the collective opprobrium of the kibbutz a second time after an inadvertent traffic violation, for which I incurred a fine. The good news was that the kibbutz paid. The bad news was that the incident was posted on the kibbutz noticeboard, with the express aim of shaming the culprit into not making the same mistake again. I was not a careless driver and I had not broken the law deliberately, but there was a surprising amount of public resentment that I had cost the kibbutz this money and behaved in such an irresponsible way.

* * *

In the latter part of 1971 a small group of us began discussing how to bring about fundamental change in the kibbutz. A fragment from the minutes of a meeting we held lists the things we discussed:

> The inevitable conflict of generations; the relationship between the economic structure and the social structure; the international youth upheaval and its consequences for us; the modern concept of the Israeli; work in the communal framework; happiness, enjoyment, play and fun; drugs; anarchism; the control of technological advance; cybernetics and automation; economic diversity as a key to happier living.

We spoke about developing a philosophical and political platform involving the younger generation on the kibbutz, not only the recent immigrants. We anticipated that response to some of the ideas 'would be hesitant and reactionary' but thought that 'with time and continual discussion many *chaverim* [members] could be brought round to our way of thinking'. In this 'movement' the 'ideas and their implications' were what mattered, not 'personalities' or 'initiators'. We decided to start a magazine, inform the 'establishment' of the kibbutz that we had been 'discussing certain ideas that have important consequences for the kibbutz as a whole' and organise a general meeting of younger people. We got as far as informing the 'establishment'.

In notes I made for an article explaining our critique of the kibbutz and how it should change, I argued that 'present day kibbutz life' was characterised by greater concentration on and awareness of material goods and personal possessions. Disillusionment with the democratic institutions of the kibbutz had set in. A 'hard core' held responsibility and power and few others participated in the running of the kibbutz. The emphasis on work as an end in itself was too rigid. Women were unable to fulfil themselves and were becoming increasingly similar to their counterparts in 'Western capitalist society'. The kibbutz had little influence beyond its gates.

I contrasted these problems with a rather idealised version of the kibbutz 20 years earlier when material possessions were few and unimportant, communal life was spontaneous and the level of social participation was high. There was mutual respect for different opinions, power was distributed more widely, men and women shared the work and 'work and life were one'. The kibbutz was 'the cornerstone of the state' and the state judged itself according to the standards of the kibbutz.

The country's economy developed. Immigrants from the Yemen, Morocco and Iraq came in huge numbers. Yet this led to a change in the character of the state, from 'predominantly white European intellectual to black uneducated'.

The importance of the kibbutz dwindled, towns grew, the army grew stronger and the borders more secure. The Six-Day War 'altered the position of many kibbutzim that were now no longer close to the border'. Their function as front-line defensive outposts became far less important.

Nevertheless, the kibbutz 'was, without exaggeration, an amazing achievement' and it was not surprising that a certain doctrinaire rigidity had developed. The pioneers wanted to 'preserve and consolidate' their achievements, but they also wanted to enjoy the life they had created for themselves and this was partly expressed in the acquisition of more material goods and personal possessions. 'None of which is bad in itself', but with the old ideological attitudes 'rapidly becoming an anachronism', nothing had come along to replace them. So young people 'learned the value of work but realised they did not have to work like their parents'.

The older members were focused on preservation and consolidation. The children of the kibbutz were 'unsure'. They had grown up in a war situation. 'Living' was vital; 'ideology, Zionism? – stupid, irrelevant, unnecessary'. And so the kibbutz declined. Attempts to deal with the problems pragmatically had some success, but the new pragmatism still served the status quo. 'Everything points to more decline. The situation dictates it.' Being 'white, Ashkenazi', the kibbutz 'holds no key to ethnic problems'; 'the older generation remain in control', 'the younger generation is losing interest'. A way had to be found '*to live justly* with material possessions' and 'to make work meaningful'.

Around ten of us tried to live according to these new ideas, as a sort of commune within the commune. But since work took up most of our waking hours, this was difficult. Occasionally, our attempts to introduce the counterculture into our lives were pathetic and farcical. On one occasion some of us went off for a long walk across the rocky fields to find a secluded spot to smoke dope for the first time. The cigarettes were already rolled and looked suspiciously like commercial fags. We lit up, passed the stuff around and waited for it to take effect. Nothing happened. We trudged back to the kibbutz, disappointed, but perhaps rather relieved.

Had we pottered along pursuing lifestyles that were merely a pale reflection of the counterculture, without thinking that we could convert the rest of the kibbutz to our ideas, I suspect no one would have been terribly bothered – in public, at least. But since we sought to introduce change and discussed our ideas with senior kibbutz members, we could not be ignored. And not only were most people aghast, they believed that our ideas were positively dangerous and subversive. We were told that discussion must be confined to practical proposals and not to abstract, half-formed ideas, which would undermine the very foundations of the kibbutz.

I am not sure that we invested very much hope in really bringing people round to our point of view. We were realistic about the possible reaction but not about what we should do if we met opposition. In the subsequent months our own personal preoccupations became increasingly important, pushing aside any prospect of 'revolutionary' change.

Coming to the kibbutz had helped Naomi and me through the transition to parenthood, but it proved less than fulfilling for her too and she found the atmosphere unsympathetic. A few months before I began my army service, we asked to be considered for full membership, but were told that perhaps we weren't ready. I wasn't entirely surprised given the incidents that brought us to the attention of members in an unfavourable light. But I was affronted and hurt and since we were not told categorically that we couldn't put our names forward, we asked that the general meeting consider us nevertheless. It did, with some reluctance, and with equal reluctance allowed us to become members. But the episode left us feeling uncomfortable. In the weeks leading up to the start of my basic army training, we began hesitantly to talk about whether we should consider leaving the kibbutz – and Israel – even if only temporarily.

*　　*　　*

As a Zionist and an Israeli citizen, I was ready to defend my new country and saw it as my duty to serve in the army. So when I was called up for basic training in January 1972, I was expecting it. While technically a conscript, I felt more like a willing volunteer. The army had a formidable reputation for toughness and I suspected it would be a severe personal test. Yet I assumed that my ideological commitment to Zionism would somehow be taken into account in the way that I, and other immigrants schooled in Zionist youth movements, were treated. In any event, as a married immigrant with a baby, I was only required to undergo the three months basic training. Evidence of a knee operation I had when I was 14 and partial colour-blindness, revealed at my army medical, cut my profile to something like 80 (out of 100). I was instructed to report to the mobilisation point in Tiveria towards the end of January to begin training in the Engineering Corps.

On the day I left for mobilisation, the weather was bitterly cold, easily penetrating my well-worn, brown duffle coat. I set off very early. Naomi held back tears as she stood holding the baby. I carried a voluminous green holdall stuffed with socks, pants, vests and various small but essential pieces of kit that old army hands on the kibbutz had advised me to take, like green nylon scouring material for cleaning my rifle. I felt a little sad and empty.

The bus journey to Tiveria was all too short. We joined the other enlisted men and were driven south through the West Bank towards Jerusalem. There we transferred to army lorries for the journey to our base camp near Hebron, south of Jerusalem. Relieved of our civvies, we were vaccinated, given army fatigues and boots, mess tin, water bottle, assigned to a *machlaka* (platoon) and taken to our dormitories. We were ordered to line up in front of the long hut and bellowed at by the sergeant major who told us what a worthless, undisciplined bunch we were and warned of the dire consequences awaiting us if we didn't immediately begin shaping up.

Sent to our hut, I scrambled for a bunk bed. I soon discovered that we were mostly immigrants in our mid to late twenties, some with families, from Argentina, France, Canada, Lebanon, North Africa, Chile, Czechoslovakia, Russia, Romania, Holland and the UK – the 'ingathering of the exiles', as called for by Zionism. But there were also a few *sabras*, mostly from difficult social backgrounds. Among us there were accountants, academics, farm workers, *yeshiva* students, drivers, hairdressers, butchers and kibbutzniks. Our officers, by contrast, were in their late teens or very early twenties, and they knew nothing of life outside school or the army.

With its rough egalitarianism, the army was a great leveller. If you weren't familiar with the kind of Hebrew you needed to know to feel comfortable on the street, you learnt it in the army. Airs and graces and complaints were like so many soap bubbles repeatedly popped by the officers. The few strictly orthodox were given time to pray but still had to complete the obligatory tasks undertaken by everyone else. If you showed the slightest weakness, the officers rewarded you with intensified humiliation.

During the first period of six weeks' training in the fundamentals of soldiering we were taught military discipline, which involved quashing independence of mind and replacing it with instant obedience to every command. If it made you feel like someone found guilty of multiple offences without even having been given a chance to defend yourself, that was how it was supposed to be. You learnt that the army was fair in that it treated you *all* as criminals, but the treatment itself was anything *but* fair. I couldn't help thinking that I didn't need to be shouted at to get me to run, march, learn how to fire a gun, throw a grenade, do as I was told. Didn't they realise this? Before January was out I wrote to Naomi: 'I'm sure that the original Palmachniks wouldn't be happy with the way things are run … it's hardly a people's army anymore.'

This did not prevent me from wanting to do all that I could to succeed, to be a model soldier. As the weeks passed I was finding the values of the army increasingly incompatible with what I understood defending and building the country was all about. And yet I couldn't and didn't abandon my objective. On 18 February I wrote to Naomi: 'I still don't find the physical side of things very hard – it's just being away from you that is so hard to bear. But I have no choice and that's the price we have to pay for being Zionists and idealists – sometimes I wonder if it is worth it. There are many things about this army that I find completely distasteful, but of course one is powerless to do anything about it. You are just "shit" as a "tiron" [recruit] and you have to suffer in silence.' In part, there was a purely practical reason for this: do as you were told, win a target practice competition, be responsible for the platoon for a week and do it well, and you could be rewarded with a weekend leave pass. For those who were family men, when things were rough leave became even more important. But there was never enough and it became the main complaint we griped about to each other and to our officers. But how could 19-year-olds be expected to understand?

I had never seen myself as particularly competitive, but in the army I seemed to accept without question the challenge of the game: to be the best at everything. I wasn't, but I tried as hard as I could. There were times when the nature of the task and the circumstances in which it had to be undertaken got the better of my intentions. On guard duty one night outside the synagogue of the local Jewish settlement, the weather was bitterly cold and damp and it snowed. Soon, my coat was sodden, my feet were like blocks of ice, my fingers were numb, and I could hardly see a thing through the steady snowfall. The empty synagogue behind me became irresistible and I slipped inside thinking I would just sit down on a bench for a brief while to recover, but I must have dozed. I was suddenly aware of a voice calling me and was struck with panic. I grabbed my Uzi sub-machine gun and practically fell through the door. It was still snowing. The voice belonged to a friend who was coming to relieve me.

Of course, it wasn't all a game. We fired live rounds in some target practices and threw live hand grenades, and in the second six-week period of training in mines we worked with live explosives. But we did all this on base, a route march through 'enemy territory' being the only time, fully armed, we really came into close contact with people outside of army personnel. That march eventually took us to a temporary encampment where we erected ragged bivvy tents and then undertook field exercises using live ammunition.

Eventually, I realised there was something of a contradiction between how I behaved in practice and what I was thinking about the army's faults. I did not question the fundamentals of Zionism, but rather saw the army as betraying the Zionist idea. At first the attitudes of the officers seemed to me to be driven largely by inexperience and *sabra* bravado. But at the level of lieutenant and above I was increasingly aware of a haughty arrogance and boastfulness, as if they were the masters of the universe and could do no wrong.

I saw this more clearly when we had to make a route march from our base to Hebron. Before we set out, our commanding officer addressed us. His uniform was immaculate. He was supremely confident and exuded a sense of power and control. Winding us up for the challenge ahead, with steel in his voice, he began describing the dangers we could face on the way. Using extreme, demonising language, he spoke about the 'Arabs' we would encounter, inciting us to believe that we would be in imminent danger at any moment during the march. As a precaution we had live ammunition in the breaches of our rifles and Uzi sub-machine guns.

Until the CO's address, I had never heard anyone in Israel talk like that about Arabs. Not that I was judging those words against an informed view of the Arab population in the West Bank, a sense of who they were or how they felt. I knew them only in the abstract as the 'enemy', both from what we were taught in the youth movement about their opposition to Zionism and from the very fact that Israel needed an army to defend itself. But the language grated with my conception of a humanistic, socialist Zionism. And even at the time I thought it hinted at a brutality that was hardly justified.

On 10 March, at a particularly jaundiced moment, I wrote to Naomi: 'I am really confused about the army and Israel now. All that has happened here not only makes me hate the army but I begin to wonder why we ever came to Israel at all. The country is being corrupted so much that I wonder what there is for us here.' As we neared the end of the course, my thoughts became increasingly confused and contradictory. I wanted clarity about our future, but I also needed to understand how my connection to Israel should now develop. Army service had exacerbated doubts and uncertainties, but at the same time a visceral sense of belonging seemed to have taken hold of me. The love-hate relationship I developed with the army symbolised my confusion about Israel and this was epitomised by my reaction to events that occurred in the days before we were demobbed.

My father's bespoke tailoring business had shrunk dramatically since the mid 1960s. This gave him an opportunity to make a new start, at 53, in the country where his two older sons now lived. When my parents decided to make this move, Naomi and I were not thinking of leaving the country, but by late April 1972, such thoughts had become ever more central to our conversations. Meanwhile, my parents and younger brother were well on their way to Israel. So while I was delighted to be seeing them again and having them close by, I already had pangs of guilt that we might be on the way out just as they were on the way in. Nevertheless, my mind was focused on just being in Haifa to greet them. They were to arrive the day before I was due to be released from the army, so I spent the last week of my service trying to persuade the officers to allow me to leave one day early. It was a struggle getting them to agree and they did so with only a couple of days to spare. This procrastination did not endear the army to me in those last days.

So much of our time in the Judean Hills south of Jerusalem had been spent under almost perpetual cloud, the fresh sunlit sky on the day of our late April passing out parade was almost intoxicating. About 300 of us lined up waiting for the company commander to address us. Having scrubbed, cleaned and polished every bit of kit that I possibly could, I was both delighted to have reached the end and satisfied that I had done my best. But I was thinking mostly about my family and the army friends I was unlikely to see again.

With the stars on his epaulets glinting in the sun, the commander began speaking. After a while it dawned on me that one of the purposes of the parade was to give the award to the outstanding soldier, *chayal mitsdayen*, on the course. It never really occurred to me that I might be in line for the overall award, though I had won the weekly award on a couple of occasions, especially as my mood towards the army had darkened considerably over the last weeks. Before I could catch up with my own thoughts, reaching me like a distant whisper on the wind I heard my name, bracketed with the words *'chayal mitsdayen'*. I froze, heard the words again only this time much louder and realised that I was being called up to the podium. In my confusion, I dropped my Uzi, which clattered to the ground, provoking laughter and a sharply worded but tongue-in-cheek rebuke from one of the officers who said dropping my gun was enough to have me disqualified from receiving the award. But I recovered the gun, ran to the podium, shook hands with the commander and ran back to my place to the acclaim of my fellow soldiers.

An intense feeling of almost childish pleasure came over me. Later on I was told that with the award came pre-demob promotion to the dizzying heights of lance corporal. And that evening I was taken aside by one of the officers who asked whether I would be ready to stay on in the army and go on an officers' course. I politely declined, though I was flattered and for a moment imagined that had I come to the army earlier in my life I might have taken up the offer. As the day wore on, my mood changed and my doubts about the army and what it represented began to replace the feelings of pleasure.

It was somehow fitting that I did, after all, leave the base camp a day early so that I could get home to the kibbutz and go the next morning to Haifa to meet my parents. Yes, I was *chayal mitsdayen*, but I avoided the farewells that came with the completion of such an experience. It's as if I said: 'Thanks, but no thanks.'

Even when I left the camp I was not fully aware of what I was leaving. I don't mean the army, but where the base was located. I knew what the place was called – Gush Etzion – and that the Jewish settlements there before the 1948 war had been overrun and destroyed by the Jordanian army. I also knew that it now contained a *yeshiva* and what I believed to be a religious kibbutz, but that's about all. And it was only some four or five years later, after I left Israel, that I learned of the place's significance.

Gush Etzion was at the very heart of the 'Greater Israel' movement to settle Jews in 'Judea and Samaria'. The members of the religious youth movement B'nai Akiva, who pressed the government after the Six-Day War to allow Jewish settlements to be revived there, were the precursors of Gush Emunim, the leading ideological force behind the religious settler movement. By 1972, there were two religious kibbutzim, Kfar Etzion and Rosh Tzurim, a village, Alon Shvut, and a *hesder yeshiva*, a seminary which combined advanced Talmudic studies with service in the Israeli army. We were there to be trained as soldiers but also to provide additional protection for the Gush Etzion settlements and the *yeshiva*.

* * *

Not long after I left the army, we decided to leave both the kibbutz and Israel. The reasons were complex and contradictory. In a letter I wrote to Naomi shortly before I was demobbed, and after a journey to Jerusalem to assist in routine security duties during the state funeral of the late Knesset speaker, I said: 'The city looked beautiful, really beautiful and I had the feeling that somehow this peculiar land was my home ... that there was something here in this country for us even if we leave for a number of years. The feeling is hard to define because all the initial baseless idealism has fallen away after experiencing town, kibbutz and the army. Maybe it's just a deep inlaid cultural urge that ties me to this land and when it came to my mind that we want to leave for a while I felt that that too was a good thing because it will give us a chance to sort out how we feel about this country ...'

I had reached the conclusion that, however worthy the cause, I did not want to spend the rest of my life as an agricultural labourer. I feared being judged irresponsible, were we to leave, and yet I was convinced that I wanted to develop my brain rather than my brawn. I still believed that higher education was the right thing for me and decided that on returning to England I would apply to Sussex University to study history.

Being unhappy in my work on kibbutz left me in an unbearable state of unresolved tension. Something had to give. But I had invested so much in becoming an Israeli. I wasn't ready to leave. Yes, I occasionally felt nostalgic for a certain kind of comfort and order Israel did not have, for England's more forgiving climate and greener landscape. But none of this outweighed the feeling of abandoning a personal journey I wanted to continue making. And that's the point. It was all very well for me to think about *my* personal journey, but I was not alone. We were three. And yet, casting a shadow over everything was a marriage turning sour. I was not ready to end it. On the contrary, I wanted to try to make it work and ultimately came to the conclusion that this could only be done by making a fresh start. The stark fact is that the main reason for deciding to leave the kibbutz and Israel was to save our marriage. Although I was certainly beginning to have ideological misgivings, what counted in the end was the personal and not the political. Had I been alone, I would not have left Israel at that time.

We knew what we had to do, but doing it was not so easy. I was worried about my parents. I felt a great sense of unease about being responsible for their coming to Israel and then, within a matter of months, abandoning them. As Israeli citizens, we needed Israeli passports before we could leave the country. But before I could get mine I had to obtain official release from the army. Guarantors had to be found for the loan we had been given by the Jewish Agency to help pay the cost of coming to Israel in the first place. And while the kibbutz undertook to pay for the transport of our few possessions back to England, I had to construct the wooden container in which to pack everything.

Apart from the practical difficulties, there was the stigma attached to leaving. We were becoming *yordim* (the collective noun for people who 'go down'), with the implication of defeat, resignation, betrayal and more. Since there were elements of failure which had contributed to our decision to leave, the charge of being *yordim* hurt. Although my desire to return to Israel at some point was genuine, I was sensitive to the implication that being unable to make a go of it, to integrate, was a result of personal, psychological weakness. Not to have gone would have been a moral failure. To go and then leave was equally reprehensible. Nevertheless, these feelings did not prevent me from leaving. But a sense of shame and confusion stayed with me for years afterwards.

Once we had made our decision to leave and informed the kibbutz officials, we felt as if we were in a kind of no-man's land as ties were cut. Justification could always be found as to why departing members were at fault and not the kibbutz itself. But even so, there was usually a sense of disappointment at being unable to increase the membership. Understandably, only close friends helped us leave. Even with them conversations were often uncomfortable and awkward. We were no longer connected to any shared future. Those remaining would continue to shoulder the responsibility for the community; in stark contrast, our departure felt like a selfish and individualistic act.

I took Naomi and Ilan to stay with my parents, who were living in Netanya, an up-and-coming coastal town between Tel Aviv and Haifa, so that I could complete packing our possessions. Eventually I slipped away, with the minimum of fuss, the good wishes of close friends and the indifference of most of the kibbutz population who seemed to have adjusted to my absence long before I physically left. Within a few years, most of the people who took part in our attempt to alter the ethos of the kibbutz, and others from the youth movement who had not, had also left.

I joined my family in Netanya and with practically no money to speak of we spent the weeks before our flight to London living with my parents and younger brother. Their flat was light and airy, but small – barely large enough to accommodate all six of us. At times I felt dreadful; guilty about imposing on my parents, concerned about what would happen to them once we were back in England, worried about my health, uncertain as to whether Sussex University would accept me.

One of the reasons why we stayed on for a while was because my younger brother was soon to have his bar mitzvah at the Western Wall in Jerusalem. It is strange to think that with all my years of intense involvement in the Zionist socialist youth movement, membership of the kibbutz and commitment to an ideology that I wanted to help modernise, Michael's entirely non-ideological path could well have resulted in him becoming a more 'complete' Israeli than me.

As the date of our departure neared I began to fantasise about life back in England, to idealise the civilised values, the orderly and calm behaviour I was soon to be part of once more. Thoughts of living a life of countercultural radicalism on the kibbutz were replaced by imagining rolling Sussex countryside, green fields, tidy streets and real pavements; a pace of life so much more gentle. Queues. No unbearable heat. Butter. Real money. The two-day weekend. And Sunday papers.

As the plane touched down at Heathrow Airport that autumn these reassuring images began to dissolve. The rain was sweeping from side to side like a machine gun spraying bullets. The tarmac was like a shallow lake. Back in north-west London, the rain was easing. Sheltering under a shop awning, I took in the scene. Time seemed to have stood still. Any changes I could identify appeared cosmetic and superficial. I felt as if I had stepped backwards into my past. Everything looked depressingly familiar. Sad, monotonous streets. Clutching suburbia. Tower blocks that reminded me of run-down apartments in Leningrad. Red buses filled with silent, red-lipped, pinch-faced passengers.

5

SEARCHING FOR MYSELF

I do not accept any absolute formulas for living. No preconceived code can see ahead to everything that can happen in a man's life. As we live, we grow and our beliefs change. They must change. So I think we should live with this constant discovery. We should be open to this adventure in heightened awareness of living. We should stake our whole existence on our willingness to explore and experience.

Martin Buber, 1972

Back in Golders Green, my immediate preoccupations were finding a job and a place to live, and waiting to hear whether I had a university place. But Israel was never far from my thoughts. Dad, who was 54, had a heart attack soon after we returned to England. It wasn't too serious and he recovered well, but it was very worrying not having money for a flight back to Israel in an emergency.

Work was scarce, so I fell back on the few contacts I had in the Jewish community and in late autumn went to work for the Zionist charity, the Jewish National Fund. I had nothing against the aims of JNF at the time, but returning to work in the Zionist world, even if only for a temporary period, felt like a soul-destroying compromise. I really needed a break from the milieu in which I had been so deeply immersed for eight years, and I saw the JNF as a form of 'armchair Zionism' with which, as a socialist Zionist, I was never comfortable. But I needed to start earning money quickly.

I didn't like the job but stuck it out as best as I could. By early 1973 I had secured a place at Sussex University to study history. Somehow, we muddled through for the next eight months, but there were moments when I was plagued by doubts and uncertain as to whether we would ever get there. Fortunately, before succumbing to these dark thoughts, we heard that the university had allocated us a campus apartment and we began to make plans to move.

When we arrived at the beginning of October I wrote of 'experiencing a feeling of relief at having squeezed through the door before it was finally closed on me', an allusion to the fact this was my fourth attempt to study for a degree. I was like a dehydrated man who had come across an oasis in the desert. Once my courses started I couldn't get enough. But my mood was soon disturbed by the outbreak of the 1973 Yom Kippur War on 6 October. Instinctively, I wanted to go back to Israel, but our family circumstances were so fragile I knew that I couldn't. Instead, I took refuge in my books. My brother and his wife had also left the kibbutz and returned to England in May 1973, but this only made it harder to think of my parents coping in wartime conditions and of friends there who would be fighting and perhaps dying. But I was aware that I had very little choice and that wallowing in my own personal turmoil was self-indulgent. The Egyptians and the Syrians had made significant advances in the Sinai and on the Golan Heights, but by the end of the month the fighting had halted after the Israeli counterattack and the game of diplomacy had begun. Thoughts of Israel receded once again as I immersed myself in my studies.

I never lost touch with Israel during my three years at Sussex and I made no conscious decision not to go back there to live. Yet I needed to put what I thought was my unfinished experience of kibbutz and Israel into some kind of perspective so that it would no longer seem like a barrier to moving forward with my studies and into a career. At least there was one less thing to worry about when my parents returned to Britain in 1974. But despite a year's psychotherapeutic marriage counselling, Naomi and I separated at the end of 1974 and early in 1975 she moved back to her home city of Glasgow with Ilan. I began adjusting to life on my own, which included trips north to visit him, moving into student accommodation elsewhere on campus, continuing psychotherapy in a group and beginning to see friends from my youth movement days.

*   *   *

I was beginning to think seriously about pursuing an academic career in British political history when unexpectedly, in May 1974, I received a letter from Gerry Kelman, my first *madrich* when I joined Habonim in 1959. Gerry was a warm-hearted, generous, kind and high-principled Scot, with a natural ability to make educating children about Israel and Zionism an enjoyable and formative experience. In the early 1960s he went on *aliya* to Kibbutz Kfar Hanassi in the north-east of Israel and returned to the UK in 1974 for two years to be the main emissary to Habonim. He wanted to know my thoughts on a project he was promoting to produce a history of the movement, an idea that was being discussed even when I was *Mazkir*.

I soon became involved in exchanges with him over what shape a book on the youth movement might take. In early 1975 I agreed to write a paper considering the problems and issues involved in producing such a volume.

I completed this in May and recommended a six-week research project that would determine whether enough material existed to produce a serious history and if so, outline the basic narrative and what would need to be done to produce it. I was then commissioned to spend part of the summer doing this. By September I had produced a detailed, 51-page document that outlined a proposal for an ambitious book, which I put myself forward to write.

Youth movements reflected the zeitgeist. Their histories were therefore of historical significance, albeit rather minor. I believed a history of Habonim was only worth writing if the movement was treated as a subject of serious historical study, rather than an excuse for extended nostalgic reflection. And I thought that writing the book would help further my ambition to become an academic historian.

I offered myself as the writer also because I believed that investigating the development of the youth movement would help me understand my experience of it and why it had become such a central part of my life. I was partly influenced to see the project in this way having spent two years in psychotherapy. And I sensed that, through this book, I might pursue more systematically the questioning of Zionism and Israel that I had begun while I was in the Israeli army. These motivations for writing the book were genuine, but they clashed with the fact that I was still in thrall to my youthful Zionist convictions. I assumed that the youth movement experience was not only positive but that its ideological patina gave it a moral superiority and therefore greater value than anything anyone else was doing at that time in their youth.

My proposal was distributed widely among former Habonim members and most approved of the plan. Gerry Kelman headed a little group set up to manage the project and it sponsored my first two-month research trip to Israel in the summer of 1976 to gather material from public archives and private individuals, and interview former movement members, especially those involved in the formative years. This would be my first visit in four years.

During the first six months of 1976, I wrote dozens of letters to people I wished to interview and made contact with various Israeli archives. Most of the responses I received were positive and helpful, though not everyone was available to meet with me. I wanted to talk to Teddy Kollek, then Mayor of Jerusalem. Originally from Vienna and a member of the umbrella socialist pioneering organisation Hehalutz, he had been a key influence in the movement during the second half of the 1930s. But he pleaded lack of time – 'Even twenty-four hour workdays are insufficient', he wrote to me on 21 June – and referred me to others. Among them were Avraham Harman, Oxford graduate and former Israeli ambassador to the US, then president of the Hebrew University, and Wellseley Aron, who founded Habonim while he was the political secretary of Chaim Weizmann, president of the World Zionist Organisation and subsequently Israel's first president, in London in 1929.

I also arranged to see many other people living in towns, villages and kibbutzim up and down the country, including some emissaries. One such who worked with me when I was *Mazkir* of Habonim was Zalman Gaster, who arrived in Israel from Romania while still a teenager. He wrote to me on 11 April 1976 (in Hebrew):

> I have now started once again to be *Mazkir* of the kibbutz, work that I am already familiar with. To my regret, the history of Garin Zayin [the youth movement immigrant group] at Amiad is quite sad. We had hoped that they would have relieved us of various kibbutz posts and responsibilities. So there's no alternative but to saddle up the old horses once again, and wait for better times which I hope will come quickly. Also in our State of Israel the situation isn't simple. You of course read the papers and even follow things a little, but as they say in England: 'For good or ill – it's my country' and one does what one can to improve matters.

Zalman's words reminded me of my own thinking and I scribbled a rhetorical question on his letter in Hebrew saying: 'And do you also have doubts?'

I never asked Zalman Gaster that question, but during the eight weeks I was there, from June to August, I put countless other questions about the past to my interviewees. Their answers mostly put flesh on the bones of a story that, by then, I knew: between 1929 and 1939, a small, British-Jewish, Palestine-centred educational scouting group transformed itself into a full-blown socialist Zionist youth movement with emigration to kibbutz in Palestine as its highest aim. The people who filled in the details from their own personal recollections were, for the most part, highly successful members of Israel's professional elites and similarly successful members of the managerial and cultural elites on kibbutzim. I also gathered a gratifyingly large amount of documentary material, which confirmed and rounded out what I had been told. But I also encountered something that took me aback.

There were two fundamental shifts in the direction of Habonim in the 1930s. The first was from being 'Palestine-centred' to fully embracing Zionism. The second was from giving equal status to the various liberal forms of the Zionist idea to adopting the exclusive ideological direction of creating a socialist society with kibbutz as its highest expression. The arguments preceding these shifts were heated and intense. Just the fact that the original founders were mostly from the established Jewish middle class and the young recruits in the East End who eventually took control of the movement were from the Jewish working class and many were involved in communist groups, illustrates the tensions that must have been present. But what I did not anticipate were the incredibly strong feelings that still existed among the protagonists 40 years later, especially the bitter resentment among those who fought hard to prevent the movement from adopting an exclusively socialist programme. This was not simply a straight split between those living on kibbutz and those living in towns and cities. Certainly, the kibbutzniks almost unanimously agreed that the socialist Zionist direction taken was the right one. But one of the most influential proponents of the adoption of socialist Zionism was Ambassador Harman who was from a wealthy middle-class family in West London. Although he never lived on a kibbutz himself, he believed it was the movement's true destiny.

While deeply immersed in this history, I was also dealing with the emotions I was experiencing being back in Israel for the first time since 1972. For the most part, I felt relatively at ease. My degree result came through in the first few days and getting a First in History felt like a strong vindication of all that I had wanted to achieve after leaving Israel in 1972. Only on a few occasions did conversation turn to fundamental questions about Zionism, but when someone said, 'Oh, Tony would probably no longer call himself a Zionist', I was rather embarrassed since at that time this was not the case.

But when I returned to the Galil with Kathy, my new partner, both to Amiad and to the other kibbutzim with English settlers, I had conflicting feelings. Friends were very kind to us and made us welcome. Others were distinctly cool. I felt as if I was being looked at as someone who had irresponsibly abandoned the kibbutz, betrayed its ideals. Painful memories of a broken marriage and a son I saw too little of also surfaced. On this, too, I imagined I was being judged.

Not everyone I met was thrilled with my approach to the book. Some did not believe it merited a serious study and wanted a collection of anecdotes, pictures and reminiscences. But most people approved and wanted to be helpful. I encountered very little disquiet or disillusionment about anything to do with Israel itself and the lives people lived there. And despite the difficulties and unhappy ending to my two years in Israel and my kibbutz membership, I felt I was in a country of which I had become a part, and which had become part of me. I had increasingly come to see Israel in more realistic terms, no longer judging everything against my former sense of the importance of the kibbutz.

*   *   *

I worked on the project intermittently for five or six years, wrote 70,000 words, but never completed the book. While I was researching and writing, I encountered various expressions of doubt as to my suitability for the task. And during this time my outlook on Zionism became more critical.

In May 1977, Gerry Kelman wrote to me:

I've received a whiff, by various half-comments or hints, of a nebulous feeling of worry or dissatisfaction as to the writing of the book, the specific approach being adopted and the writer. I'm not sure how strong this undercurrent is, or if it is even worth thinking about. In some cases ... it is nothing more than sour grapes but at various points in time I've heard apprehension that you are not a chaver kibbutz [kibbutz member], or (even more criminal!!) you are a 'yored' or that you have a very pessimistic view of the present-day movement.

When my work on the book seemed to be faltering, Gerry wrote to me in June 1979 to ask whether I had 'basically changed my mind about the whole project'. I replied: 'Not as far as whether it should be done is concerned. I have certainly changed my mind about the subject matter but that is perfectly natural when considering a subject over a number of years – especially a subject that, at root, is still topical and controversial ... This simply means that I have become more critical as time has passed. Don't get me wrong – my own shift is not so great.'

Where my thoughts on Zionism were going can be gauged from the last chapter of the uncompleted manuscript: 'The English [Jewish] attitude to Zionism loudly echoed the tenets of British Imperialism', I wrote. 'Not only was Palestine seen as an undeveloped country with an ignorant native population lacking any national identity, but colonisation was also seen as the solution for co-religionists who were unable to survive in their present environments – the same solution was proposed by Imperialists for Englishmen who were unemployed and was seen as an answer to overpopulation and a rising birth-rate.' The Habonim Handbook referred to Jaffa as having 'remained enslaved for 2,000 years until it almost forgot what it was to be free', and to the Mediterranean as having 'once more become what it was two thousand years ago, simply ... the national Jewish sea'.

Neither as a youth movement member nor as an Israeli citizen had I ever seriously asked questions about Palestine's Arab population, but I now began to ask them as I studied the educational documents and the summaries of discussions among the leadership in the 1930s. 'It hardly seems probable that the early Habonim settlers gave much thought to [the Arabs] at all', I wrote. 'When settlements were attacked, and there were riots and disturbances, the individual Arab lost his identity and was submerged in the marauding mob. He was seen as an ignorant peasant, easily influenced and led by unscrupulous leaders. Zionism was clearly envisaged as being a civilizing instrument which the Arabs should welcome because it would lift them out of squalor and poverty. But it was not the primary task of the Jews to reform

Arab society. Even the intending Halutzim [socialist Zionist pioneers] realised the exclusiveness of Zionism.'

The Jewish emissary from Palestine in the mid 1930s, Eliyahu Werbner, said 'that it was necessary to "drain the Arab social swamp so that the Jewish National Home should be free from bad influences emanating from an unhealthy society in its midst"'. In 1937 a senior member argued in the movement's periodical that Zionism was not the tool of British Imperialism but was bringing socialism to the Arab masses, which Arab Imperialism did not permit. I wrote: 'It did not seem to occur to the writer of the article that national feeling, whether inspired and generated by corrupt ruling cliques or not, can render ideas of Socialism and equality completely irrelevant. He was also not aware that his analysis implicitly allowed for the existence of Jewish nationalism but not Arab nationalism.'

Back in England, I began working on a doctorate at the London School of Economics, determined to carve out a career in academia. But as the year passed I began to feel that I was losing direction. The LSE felt like a factory. Working on an entirely research-based PhD I had virtually no contact with any other graduate students. Appointed to a part-time lectureship in history at Brighton Polytechnic for 1977–78, I decided to defer my PhD place for a year and concentrate on finishing the youth movement book. At first, the change seemed to help. I made good progress and managed to cope well, delivering lectures and running seminars. But doubts persisted and when I returned to Israel in the summer of 1978 to gather enough research material to finish the book, I was unsure what path I was travelling. One fact I particularly wanted to determine, which was only marginally related to the book, was whether an Arab village existed on the site that was now present-day Kibbutz Amiad. A friend put me in touch with a sympathetic official at the Lands Administration office who was fairly sure there had been such a village, but I never followed up on my enquiry.

I was far more conscious of the political climate in Israel and of the views and feelings about the country of people I met. Steve Israel, an Oxford History graduate in his early twenties whom I knew from Habonim, had recently finished his basic army training and was a member of Kibbutz Bet Haemek. He had a brother living on Kibbutz Mevo Hama on the Golan Heights, in occupied territory. We met in Jerusalem while he was on leave.

Steve was critical of the army. He suggested that it did nothing to strengthen Zionist feeling, rather the opposite. He seemed weighed down by his concern about Israel's situation and was soon to go to a settlement in the occupied territories. He confessed to a certain sense of excitement when thinking about the prospect in isolation, but he opposed government policy on creating settlements and said that he was certain that he would not be going there at all were it not for the army. And yet he spoke of the territories as something no one would want to give back anyway. A number of other members of his unit harboured similar doubts about serving in occupied land, but like him, they were all new immigrants and older than their officers who seemed not at all concerned about such questions.

He sympathised with the Peace Now movement, founded earlier in 1978 after Israel invaded Lebanon in the Litani Operation in which 1,000 Lebanese and Palestinian civilians were killed and 150,000 civilians were forced to flee their homes in Southern Lebanon. But he could not understand the 'ridiculous arguments about a "secular democratic state" that go on among left-wing groups in Britain' because it was irrelevant to the reality in Israel. He thought it was one manifestation of unwarranted interference in Israel's affairs by diaspora Jews.

Two older Scottish immigrant friends I talked with had lived in Israel for 15 and 11 years respectively. Gerry Kelman, who remained closely engaged with the book project, had recently left his kibbutz and was working as an agricultural economist in the development town of Arad in the Negev desert. Yigal Levine was a professional Zionist who worked for an organisation assisting in the absorption of British immigrants and lived in a comfortable part of Tel Aviv. We discussed the prime minister, Menachem Begin, and the peace initiative of the Egyptian president, Anwar Sadat, who had made his dramatic visit to Jerusalem in November 1977. Talks were to begin in early September 1978 at Camp David to hammer out a peace treaty between Israel and Egypt. Both were critical of Begin. And yet both felt that despite being an important step, Sadat's gesture was not realistic and had not been backed up by any positive plans – as if merely by flying 'unexpectedly' to Israel, the entire conflict would be solved at a stroke. They saw the possibility of a separate agreement with Egypt as a first priority and criticised Begin's continuing settlement policy, but argued that the settlements were pawns in the negotiating game and that Sadat should realise that and play along.

I was given a much more complex and pessimistic view of what was going on in Israel by Shimon Applebaum, a 50-something professor of archaeology at Tel Aviv University who had studied at Oxford. He was deeply critical of the situation and spoke of the state more or less cracking up from the inside. Back in 1961 he had written about the corruption in Israeli society and the weakness of Israeli democracy, so this was not a new development. The failure of the left in the last elections was symptomatic of the problems. He thought few people cared about democracy enough to fight to keep it alive. The danger had become very real since Begin came to power because 'the revisionists don't give a damn about democracy'. He believed that the Labour Alignment should have gone to the electorate on the basis of a full socialist programme. Pragmatism might have been fine in pre-state days but now it was destroying the fabric of the state.

Despite this pessimism, Shimon Applebaum still called himself a Zionist, 'but in a critical sense'. He saw nothing in Sadat's visit that changed what the Arabs were offering and believed that Begin had so far made all the concessions. He believed that the 'West Bank Arabs' did not want to return to be part of Jordan, nor did they want to be part of Israel. Yet their prosperity was tied to what Israel had done for them, even though they had been reluctant to take things like electricity and water. But they now believed that Israel would soon be pulling out so they were taking advantage of linking up to Israeli utilities.

More revealing perhaps were a few chance experiences of the reality of modern Israel. Three incidents I witnessed disturbed me, the first when I was at a petrol station with a friend, Tessa, with whom I had been staying in Jerusalem. An Arab attendant came to fill the car's tank and accidentally broke the lock on the petrol cap. The manager of the station refused to take any responsibility and forced the Arab to sign an admission of negligence. He meekly agreed. Tessa was furious at the manager and angry with herself because she did not want to get the attendant into trouble.

A few days later I was travelling by bus in the Negev desert from Arad to Beer Sheva when two Bedouin women carrying very young children climbed aboard. A young boy, probably about ten, had been sitting next to a soldier, shooting him excited and admiring glances, but the soldier then vacated his seat for the women and moved down the bus. One of the Bedouin women moved to sit in the vacant seat but the boy tried to stop her. The boy's mother insisted that he let the woman sit down, but he angrily refused. We, the passengers, all insisted that the Bedouin woman be allowed to sit, but the boy still angrily refused to sit next to her and pushed past her to sit somewhere else. He spent the rest of the journey mocking the woman's Arab accent.

The third incident occurred when Tessa drove me to an appointment and on the way we stopped at the cemetery in Rehovot, where her father had been buried earlier in the year, so that she could water the flowers on his grave. When we got to the graveside, she noticed that the year of his death, '1978', had been roughly removed. We found one number, '7', on the ground. Tessa called over a cemetery attendant who was very sympathetic and said 'It must be Arabs who did it.' She asked him some questions and we learned that the gates to the cemetery were not locked at night. Back in the masonry workshop, the mason agreed with the attendant and blamed the vandalism on 'Arabs'.

*   *   *

Back in England, I resumed my doctoral studies and lecturing in October, anxious to get my academic career back on track. But the teaching was unrewarding and the research going nowhere. I continued working sporadically on the youth movement book. But as I looked back over what I had already written, I was more conscious than ever that I had not sufficiently questioned my own assumptions about the subject matter.

In late January 1979, my mother, who was only 59, died in the middle of the night, of a massive and unexpected heart attack. The following morning close family gathered at my parents' house. It was a bitterly cold day, one of those days in the depths of winter that seem made for death.

Not long after she died I decided to abandon my doctorate and discontinue teaching at Brighton Polytechnic after the end of the academic year. I'm sure her death had something to do with my decision. In almost unseemly haste I applied for a job as research officer at the Institute of Jewish Affairs (IJA), a body I knew nothing about. The post involved research and writing on issues affecting Jews throughout the world, editing and publishing responsibilities, as well as assisting in the management of the research programme. But this move was not as impulsive as it seemed.

Over the previous months I had been giving a lot of thought to how I might renew my academic ambitions and, for a while, I considered looking at the rise of antisemitism in Germany, specifically the influence of Richard Wagner on the development of Nazism. After much thought and discussion, I came to the conclusion that it was impractical, but the exercise was helpful; I realised how much more energised I felt about working on a subject that had some meaning for me personally. By pursuing a career in researching modern historical and contemporary issues affecting Jews, I could combine my writing and academic interests. Against this background, my decision to apply for the post at the IJA made much sense.

I was called for an interview and learnt in May that I had been successful. I then faced an immediate crisis of conscience as to whether to accept the offer of the post. Perhaps it was a need for a more structured existence, for the chance to throw myself wholeheartedly into one fulfilling project, which finally led me to say yes. Or perhaps I thought my mother would have approved.

The IJA was the research arm of the World Jewish Congress, the body founded in 1936 to represent the political interests of Jewish communities worldwide. The WJC's Geneva representative, Gerhart Riegner, became internationally known for alerting the world in August 1942 to the Nazis' plans to murder the Jews of Europe. He was appointed secretary general of the WJC in 1965.

Established in New York in 1942, the IJA's main tasks were documenting the effect of the Nazi onslaught on Jews and developing the legal principles for obtaining post-war reparations from Germany for its crimes. The reparations agreement that Nahum Goldmann, the WJC's president, concluded with the German Federal Republic in 1952 was based on the IJA's work.

The IJA was moved to London, after a decision to close it was reversed, and it reopened in 1967 in Jacob's Well Mews in the West End near Baker Street. The head of the WJC's European branch, Dr Stephen J. Roth, an expert in international law, was appointed director. Born in 1915, Roth was from the provincial Hungarian town of Gyöngyös and held a doctorate in law from Budapest University. When the Germans took control of the country in 1944 he became active in the Zionist underground, helping to organise the escape of Jews across the border to Romania. He was arrested by the Gestapo, taken into custody and held for three months. He narrowly escaped being sent to Auschwitz and was released in September. After the war he became director of the WJC office in Budapest and in 1947 he moved to Britain to become general secretary of the WJC British Section.

Roth had a sharp mind, an immense capacity for work and a furious temper. From 1967 to 1980 he had a dual role as professional head of the WJC in Britain and Europe. He was also a major player in British Jewish politics as an elected official of both the Board of Deputies of British Jews (BoD) and the British Zionist Federation (ZF). An astute political operator, he developed an agenda for the IJA that enabled him to work independently with high-level Jewish and non-Jewish academics and political figures in the UK, continental Europe, Israel and America. The key to his independence, which was resented by British Jewish leaders and by leading American figures in the WJC, was the fact that almost the entire budget for the Institute came from the WJC (though part of it was from the World Zionist Organisation, WZO), which provided the funds, year after year, with only the minimum of variation and little scrutiny. Moreover, despite being an independent registered UK charity and a not-for-profit company limited by guarantee, the IJA's governance structures were purely formulaic.

Roth's programme of research, publications and public activities dealt with a wide range of Jewish issues including Israel's international position and changing perceptions of Zionism. The problems facing Jews under communism, new developments in Christian-Jewish relations and the state of antisemitism were covered in three semi-academic journals. He set up a high-level experts' panel to discuss human rights in international law. Practically every month there was a well-attended lecture at Chatham House. Current affairs seminars were held at Jacob's Wells Mews. And in an attempt to play a role in policy-making, Roth set up a Policy Planning Group in the late 1970s chaired by the late Stuart Young (chairman of the Board of Governors of the BBC from 1983 to 1986 and brother of Lord David Young), which included prominent Jewish businessmen, politicians, academics and community leaders.

To oversee the research work of the institute, Roth established a research board. Its first chairman was Sir Keith Joseph, but he resigned when appointed a minister in the Thatcher government. Choosing Joseph was no indication of Roth's politics. Stephen was schooled in a political context which demanded that Jewish concerns be pursued through good relations with all mainstream political forces. Joseph was replaced by Lord Lever, the former MP, Treasury minister and millionaire Labour peer from Manchester, who lived in style in Eaton Terrace.

The Research Board was stacked with academic luminaries including the historian Professor Elie Kedourie, the legal expert Professor Herbert Hart and the scientist Professor Albert Neuberger. In those early days of my role at the IJA I found it difficult to understand how Kedourie could reconcile his opposition to nationalism with membership of a group most of whom I took to be strongly inclined towards Zionism. But I soon realised that he had no sympathy for Arabs and that not all the members of the Board were as Zionistically-inclined as I had at first assumed.

As I learnt more about these unfamiliar worlds I became increasingly aware of and stimulated by the diversity of diaspora Jewish life. The IJA enabled me to engage with intellectual and academic issues of Jewish interest without needing to declaim my allegiance to Israel or Zionism. I was still a Zionist. But having been involved, on a very personal level, for ten years in the theory and practice of Zionism, and feeling that the whole episode had left me confused and rudderless, I didn't want to be part of anything that involved the *promotion* of Zionism.

The national origins of IJA staff reflected the fate of the European Jewish diaspora: most were Eastern and Central European Jewish émigrés, who had been forced out of continental Europe either by the Nazis or later by the communists. Roth's deputy, Dr Elizabeth ('Ergie') Eppler, was a tough, chain-smoking Hungarian Jew, who managed to escape from Hungary with her mother before the Auschwitz deportations began. Dr Lukasz Hirszowicz was head of the Soviet and East European department. A brilliant Polish-Jewish intellectual and academic who lectured part-time at the LSE, he was fluent in at least six languages. Formerly a dedicated communist, he spent the war years in Palestine at the Hebrew University, Jerusalem. After returning to post-war Poland to build a new communist society, along with 20,000 other Jews he fell foul of the thinly disguised antisemitism of the Polish regime in 1968 and was forced to leave.

As in all small institutions, daily life at the IJA was a soap opera, made peculiarly complex because of the almost bewildering mix of languages, accents, customs, habits and cultural preferences. But, though a cliché, it was also like attending the 'university of life'. I benefited from the knowledge, wisdom, judgement and mental agility of some of my colleagues in ways that I only came fully to appreciate years later.

Of all the staff, the only seriously active Zionist was Roth. As for the rest, some felt strongly connected to Israel – Ergie Eppler went to live there when she retired in 1983 – but for the most part, Israel and Zionism did not seem to dominate their lives. After being forced to leave their countries, all the émigrés had the choice to go to Israel to live and the fact that they chose not to indicates that they didn't have Zionism knocking on the door of their Jewish identities in the insistent way in which it had been, and still to a certain extent was, knocking on mine.

I thought my stay at the IJA would only be temporary, a stepping stone to something else. This seemed likely as I began to understand the organisational, personnel and leadership weaknesses of the place. They left me angry and frustrated but also posed a challenge, and I found myself becoming very involved in my work, regularly putting in extra hours. At first, I was commissioning and editing research papers, then I began revamping the entire publication programme. I also felt that I could produce better work than some of the writers and academics we engaged, and by early January 1980 had a list of ideas for papers I was interested in writing, including such topics as Arab aid to the third world, Islam's image in the West and the worldwide religious revival.

Gradually, Israel's hold on me was loosening but I felt no anger or bitterness about the past. I was more concerned with forging a career, remarrying, setting up a more permanent home and encountering new questions about the Jewish elements of my identity. Israel was a constant presence but one that I was now contemplating from outside the bubble. I understood more about where the country was located in the international arena and how others saw it, especially the Arab, Muslim and third worlds. And yet my emotional connection to the country was still strong and complex. Although I had no difficulty working in an environment in which, for a few people, Zionism was a central part of their lives, I felt very uncomfortable whenever I was expected to represent the IJA in any Zionist activist circles. When asked to do so I said I would only go on the understanding that I was there to listen and report back. To his credit, without hesitation Stephen Roth accepted my position and the role I said I could play.

But I was soon thrown into working on a project dealing with public perceptions of Zionism and Israel. This arose out of increasing concern among the Institute's key academic and intellectual advisers about the changing status of Israel and Zionism among Britain's thinking classes. In June 1980 Stephen was organising a high-level discussion on 'The erosion of liberal support for the Jewish position'. I was asked to set out the basic proposition and examine its validity in a background paper for the gathering. I maintained that the general Jewish perception was that 'support for Israel was not only automatic in liberal circles and among social democrats but Israel was also seen as an example of the strength of liberal pluralistic and social ideas'. But many felt that an attitude had developed that claimed that 'Israel and Jews throughout the world cannot continuously rely on European feelings of guilt regarding the Holocaust to ensure support of positions which are politically and morally unacceptable to the rest of the world ... Rather, there is now a clear tendency for liberal opinion to swing towards groups who openly oppose Israel, Zionism, the notion of Jewish nation and statehood, on the grounds that such groups also have legitimate rights which must be satisfied.' Nevertheless I doubted whether 'liberal support for the Jewish position' had ever been what was implied in the phrasing of the subject for discussion. 'It might be argued', I wrote, 'that such a notion was always largely theoretical. Jews have helped themselves – support or no support.' I then argued that the way the subject had been formulated was 'a thinly disguised way of claiming that support for Israel is no longer forthcoming – support for Israel's enemies is increasing', and I urged that, if this were so, we should look for an explanation both in what Israel and Jews were doing and in developments in the wider world. I suggested that Jews themselves were becoming more conservative, and that the liberal position in general had increasingly come under attack.

I was trying to indicate that if indeed there was a distancing from Zionism, it was partly justified: 'there is still very much the notion of "enlightened self-interest" at the root of the liberal position, [and] the move towards recognition of Palestinian rights satisfies principle and pragmatism at the same time'. But what was happening was to a great degree self-inflicted. 'The formulation [of the subject for discussion] actually reflects Jewish insecurities and uncertainties', I wrote, and the way forward was 'to confront ourselves', 'to move away, as far away as possible, from any notion of a monolithic "Jewish position" and rediscover and re-emphasise a Jewish pluralism which is not false consensus but represents genuinely differing points of view about the form, structure and values of possible Jewish societies – and this involves the development of a new relationship between Israel and the Diaspora'.

Others were also taking another look at Zionism in the light of changing world conditions. Towards the end of 1980 the WZO was planning to establish a series of international seminars to re-evaluate and regenerate Zionist ideology. Responding to this idea I wrote that 'for [an] ideology to be revalued, regenerated from within' could be said 'to be [a] contradiction in terms.' An organisation concerned with its survival did not seriously want to rethink its basic ideological premises but to stick with them and develop them in a new way according to new conditions. If the exercise was to have any meaning, I argued, it would need to ask very basic questions about the reality of the Jewish people's position today, 'the conditions of its existence', the actual nature of Israel-diaspora relations, how Israel has influenced the situation of Jews throughout the world since 1948. The answers to these questions would produce a very different picture of Jewry than the one that faced the Zionist thinkers of the past. 'Given this', I wrote, 'how is it possible that an ideology which derived from a certain set of conditions be of any validity for us today?' The establishment of Israel had resulted in Zionism becoming an arm of the state. 'This gells with my own notion of WZO being essentially a glorified travel agency, and turning all its outlets into travel agencies too ...The WZO has a product to sell ... and the seminar ... can even be seen as a sophisticated PR exercise.'

Further discussions involving Professor Julius Gould, the right-wing sociologist from Nottingham University, and the historian Professor Chimen Abramsky, head of the Department of Hebrew and Jewish Studies at University College London, and a former communist, prompted me to record more thoughts on Zionism and Israel-diaspora relations. 'The trappings of the Zionist movt. may have remained in existence after 1948 but the nature of the ideology upon which the movement depends for its *essence* changed irrevocably', I wrote. With the aim of establishing a state having been realised, 'the differences between [Zionist] groups only retained their validity within the framework of the society whose autonomy they had sought to achieve. In the Diaspora those differences rapidly came to lose their significance.'

My final comment in that 1980 paper was a modest plea for giving priority to Jewish universalism: 'Jews must make a more conscious contribution to finding solutions to the problems which afflict contemporary society, thus giving substance once again to the basic principles which liberals adhere to.'

*   *   *

I returned to Israel for two weeks in January 1981, this time as part of the staff running the quadrennial plenary assembly of the WJC. A transfer of power was taking place from an essentially European to a New York Jewish leadership that was very different, more aggressive and assertive. The ageing and infirm WJC president, Nahum Goldmann, had stepped down leaving the organisation rudderless and $40 million in debt, or so we were told. Standing in the wings, and eagerly promoted by US Jewish officials of the WJC, was

Edgar Bronfman, head of Seagrams Corporation, the drinks conglomerate. The main purpose of the assembly, which was held every four years, was to elect Bronfman to the presidency. 'This is assured', I wrote, 'since Edgar is paying for the lot ... But Edgar is no fool, neither does he seem to lack vanity. As he told us sitting round the hexagonal table in [Stephen] Roth's office (the table-top creaking and heaving throughout), "I don't just want to be elected, I want to be elected with *enthusiasm.*"' And indeed, the key purpose of the assembly was achieved. Not only was Bronfman elected unanimously, but Dr Israel Singer, Bronfman's close aide and adviser, became the WJC's executive director, eclipsing Gerhart Riegner, who remained secretary general in Geneva, but shorn of most of his power.

The organisation of the assembly, held in the cavernous Binyanei Ha'uma conference centre on the edge of Jerusalem, was completely chaotic. After three days confined in the tiny area encompassing the charmless and unappealing Apartotel in which we were staying and the brutal-looking conference centre, on the Saturday before the Assembly began we were able to get out for a long walk around the Old City and eat dinner at the Masswadeh restaurant in East Jerusalem. The place seemed remarkably peaceful. We walked everywhere in the Old City without any feelings of apprehension.

The experience of being back in Israel did not trigger any immediate new thoughts about my relationship with the country or my attitude towards Zionism. I was preoccupied with coming to terms with and negotiating my place in the wider WJC hierarchy. Assimilating these new circumstances seemed to take precedence over any reflective thinking. But it wasn't long after returning to the UK that I was once again exploring new ways of understanding Zionism and Israel.

In 1982 I reviewed a book by Professor Shlomo Avineri for our house journal *Patterns of Prejudice* (vol. 16, no. 3) and returned to the link between Jewish universalism and the aims of Zionism. In *The Making of Modern Zionism: The Intellectual Origins of the Jewish State*, Avineri argued that the 'founding fathers' of Zionism all saw the solution to the crisis of the Jewish people in universalistic terms. '[T]he crisis of the twentieth century is posing a threat not only to Jewish people but to the world at large. Therefore the solution to this crisis cannot just be a particularist redemption of the Jews; it will have to involve a universal redemption', Avineri wrote.

I thought the book was important because it clearly set out to show that the Zionism of Menachem Begin, Israel's prime minister and heir to the legacy of Jabotinsky, was antithetical to the fundamentals of Zionism. When Avineri wrote in the preface that 'the politics of the day sometimes push Zionist propaganda into apologetics and rhetorical self-righteousness, both of which do injustice to the profound historical and theoretical sources of Zionism', this was an unmistakable reference to the particularist political path that Begin's Likud government was following.

Avineri also confronted the question of the role that Palestine's indigenous Arab population was assigned in Zionist thought. He argued that some thinkers allowed for an Arab nationalist movement and some didn't. But Zionism was a complex idea, an ongoing and 'far-reaching *social* revolution', so it would eventually accommodate Palestinian nationalism too. It was an ideology that championed 'the supremacy of the public, communitarian, and social aspects at the expense of personal ease, bourgeois comfort, and good life of the individual.' Consequently, Zionism was a 'permanent revolution' that 'has ultimately no chance unless it constantly revolutionizes Jewish life in Israel and stops it from coagulating into the traditional historical moulds of Jewish social and economic behaviour'.

Avineri clearly felt that the Zionist movement had drifted from the central core of Zionist ideas and that re-evaluating the essence of Zionism – as he defined it – would help bring it back to its true purpose. If it were true, as I believed, that 'Zionism [has] become the ideological arm of the government of the state of Israel', I wrote in my review, Avineri's '"permanent revolution" has certainly lost its way or has been swallowed up by the bureaucratization of the state and the Zionist movement. It is, frankly, difficult to conceive of established institutions being in a state of permanent revolution.'

I was still fundamentally sympathetic to the idea of an active Zionist movement, though I personally did not want to be involved in it, and therefore part of me wanted to believe that Avineri was correct in seeing Likud Zionism as an aberration. And yet I thought that the reality of Israel just before the 1982 Lebanon War proved the opposite, so I found Avineri's central argument unconvincing. The war, and in particular the Sabra and Chatilla Palestinian refugee camp massacres in September 1982, seemed far removed from Avineri's 'far-reaching social revolution'. The public backlash against Israel was severe. The view in the Jewish community was that the media had been particularly harsh on Israel and extremely biased, having published distorted and misleading stories and pictures. But there was also deep concern about the criticism of Israel coming from intellectual and academic sources, and growing worry that it was antisemitic. By 1983, disquiet about attitudes to Zionism, and in particular the growth of anti-Zionism, had intensified.

In response to these developments, Stephen Roth decided to set up a small working party that year to plan a study of anti-Zionism, but with the principal aim of exploring the connection between anti-Zionism and antisemitism. The chairman of the group was Professor Sammy Finer, the Gladstone Professor of Government and Public Administration at Oxford University and one of the UK's leading post-war political scientists. There were three others: Stephen

Roth himself, Julius Gould and Lord Max Beloff, the prolific historian and former principal of the University College of Buckingham, a vain and highly opinionated right-wing public intellectual. I was attached to the group to record its discussions.

The group displayed a great deal of realism about the issue and at the first meetings made it clear that they thought there was no point in producing a book on anti-Zionism without considering what had happened to Zionism during the years that anti-Zionism had 'assumed such widespread dominance'. This was because everyone had deep reservations about what they called 'Begin's Zionism'. But the question was: How should this be done? I thought it would be wrong to see Zionism as a passive victim of an increasingly hostile world. Anti-Zionism would certainly have developed differently had there been no Six-Day War, no prolonged occupation, no building of permanent settlements on the West Bank, no Israeli government insisting that certain territories occupied in the Six-Day War were eternally part of Israel, no war in Lebanon, and so on. So to rescue Zionism from growing opposition was no simple matter.

In a proposal for the book I suggested looking specifically at the policies of the Begin government since 1977 and considering the extent to which they lay within mainstream Zionism. With Shlomo Avineri's thesis clearly in mind, I wrote: 'If it could be shown that Begin's Zionism is not true to the *essence*, the *core* of Zionism, it is then possible to say, or for the appropriate conclusion to be drawn, that Zionism cannot be held responsible for the excesses of the Begin government.' But I concluded, quite categorically, that 'it is impossible to suggest that Begin's Zionism is so far outside the mainstream of Zionism that it cannot even be considered legitimate. The history of the Zionist movement simply does not support this contention … Avineri's argument is a powerful presentation of the case for a *dominant* trend in Zionism but I do not believe it can be used to ostracise Begin's Zionism.'

The key problem, I suggested, was that there was a great deal of confusion as to precisely what both anti-Zionism and Zionism were – anti-Zionism was used both to describe opposition to Zionist ideology and opposition to the policies of the government of the state of Israel, and the two were clearly not synonymous. But certainly the state of Israel's 'tool for realising Zionism is the *Zionist movement*.' As for Zionism, with the Zionist movement now an arm of the government of the state, 'its primary functions, as manifested in Zionist federations and official Zionist groups throughout the world, are to defend the interests of the state, to act as a public relations firm for the state and to encourage immigration. There is nothing independent or spontaneous about the Zionist movement. Its structure was, in effect, frozen in 1948.'

To cut through this confusion, I argued that we should establish a stripped-down descriptive definition of Zionism that encapsulated the essence of the ideology. The state of Israel had been established so 'one can no longer say that Zionism is the *idea* of establishing a Jewish state in Eretz Israel'. I suggested this definition: '*Zionism is the principle that the State of Israel belongs not only to its citizens but also to the entire Jewish people.*'

It now seems bizarre that I seemed to see no confusion between talking about a country belonging to its citizens, a significant proportion of whom were not Jewish, and at the same time belonging to Jews who didn't even live there and had no intention of doing so. But I was transparent about what I was aiming to achieve. 'I believe this is a very useful definition as far as our purposes are concerned', I wrote in my paper for the group. 'It highlights the neutrality of the essence of Zionism. It clears the way for identifying precisely what anti-Zionism is. It makes clear that the policies of the government of the State of Israel have to be judged according to the criteria whereby all democratic political systems are judged and not according to the purity or otherwise of its Zionism. It shows that the major ideological debates in Israeli society – about the territories, the character of the society, the question of religion and state – are not debates about Zionism but about the kind of issues which are fundamental to any pluralistic society.' Some of these statements are precise opposites of the truth – Zionism isn't 'neutral', ideological debates about Israeli society *are* about Zionism – but the central point about judging Israel's policies on the basis of universal democratic norms was then, and remains now, fundamentally valid.

The first chapter of the proposed book would establish the minimalist definition of Zionism 'which allows us to take the policies of the Israeli government out of the debate – we neither have to justify these policies nor condemn them, because they have nothing to do with the essence of Zionism' – thereby avoiding providing ammunition for antisemites, the fear expressed by Finer and the others at the outset. The rest of the book would be a study of anti-Zionism, not of the relationship between anti-Zionism and antisemitism – although this would 'clearly figure significantly in the study since in classifying forms of anti-Zionism it will be necessary to identify whether or not they are antisemitic ... [T]he distinctions will serve to show Jews and genuine anti-Zionists that thinking Jews are indeed aware that not all criticism of Zionism and Israel is antisemitic, and furthermore that only certain kinds of criticism should actually be labelled anti-Zionist in the first place.' By a tortuous route, I finally arrived at a position which I believe holds to this day.

I was obviously desperate to find a frank and realistic way of criticising actions of the State of Israel without throwing the baby – Zionism – out with the bathwater. When the group discussed my paper, Finer accepted my proposed approach without question. Gould, on the other hand, dismissed my entire argument as 'procedure' and lacking any 'intellectual merit'. He pressed his view so strongly that Finer gave in. Roth did not want to take sides. (Beloff couldn't attend the discussion.) The book proposal was shelved and instead Roth and some academic colleagues in the US and Israel decided to hold a conference on anti-Zionism and antisemitism, which took place later in 1983. Out of that conference eventually emerged (in 1990) a book of essays, *Anti-Zionism and Antisemitism in the Contemporary World*, edited by one of the participants, Robert S. Wistrich, who, at the time of publication, was Professor of Modern European and Jewish History at the Hebrew University Jerusalem. Gould's essay in the book, originally published in *Survey of Jewish Affairs 1985*, reveals why he was so opposed to my proposed plan in 1983: essentially, he believed that most anti-Zionism *was* antisemitism since it was 'a form of collective discrimination against the Jewish people that recalled past (or present) denials to *individual* Jews of equality of citizen-rights' (p. 188).

*   *   *

During the early 1980s I began researching and writing on Middle East issues, international politics and global Jewish concerns. The Institute's approach was to analyse these matters in an objective, academic manner, from the perspective of how they affected Jews worldwide and Israel. In theory we were free to reach whatever conclusions to which examination of the data led us. And to a large degree, this is how things worked. But there was a limit, never formally defined, beyond which we could not go. The welfare of the State of Israel was a paramount consideration, the assumption being that most criticism on the international stage was illegitimate. Where issues like the position of Jewish communities worldwide, antisemitism and the situation of Jews under communism were concerned, there were no similar kinds of defensive assumptions being made. Overall, this meant that as a researcher, I was not under any pressure to pursue an overtly propagandistic line. I could more or less follow my nose and go where the material took me. As a result I developed a perspective that did not automatically interpret every statement or stand on Israel by international, Arab, Islamic and third-world bodies as based on prejudice and unjustified vilification.

In effect, I was educating myself about Middle East politics, the position of Israel in the world, the state of world Jewry, the image of Jews and Israel in the media and the rise of political Islam. Apart from the material produced by the BBC at Caversham, which gave a perspective on the Arab, Muslim, non-aligned and third worlds that it was impossible to develop just from reading the mainstream press, it was my responsibility to scan numerous periodicals from *The Economist, Foreign Affairs*, the *Near East Review* through to *MERIP*, the *Arab Voice* and the *Journal of Palestine Studies*. While the brief was to look for negative material on Jews and Israel, the effect of absorbing information and analysis from these periodicals was to give me a broader perspective and enable me to understand the motives and positions of 'the other side', while not neglecting or minimising the concerns of Israel.

But my autodidactic experience continued beyond the formal responsibilities I had at the IJA. In 1982, I offered to share my office in the Institute's new premises in Hertford Street, Mayfair, with the former editor of the *Jewish Chronicle* (*JC*), William Frankel, a major figure in British Jewry. He had persuaded the WJC to fund the publication of a yearly volume of essays entitled *Survey of Jewish Affairs*, of which he would be the editor. It seemed like a good opportunity to become involved in what was an interesting publishing project that might help my career. I offered my help and William was delighted. This was the beginning of a friendship that lasted until William's death aged 90 in 2007 and had a major impact on my life.

I ended up editing most of the essays in the *Survey*, liaising with the writers, and suggesting topics for William's introduction, which he wrote himself during the first few years, but which later I drafted for him. Much of the material we published was of a very high quality – generous fees were paid – and far from propagandistic. It certainly broadened my horizons and brought me into contact with scholars, authors and journalists from the US, Israel, France, Germany, Italy and elsewhere. In 1988 William agreed to appoint me as assistant editor.

It was through William that my self-education in Jewish affairs and more specifically Middle East realities continued in another way. He introduced me to his successor as editor of the *JC*, Geoffrey Paul, just as Geoffrey had hired an editor for a new analysis section of the paper called 'Middle East Mirror'. David Spanier of *The Times* was an international affairs expert who loved playing and writing about poker. Affable and easy-going, David was looking for informed Jewish writers and in May 1982 commissioned me to write a piece on the restoration of Israel's diplomatic ties with African states, which had been cut at the time of the 1973 Yom Kippur war. David liked my work and I wrote regularly for him – a piece virtually every two weeks for six months. I enjoyed the exposure and the discipline of producing work of a specific length by a set deadline. What I wrote was intelligent, balanced and readable; nothing startling or radical. And I learnt a great deal from the reading, research and thinking I had to do for the articles. Eventually, for reasons of lack of space and a drop in advertising revenue, the 'Middle East Mirror' pages were axed and David Spanier ceased to work for the *JC*. I also heard that there was considerable disquiet among in-house journalists who were miffed that freelancers were getting these commissions.

Meanwhile, a third avenue of extra-mural enlightenment opened up. My IJA colleague Michael May and I created the Younger Generation Group, together with Gordon Wasserman, a senior civil servant who was a member of the Central Policy Review Staff, the in-house government think tank set up by the former Labour prime minister Jim Callaghan, which Margaret Thatcher was about to axe. This was an informal group of Jewish academics, community workers, writers, professionals, rabbis and political activists, aged between 25 and 45, who came together once a month for frank discussions about political, communal, international and religious issues affecting Jews. It appeared impossible to hold these elsewhere in the Jewish community, not because discussion was censored but rather because the prevailing view was that most ideological and political issues affecting Jews had been settled. Everyone was said to be uniting around Israel. It was quite clear from the enthusiasm and interest shown in our group that these matters were by no means done and dusted. For the first time, I came into contact with anti-Zionists and a sustained critical discourse on Israel.

6

ROCKING THE BOAT

Tony Lerman ... has fallen foul of a power-mad cabal who got him the chop [as Editor of the Jewish Quarterly] because he didn't conform to their particular, paranoid way of looking at things.

Bernard Kops, 1985

Antony Lerman combines Jewish self-hate and loony Leftism in a blanket attack against the Anglo-Jewish community in general and in particular against those of us who have taken a stand against anti-Israel bias and the new Left-wing antisemitism in the British media.

Sir Alfred Sherman, 1986

Towards the end of 1983, I became involved with a group of people who were trying to provide support for the ailing Jacob Sonntag, the editor of the *Jewish Quarterly* (*JQ*) magazine. Founded by Sonntag in 1953, the *JQ* represented one of the very few outlets for Jewish cultural expression and political thinking in Britain. Sonntag dedicated his life to the magazine and constantly struggled to obtain financial support. Contributors were paid intermittently. Most people, including prominent writers, wrote for free. The ever-present financial problems were unsettling but consonant with the image of the magazine as an outpost of free-thinking, left-of-centre ideas. Although Sonntag was a stubborn, intensely serious and sometimes difficult man, writers were loyal to him and he commanded great respect. In his person, life and work he bridged the rich cultural world of East European Jewry and contemporary Jewish life in Britain. 'He believed in the need to continue, somehow, in this country, the tradition of European Jewish intellectual life that had been shattered by the Nazis', wrote Renée Winegarten in the edition of the *JQ* marking his death in 1984. 'He believed that there must be, here, a forum for serious and carefully considered discussion where thoughts and feelings could be discussed without fear or favour.'

Sonntag always ran the magazine largely single-handed and continued to do so despite being ill. The immediate need was some practical help in editing, production, distribution and fundraising. I could offer help in the first two areas and soon found myself working directly with Sonntag on the current issue. If he was aware how ill he was or how much he needed editorial help, he certainly didn't show it.

Sonntag died on 27 June 1984. With the trust and support of Jacob's wife Batyah, his daughter Ruth, and the backing of his long-time collaborator, Rafael (Felek) Scharf, an art dealer who had done more than any other person associated with the magazine to keep it alive, I was soon formally appointed editor. Together with Michael May, Colin Shindler, a chemistry lecturer and Soviet Jewry activist, and Ruth, I produced the edition of the *JQ* marking Sonntag's death. The cover image was a copy of his portrait painted by his friend, the artist Josef Herman. The issue carried his last editorial, which was devoted to Israel's failure to live up to the promises of its founding ideals and to the hope that those ideals could still be fulfilled by 'those in Israel who are working towards genuine peace and real progress'.

In my first editorial in the issue produced at the end of 1984 (vol. 31, nos 3–4), I set out what I wanted the magazine to be, stressing that it had 'always functioned according to the fundamental principle that pluralism and tolerance must prevail in the Jewish community – a principle that is not greatly favoured in some sectors of Anglo-Jewry today'. I reviewed how the position of Jews had changed since 1953 when the *JQ* was launched and how this was reflected in what had happened to Israel:

> Since 1953, the state of Israel has fought four wars – the last war bringing to the surface deep divisions in the Jewish world and producing new tensions in the already problematic relationship between Israel and the Diaspora. Inside Israel there is a far-reaching debate about the nature of the state, a debate thrown into sharp relief by the election of an outspoken Jewish racist to the Knesset. In 1953 Israel was widely seen as a beacon of progress and enlightenment; today much of the public discourse of international affairs contains ritual condemnation of the state and a permanent attempt to undermine its legitimacy. Zionism has become a dirty word. How far this attack on Zionism is a disguise for old or new antisemitism and how far it arises from a genuine disagreement with and a critique of the present character and policies of the state is a question Jews must urgently seek to answer. It is far too easy to raise the spectre of antisemitism, call for unity and thereby ignore the changes in the Jewish position in the world that these developments represent.

Referring to the Holocaust and how politicians and ideologues feel free to make political use of this 'tragedy of tragedies', I wrote: 'The perceived threat of another attempt to annihilate Jewry is too readily invoked for the purpose of stifling genuine and crucial differences of opinion. Jewish life is not only about survival.'

In my second editorial, published early in 1985, entitled 'The politics of antisemitism', I spelt out the arguments then gaining ground that the attacks on Israel and Zionism were examples of a new antisemitism and proceeded to explain why they were flawed. I conceded that 'Some who wish to deny Israel any basis of existence are certainly antisemitic and their speeches in UN forums show this clearly by the Stürmer-like imagery they employ.' But, I argued, only a very small number do this: 'The fact is – and this is rarely stressed – opposition to the ideology of Jewish self-determination is unacceptable on its own terms and can be proved to be so. Calling the attempt to delegitimize Israel antisemitic is effectively an escape from the need both to argue the case for Zionism and to destroy the anti-Zionist case by attacking its premises.'

Prefiguring arguments that would become common in the first decade of the twenty-first century, I wrote: 'Anti-Zionism as a credible threat to Western civilization is an exaggerated notion ... The danger in seeing anti-Zionism as a form of antisemitism is that we impute to the anti-Zionist argument a power it does not possess and an effect it has not achieved.'

> The real crises [for the Jewish people] are in Zionism, in the nature of the Jewish state and in relations between what should be an independently-minded and assertive Diaspora and Israel. It is because these issues are so troubling and so difficult to confront that the source of anxiety is sought in the age-old common enemy: antisemitism. In Israel the debate on these issues goes on daily in the newspapers. Here, the debate is avoided. Rather than concede that the Arabs have an ideological case, we treat their anti-Zionism as prejudice. Rather than admit that Israel's mistakes fuel anti-Zionism, we prefer to brand critics as antisemites.

I wanted to highlight the damage this was doing to how Jews saw themselves:

> What we are now witnessing is the use of the politics of antisemitism as a means of legitimation, a form of self-definition. This holds true as much for the political right as it does for the political left. It is almost as if making a stand on antisemitism the central feature of one's general position in the Jewish world is a *sine qua non* of contemporary Jewish identity. Israel has been called 'the organizing idiom of Jewish self-definition' but it sometimes seems as if this is more truly the function of antisemitism.

Presaging the devaluation of the term antisemitism two decades later, I wrote: 'Antisemitism has not disappeared. It exists on many levels and must be watched and fought. But it does that fight no service, and painfully reduces our much needed possibilities for self-understanding, to use the word so widely that, at one and the same time, it means everything – and nothing.'

Before becoming editor of the *JQ* I had hardly said anything in public about my views on the politicisation of antisemitism or on Israel and Zionism. The editorial changed all that. I was not consciously aiming to have an impact outside of the small and select readership, but I knew that my views were certainly not 'mainstream'. Nevertheless, I did not think that they would generate political controversy even though the magazine was read by some in the Jewish establishment.

It therefore came as a surprise to hear that the editorial, and an article I published in the same edition by David Rosenberg of the Jewish Socialists Group (JSG), entitled 'Racism and antisemitism in contemporary Britain', had angered members of the Board of Deputies of British Jews (BoD). Eric Moonman, the former Labour MP for Basildon and chairman of the Board's Defence Committee, which oversaw the community's efforts to monitor and combat antisemitism, raised the matter at a BoD meeting. Moonman was the director of Group Relations Educational Trust (a body raising funds for Jewish defence work). Stephen Roth, who was very involved with both the BoD and the Zionist Federation, told me and my colleague Michael May that he was very unhappy about the possibility of this controversy having a negative impact on the IJA. I was bemused by all the fuss and had no idea that the affair might develop into a major communal controversy. But I soon learned that at the full meeting of the BoD on 28 April, where Moonman raised the matter, the Israel Committee chairman, Arieh Handler, leader of the orthodox Mizrachi Zionist movement in the UK, had promised that it could be discussed at the next meeting of his committee. This took place on 1 May, with Eric Moonman present, as well as some other members of the Defence Committee, and attending by invitation was Mr H. Bar On, deputy director-general of the Israel Foreign Ministry. The two vice-presidents of the BoD, Dr Lionel Kopelowitz and Martin Savitt, were there, together with other BoD officers.

In the afternoon of 1 May, a BoD official called and 'invited' me to attend. Aware that I would be reprimanded by the committee, I declined. I knew full well that it was likely to take the form of a McCarthyite tribunal. And I did not believe that they had any right whatsoever to discuss the *JQ*'s editorial policy.

The minutes of the meeting provide only a very cursory and bland summary of what was agreed. The premise of the discussion was that the BoD should 'take a stand on the current issue of the magazine'. The chairman 'stressed that the Jewish Quarterly was an independent magazine, in which those who wished to express their views were free to do so. There was, however, concern over the editorial and an article in the current issue.' Eric Moonman proposed a resolution which was adopted by the committee: 'The Israel Committee and the Defence Committee of the Board of Deputies, after a full discussion, express grave concern at the recent editorial and the article by David Rosenberg in the Jewish Quarterly, which can only hinder the efforts and credibility of the Board of Deputies and the Jewish Community generally, in its campaigns to fight anti-semitism and anti-Zionism.'

Only one member opposed the resolution, the elderly and learned Dr Schneir Levenberg, the UK representative of the Jewish Agency. In response the chairman said the BoD 'should be seen to be taking a lead on these matters so that the Community would know where the Board stood and where it did not stand'. He added that the 'discussion and the resulting resolution were not for publication'.

As I learned a few days later from a furious letter from Stephen Roth, addressed to me and Michael May, the *JQ* matter was the principal and most lengthy subject discussed at the meeting. Many members present demanded that Michael and I be asked to resign from the IJA and there was very strong condemnation of the offending issue of the magazine. But more worrying for Roth was a letter he had received, dated the day of the meeting, from one of the vice-presidents, Martin Savitt: 'Further to our conversation regarding the Rosenberg editorial [*sic*] in the current issue of the Jewish Quarterly, apart from my own views that David Rosenberg was given the platform that he seeks to attack the Board and Israel, I have received numerous complaints from members of the community. Most are concerned that Officers of the IJA are using the Jewish Quarterly to express political views and surely this cannot be right. I would hope that you look into this matter, because I have to say, from a personal point of view, I would not continue my membership with the Institute if policy matters were to be changed.'

In his letter to us, Roth insisted that our roles at IJA were incompatible with our roles on the *JQ* as long as the magazine dealt with 'political matters'. Only if the magazine reverted to its 'cultural/literary' role would he continue to allow us to retain our *JQ* responsibilities. We pointed out that the accusation that we had 'turned the *Jewish Quarterly* into a political magazine' was nonsense. It had always dealt with, and expressed editorial opinion about, political matters, including Israel and antisemitism. We strongly criticised his reaction to the criticisms of us and the IJA being made by Jewish establishment figures. One of the things that made us particularly angry was his attitude to the substance of what I wrote. As our letter put it: 'you have told us both directly within the last fortnight or so – that you yourself agree with the views expressed in [the editorial]. Indeed, what Tony has written there stems directly from everything we feel we have learned, under your guidance, at the IJA. And yet, astonishingly, you make no reference to this in your letter. Instead, you appear to distance yourself from such views.' We also pointed out that the yoking together of my editorial and the article by David

Rosenberg, as if they represented the same views and were part of a concerted and coordinated attack on Israel and the leadership of the community, was completely unjustified. One of my aims was to refute a principal tenet of Rosenberg's position: 'Rosenberg's case is predicated on precisely the increase in and exaggeration of antisemitism against which Tony argues in the editorial ... Quite a number of people immediately realised that Tony was arguing against the Rosenberg position and singling [the JSG] out as one of the groups that use antisemitism as a means of legitimation. Strange how certain people on the Board of Deputies have not recognised this.' But on one important point we made it clear that we agreed with David Rosenberg: 'that there should be open debate about the question of antisemitism'.

There were four substantive issues raised in this controversy: what could be said critically about Israel; whether communal policy on antisemitism could be openly discussed and criticised; whether the leadership of the Jewish community could be subjected to scrutiny and criticised if necessary; and whether all of these things could be done by someone working for what was considered a mainstream Jewish organisation. But there were other, more complex communal factors that affected the way the controversy unfolded, principally the impending election of a new president of the BoD.

One of Roth's closest allies was Martin Savitt, one of two BoD vice-presidents. Much of his support came from people active in the defence arms of the community and from the Association of Jewish Ex-Servicemen (AJEX). Savitt therefore saw that the *JQ* affair might easily damage his chances of becoming president unless he was seen to take a very robust position against the editorial and the Rosenberg article. In addition, given that the IJA had become implicated in the whole affair, Savitt, in his 1 May letter, felt it necessary to read the riot act to Roth as a sop to those whose knives were always out for the IJA director, but not in such a way as to jeopardise the support Roth was giving Savitt in his run at the presidency. The other candidate, Lionel Kopelowitz, was as furious about the *JQ* editorial and Rosenberg article as Savitt, but he drew his support from centre-right and orthodox Jewish circles and simply had to make clear his position in order to benefit from the affair. In the event, much to everyone's surprise, not least Martin Savitt's, Kopelowitz won the election and presided over probably the most ignoble and demeaning period in the BoD's history.

The *JQ* affair would not have become such a major communal controversy without the political background of the election of the new BoD president. But it also clearly showed the extreme sensitivity that prevailed in relation to what could be said about Israel and by whom. I was seen as giving succour to antisemites and anti-Zionists, and doing so within an establishment Jewish organisation. The JSG, which had a membership of about 100, was regarded as a kind of fifth column. Its vilification by the establishment bore absolutely no relation to its influence in the community. What riled the BoD was the fact that anyone could still follow the ideas of the pre-war Bund, the most popular Jewish political group in Eastern Europe. The Bund opposed Zionism and argued for diaspora autonomy, based around Yiddish culture in a wider socialist society, but it was virtually wiped out in Eastern Europe during the Holocaust. And after the war the Holocaust became the clinching argument for Zionism. The very idea that the Bund could continue to exist was a constant reproach. Zionism and Israel had become so integral to the Jewish community's self-perception, no challenge could be tolerated. But it was one thing to dislike the ideology and politics of the JSG; quite another for a large, well-established organisation like the BoD to develop such extreme paranoia about a small group of thoughtful people with radical ideas but practically no power.

The BoD had their say and the exchange of correspondence between May and me on the one hand and Stephen Roth on the other resolved nothing. As the weeks went by I felt under constant pressure. Combining the editorship of the *JQ* with my IJA responsibilities was increasingly difficult. It seemed 'impossible to do one thing or the other properly', I wrote in my diary. Although friends and colleagues who worked with me on the magazine were very supportive, I felt isolated and alone. And the continued reinvigoration of the *JQ* was in jeopardy.

Roth continued to put pressure on me. He simply could not tolerate any member of staff expressing views on antisemitism and Israel which might have a negative effect on the IJA's image in the community and his position in the BoD and the ZF. He insisted that my editorship of the *JQ* was not compatible with my duties at the IJA. I began to feel that I was being backed into a corner. My livelihood was now at stake. I was coming round to the view that I would have to resign. I wrote in my diary:

> I believe that this affair has brought to the surface the very worst aspects of Jewish life in this country: the inability of the self-styled establishment to allow the free expression of views on issues of Jewish importance; the attempt to suppress such expression by underhand, behind-the-scenes methods; allowing an unrepresentative handful of reactionaries to determine the nature of political debate within the Jewish community; threatening employees of Jewish organisations with the loss of their jobs because they express their views on political matters in print; the autocratic, fundamentally undemocratic nature of Jewish institutions; attacking an individual using hearsay, innuendo and unsubstantiated allegations; the imputation of guilt by association.

In a letter I wrote to my *JQ* colleagues I said: 'It frankly annoys me that the Jewish Chronicle, which knew about the goings on at the Board almost from the very beginning, has chosen not to publish a story about the affair.' Privately I wrote: 'I find it difficult to express the strength of my feelings about the behaviour of certain individuals within the Board of Deputies. Their behaviour has been bigoted, despicable and hypocritical.'

On 1 July I wrote to Roth informing him that I would resign from the editorship of the *JQ*. I told the trustees of the Jewish Literary Trust, which was responsible for managing the affairs of the magazine, and it was agreed that Colin Shindler would take over. Everyone knew of the pressures I faced, both political and personal, but at the meeting of the Trust where the decisions were taken, we did not dwell on these aspects and agreed that a press release would be issued which would give as my reasons for stepping down 'increased responsibilities at the Institute of Jewish Affairs'. This referred to the fact that I was being appointed editor of the Institute's journal on racism and antisemitism, *Patterns of Prejudice*.

Issued on 11 July, the press release included a statement from the chairman of the Trust, Louis Littman: 'Mr Lerman's decision was accepted with regret and reluctance ... The magazine has made marvellous progress in the last 15 months ... more than doubling its subscribers and generating lively interest in cultural and controversial issues. Tony Lerman has played a central role in achieving this progress.'

The *JC* carried the story on 19 July. After a perfunctory mention of the reasons given in the press release, the reporter got to the heart of the matter: 'The last issue to be edited by Mr Lerman aroused furious anger in some sections of the community. They were outraged at the editorial ... and at an article by Mr David Rosenberg, of the Jewish Socialists Group ... It was felt that Mr Lerman should not have allowed the publication of views contrary to official communal policy while at the same time working for a communal organisation, the IJA.'

The story sparked a war of words on the letters pages of the paper which went on continuously for seven weeks and – after a break for the Jewish festivals – into an eighth. Louis Littman and Colin Shindler separately took issue with the sensationalist tone of the *JC* story. Dr Lionel Kochan, a leading Jewish academic, wrote of his 'feeling of unease at your report ... that the editor ... has been replaced after publishing material that apparently displeased certain sections of the community', and raised doubts about what it meant for the independence of the magazine.

On 2 August a long lead letter expressed outrage and lambasted the BoD and 'the guardians of "official communal policy"', and said that my resignation 'can only cause dismay among those who value the cultural vitality and intellectual integrity of Anglo Jewry'. This was signed by the literary critic, Professor George Steiner; the novelists Bernice Rubens and Clive Sinclair; the historian of modern Israel, Dr Noah Lucas; the writer on Jewish theology, Hyam Maccoby; the publisher, editor and poet, Anthony Rudolf, and the writer and television producer, David Herman. A clutch of young, up-and-coming academics – David Cesarani, Bryan Cheyette, David Feldman and Steven Zipperstein – all of whom are now leading professors in their fields of history and literature, also signed. 'Once again', the signatories wrote, 'the official community has taken a step towards enforced conformity, crudely imposing a monopoly over the right to represent Jews and Jewish opinion.' Rabbi Julia Neuberger insisted that instead of attacking me, communal leaders should have 'defended to the last' my right to publish the editorial and the Rosenberg article. 'Instead, the reaction within the Board of Deputies and elsewhere seems to be a sign of precisely that paranoia which the offending editorial described ... For a long time now we have been told about "Jewish solidarity" and begged not to rock the boat in public. That was always reprehensible and distasteful. But the denial of a free press is quite different, for it implies a totalitarian view of the Jewish community where the expression of only some views is acceptable. I reject that view and despise it. And I am sure that I am not alone.' The playwright Bernard Kops wrote: 'Tony Lerman ... has fallen foul of a power-mad cabal who got him the chop because he didn't conform to their particular, paranoid way of looking at things.' The novelist and poet Emmanuel Litvinoff, who was not especially impressed with my editorial, was unequivocal: 'The Board of Deputies has no right whatever to summon [the *JQ*'s] editor and demand an explanation ... Nor has the Institute of Jewish Affairs any right to lean on him to resign on the grounds that it is his employer.'

But the reaction against me and these letters of support was strong too, even if extremely defensive. The chairman of the Israel Committee of the BoD, Arieh Handler, simply dismissed accusations that it wanted to censor views. He wrote: 'there would be little or no respect for the Board and its deputies if they did not take a stand on issues of concern to them, and to the community which elected them'. The chairman of the Defence Committee, Eric Moonman, was even more robust, claiming that nothing the BoD had done, in the 'one brief item of discussion at a two-hour meeting of the Israel Committee', had anything to do with my resignation. The outspoken right-wing lawyer Lionel Bloch attacked the correspondents: '[The radicals] are ready to fight to the last for the right of anti-Zionists to spout their tendentious splutterings, but I don't remember when any of them got exercised because those who disagree with them are denied space in the publications of the Left.'

I was able to supply sympathetic letter writers with facts because I had a copy of the so-called 'confidential' minutes of the Israel Committee meeting and the BoD employee who was secretary of the Committee, Paul Usiskin, who later became Chairman of Peace Now UK, had taped the proceedings and secretly given me a copy. The issue eventually became almost exclusively a matter of freedom of speech and whether the BoD had any business whatsoever in treating what was published in the *JQ* as a matter for concern. The issues that provoked the ire of the establishment – Israel and antisemitism, and whether someone working in a major communal organisation had a right to express view on these subjects that were not considered mainstream by the establishment – were pushed aside. Some people called on the *JC* to republish the offending editorial, but the editor, Geoffrey Paul, declined to do this. All along, he refused to take an editorial position on the controversy. He simply held the coats while everyone else slugged it out.

With the BoD elections out of the way and Savitt defeated, Roth wrote a very long letter to the *JC* portraying my appointment as editor of *Patterns of Prejudice*, the IJA's house journal, as the *real* reason for my resignation as editor of the *JQ*. No longer constrained by his backing of Savitt for the presidency he turned on the Board using his own inside knowledge of what had happened:

> The views [expressed in the journal] were simply condemned as heretical by those who feel they are the repositories of the only possible 'correct' interpretation of Jewish policies.
>
> Instead, the full authority of the Board of Deputies was sought to be brought down on the 'guilty' editor. Moreover, the deputy who started the attack [Eric Moonman] by raising the issue in the full publicity of a Board session referred to the fact that the editor and associate editor of the 'Jewish Quarterly' were communal officials, implying that they are thereby more subject to censorship; and while the outcome of the Board's Israel Committee was as innocuous as Mr Handler has described it, it is a fact that at that meeting the dismissal of Mr Lerman by the IJA (!) was demanded.

Stephen's letter was disingenuous and hypocritical. There was barely a hair's breadth between him and other members of the BoD on what discourse about Israel should be given space in the communal mainstream. It was about this time that he told me that there were no longer any serious ideological debates within the Jewish world since Zionism had become so dominant and all other ideologies of Jewish existence were irrelevant.

The *coup de grâce* was delivered the following week, on 30 August, by Dr Schneir Levenberg, who had been chairman of the Israel Committee and a BoD vice-president. Ponderous, but well-respected, Levenberg wrote: 'I strongly warned the Board's Israel Committee not to get involved in an issue which is not their concern; not to create a dangerous precedent of interfering in the editorial freedom of Anglo-Jewish publications. Those who pushed through an unfortunate resolution or kept silent must bear responsibility for an incident which brought damage to the representative body of British Jewry.'

In the autumn, the journal of the Reform Movement, *Manna*, devoted its editorial to the *JQ* affair, mounting a strong defence of freedom of speech and attacking the notion that 'we are a community with a single voice, united on all important issues'. 'Tony Lerman's offending editorial', it said, 'suggested that the community over-estimates the prevalence of antisemitism in the world and uses the cry of antisemitism to evade discussion of difficult issues relating to the policies of the State of Israel and the current direction of Zionism. A radical position. But may it not be stated?'

Early in 1986, the *Guardian* published an article by Walter Schwartz about how far British Jews should go in publicly criticising received ideas in the community. Asking 'Is anti-Zionism antisemitism?', and quoting the editor of the *JC* and the leading Reform rabbi of his day, Hugo Gryn, who both said 'yes', Schwartz wrote: 'This view is so entrenched that when it was refuted in the left-leaning Jewish Quarterly last year the editor, Tony Lerman, felt compelled to resign in the furore.' Schwartz continued: 'At a sad symposium on "intellectual freedom in the Jewish Community" recently organised by the same magazine, Lerman was honoured as a martyr and the uniquely outspoken Liberal rabbi Julia Neuberger said: "For many of us intellectual freedom exists because it is very difficult for us to be silenced."'

That 'sad' symposium, held on 15 December, was addressed by Steven Zipperstein, a lecturer in modern Jewish history at Oxford University. His remarks were published as a feature article for the *JC*, and subsequently in the *JQ* itself (no. 2, 1986). Zipperstein was critical of Anglo-Jewry's rigid tendency towards centralisation fed by constant fear of a Holocaust that the community never experienced. Unwilling to acknowledge the real diversity among British Jews, the establishment tried to marginalise people with unconventional views. 'Highbrow Jewish magazines, provocative editorials, Progressive rabbis who insist on speaking about the Middle East to audiences that do not already agree with them, curiously unpredictable Jewish intellectuals, and whoever else does not sullenly toe the line – all of these are marginalised and written off. If possible, as in the case of Tony Lerman ..., they are forced to quit.' Zipperstein argued strongly for the need to publish 'sometimes unpopular views':

> Let us not fool ourselves about this. If the Jewish Socialists' Group is anathematised because it promotes views that at one time, and not too long ago, captured the allegiance of far more East European Jews than did Zionism;

if Tony Lerman is forced to resign because he allows the 'Jewish Quarterly' to publish one article airing neo-Bundist views (along with an editorial intelligently and subtly criticising them), this does not mean that the Jewish communal leadership is merely obsessed with socialists.

Much more importantly, it means that it is fixated on unity and willing to sacrifice anyone, anything, any institution, any editor, any intellectual that stands in the way of unity. Intellectual exchange cannot flourish in such an atmosphere. This is probably of little concern to those who pushed Lerman out of the 'Jewish Quarterly'. But it should be of great concern to the rest of us.

In the following year, Julia Neuberger returned to the story in an article she wrote for *Index on Censorship*, prompted by the question of Jewish vulnerability to perceived manifestations of antisemitism and how in some curious way 'Israel lies at the heart of this debate'. She saw the *JQ* affair as an example of the way 'powerful Jewish organisations, on both sides of the Atlantic', which increasingly interpreted criticism of Israel as being antisemitic, were also regarding internal criticism as dangerous, 'if publicly exposed'. She continued: '[The] people who rock the boat, the ones who cannot quite be described as "self-hating Jews", nor even as anti-Zionists [the ones who] do not toe the line [– this spells danger to] the leaders of the community convinced that unity must always be displayed to the outside world ... And their reaction is to fight. It is a story that is likely to reflect ill on Anglo-Jewish institutions and their leaders.'

Rabbi Neuberger then asked why there was such sensitivity resulting in attempted censorship or self-censorship and gave four reasons: Accusing critics of Israel of antisemitism meant that the reasons for the accusation 'need not always be answered'. Fear of a repeat of the Holocaust. Fear that a world that allowed the Holocaust to happen could also allow another to take place, 'the unmentionable (but no less possible for that) destruction of the State of Israel'. Finally, many Jews admitted Israel did wrong, but this was only legitimately expressed in private: 'public and published criticism is an acute danger'.

I was naturally pleased that the message I had tried to convey in the editorial had spread far wider than I could have ever imagined when I penned it. Those who defended me and also validated my original argument were sufficiently independent not to have to succumb to pressures to keep quiet, nor to censor themselves. I envied them and felt deeply upset that I could not tell my side of the story. That is, I could have told it, but only by resigning from the IJA, and I was in no position to do that. The fact that in the end I felt compelled to resign the editorship of the *JQ* left me feeling ashamed for years afterwards. While the arguments against my resigning from the IJA were decisive, this still did not prevent me from feeling that I had let down my friends and therefore also myself. But I was convinced that had I not resigned the editorship, Roth would have found some way of forcing me to leave.

Although this episode was a significant point in the crystallisation of my thoughts about Israel and antisemitism, and marked my entry into public debate as a controversial figure, regarded even then as on the side of anti-Zionists and other enemies of the State of Israel, I was ill-equipped to understand the significance of what was going on. I never intended to put myself in that position and rejected the way I was being characterised. I was critical of the establishment but always saw myself as located within the broader communal consensus. I was still a Zionist. I had chosen to work within the confines of the organised Jewish community. I had had my fill of official Zionism, yet I was no more critical than those in the Peace Now movement and had in fact attended the first public meeting of the British Friends of Peace Now.

*   *   *

In May 1986, I was asked to attend a conference in Toronto examining media coverage of the Middle East conflict, organised by Canadian Professors for Peace in the Middle East (CPPME). I had been following this issue since the 1982 Lebanon War when accusations of media bias against Israel were widespread. The IJA organised a symposium on the issue at Chatham House, chaired by William Frankel, at which emotions ran very high. Journalists like Robert Fisk and Tim Llewellyn (then with the BBC) were in the packed auditorium and members of the audience repeatedly let their anger get the better of them and shouted comments from the floor. My own sense of things at the time was that claims of media bias were exaggerated.

When I started doing research for the paper, I came to realise that much of the literature, especially in relation to the Middle East conflict, showed that bias was in the eye of the beholder. In one experiment, the same filmed news coverage of the conflict was shown to separate groups of Jewish and Arab students: the Jews concluded that the material was biased against Israel; the Arabs that it was biased against the Arabs. I thought the main problem with the media was not the occasional distortion but, rather, poor journalistic standards, the increasing tendency to sensationalise and a sometimes over-zealous identification with the underdog. I tried to reflect these views in my paper.

But this was not an academic conference and when I arrived I learnt that quite a few serious academics had declined to attend since they feared that the proceedings would be dominated by people exchanging propagandistic insults. Israeli loyalists regarded the CPPME as leaning too far towards sympathy with the Arabs and the Palestinians, although I saw no particular evidence of this at the conference. It was clear, however, from one or two of the Israeli participants, like Yossi Olmert, who went on to become head of Israel's Government Press Office, that even staging such a conference with the participation of Arab academics and raising the idea that there might *not* be bias against Israel, was beyond the pale.

On returning to London, I wrote a report on the conference for the *JC*, which was published on 18 July under the title: 'Are the media really biased?' In it I cast doubt on the emphasis placed on influence of the media in shaping opinion about the Middle East conflict. This did not go down well with the sizeable cluster of people who were assiduously 'monitoring' the media for anti-Israel bias. One well-known scourge of Jewish leftists, and a vociferous defender of Israel at the BoD, Raymond Kalman, wrote '[A]fter much academic huffing and puffing [Lerman's article] came down to the fact that not all anti-Zionist media reporting was necessarily anti-Jewish – which anyone with half a brain in his or her head already knew and acknowledged. And which it really did not take a conference in Canada to produce. May I suggest that the same time and effort be brought to bear upon the *fact* that some anti-Zionist media reporting *is* anti-Jewish. In addition, to report as Tony Lerman and his colleagues did actually legitimises our opponents' propaganda.'

The *JC* played a significant part in feeding Jewish concern with the media through its weekly media column, written by Philip Kleinman. Kleinman, a Cambridge graduate who lived in Israel for a while but returned to the UK and became a journalist, was engaged to write his regular piece in 1974. A fierce critic of media coverage of Israel and Jewish matters, Kleinman's robust approach brought him a large following among readers. Shortly after my article appeared, I was very surprised to get a call from the editor, Geoffrey Paul, telling me that Kleinman was taking a two-month sabbatical and asking whether I would fill his spot in the paper until he returned. I found it hard to believe that he asked me to do this without realising, from my recently published article, that my point of view would be rather different from Philip's. Nevertheless, I jumped at the chance, although Roth was not entirely happy. Kleinman extended his sabbatical, so I wrote the column for four months in all.

My first column appeared on 5 September and I immediately put down my marker: 'There may be more time and space devoted to the Middle East [in the media] than to other issues of Jewish concern. But the excessive Middle East watching that that coverage draws from Jews has a distorting and stultifying effect on the self-perception of the [Jewish] community.' This comment and whatever else I wrote in my columns, which rapidly attracted the ire and outrage of some correspondents, needs to be set in the context of the things being said by my fellow-columnist on the same page of the paper: the incomparable Chaim Bermant. Bermant, like Kleinman, had been enlisted by

Frankel as a columnist. Wickedly funny, steeped in Jewish learning, brilliantly incisive and fearless, for almost 40 years he symbolised everything that was good about the *JC*. People frequently took issue with his views, but his columns became indispensable reading, a wry reflection on the community's strengths, weaknesses and idiosyncrasies. It was a great honour to have my picture parallel to his at the top of the page, me with closely cropped beard and he with beard of a more rabbinic length and heft.

In his column of 5 September he wrote about the corrupting effect of the occupation of the West Bank and Gaza on both Jews and Arabs, after having seen a preview of a television documentary on the subject by Victor Schonfeld, *Courage Along the Divide*. The words of a young soldier describing the brutalising experience of serving in the West Bank had come back to him as he watched the film, 'with its scenes of petty harassment, bloody-mindedness and outright thuggery. It should end once and for all the claim that the Jewish occupation is benign. It may have been so at the beginning, but it hasn't remained so, for it is not in the nature of occupations to remain benign. But the film is more than an atrocity story,' Bermant continued. 'It also shows Jews and Arabs who are aware of what the occupation is doing to their people and who are trying to do something about it.' He then quoted the words of IDF Colonel Meir Pail, 'a distinguished soldier'. With frightening prescience Pail says: 'If Israel's rule continues on the West Bank and in the Gaza Strip ... the Arab terror will grow ... and the Jewish terror will grow ... In much less than a generation the State of Israel will resemble both South Africa and Northern Ireland. We mustn't run away from harsh reality, we must live in it and struggle to change it from within. The only way to progress is to return the territories we conquered for peace.'

Set alongside Bermant's words, my comments on the media hardly seem radical, and yet the letter writers who responded to my columns in the subsequent weeks thought otherwise. I wrote about the documentary a week after Bermant and took issue with Jewish leaders who accused the makers of being biased. In the subsequent issue of the *JC*, both Bermant and I were taken to task in separate letters. Bermant was criticised for his endorsement of the pessimism expressed by Pail in Schonfeld's film. I was accused of being 'complacent' and told that my view was 'an irrational and dangerous one that should be challenged'. (In a letter to the editor, Wally Leaf, vice-chairman of the Public Relations Committee of the BoD, baldly stated: 'we wanted cuts'.)

I did not always defend the media in my columns. I was critical of the ways in which Israel was sometimes represented and argued that a more diverse media environment would produce a more balanced view of Israel and Middle East developments. But I was deeply suspicious of so-called 'media-monitoring units' that claimed to have 'scientific' evidence of pro-left-wing and anti-Israel bias. When I defended the BBC after the Tories attacked it for 'pro-Gaddafi' bias in its coverage of the US raid on Libya, I was taken to task by Sir Michael Hadow, former British Ambassador to Israel, and by others. In his letter to the *JC* on 14 November, he expressed surprise at my 'stout defence' of the BBC: 'I thought his column was designed basically to analyse anti-Israel or antisemitic bias in the British media ... All I can say, as a confirmed Israel-watcher over the years, is that the BBC has shown considerable bias against Israel and Zionism.' It was against *JC* policy for columnists to answer critics in their columns, so I wrote my own letter to the editor instead (28 November). I disputed Sir Michael's view of the purpose of the media column: 'What a narrow and distorted view of the world Jews would have if they looked at the media only for that reason.'

I also hit a raw nerve in my column of 19 December when I argued that 'Black protests at [negative media] treatment rarely seem to find an outlet in the national press. Yet there never seems to be a shortage of members of our community ready to weigh in, publicly or behind the scenes, with ill-found charges of anti-Zionist bias or antisemitism.' I concluded: 'Another problem is a certain ambiguity about racism and race relations generally – Jewish racism being the dirty secret of our time.' Sir Alfred Sherman, one of Margaret Thatcher's key right-wing, free market gurus, and a former communist, let fly (2 January 1987): 'Antony Lerman combines Jewish self-hate and loony Leftism in a blanket attack against the Anglo-Jewish community in general and in particular against those of us who have taken a stand against anti-Israel bias and the new Left-wing antisemitism in the British media.' He continued: 'Mr Lerman uncritically reproduces the Leftist slander against the Jewish community, "Jewish racism [is] the dirty secret of our time," without any evidence except our failure to support a fringe body, the self-styled Jewish Council for Community Relations.' And he characterised me as being among the 'rabidly anti-Zionist' Jews, 'stridently haranguing and slandering our community'.

Another letter writer, Ruth Willers, reminded me of the Holocaust, arguing that it all began with a few anti-Jewish cartoons and stereotyping of Jews in the press: 'I should have thought that the duty of the "JC's" media columnist lies in alerting us to any incidents where antisemitism (be it in its original form or disguised as anti-Zionism) raises its ugly head so that it can be branded immediately and rooted out before it takes hold in public opinion. But Mr Lerman seems to make every effort to lull us into complacency. His concern for his Arab friends, on the other hand, is most touching: it makes me wonder if he is in the right job and also what and whose game he is playing.'

In my last column (26 December), I summed up the overall approach I had taken by quoting from research by Dr Michael Tracey, head of the

Broadcasting Research Unit at the British Film Institute, that cast doubt on the notion that content produces a predictable effect – that is, that content described as pro-Arab, or critical of Israel, will result in a damaging influencing of opinion. But I suspect that many readers agreed with a Mr S. Lewis of Bournemouth whose 21 December letter to the *JC* was sent on to me, though not published: 'You waste your space on Left-wing drivel. This week was the limit. I do *not* buy the Jewish Chronicle to read about the Black community ... The Times has a bit from Israel every day mostly nasty. I hope Mr Philip Kleinman takes over very soon as he wrote about *news*, not rubbish ... We should be pleased the Arabs in cartoons are like that. It used to be *us*. Maybe that was before your time. I couldn't care less about the Blacks since they expelled the Israelis. It is not *our* problem.'

I had the distinct impression that Geoffrey Paul was happy to see the back of me when my stint was over. Nonetheless, I was satisfied that I had conveyed my view that while being oversensitive was understandable, it was counter-productive: it only exacerbated the community's tendency to fear the way it was portrayed in the wider world and it was not helpful to Israel because it reinforced the tendency of Jews to avoid unpleasant facts about what the Israeli government was doing. But the responses to my column revealed just how reluctant was a certain concerned sector of the Jewish population even to listen to a different interpretation of the position of Jews and Israel in the world. And it was the first time that I had come across people who found this new narrative so threatening that they were ready to brand the person telling it an enemy of the Jewish people, a self-hating Jew. I was quite shocked by this reaction given that I was still a Zionist and was making a career for myself in the Jewish community.

More important, writing the column gave me an opportunity to clarify my own thoughts on Israel's position in the world, the relationship between Jews and Israel and where Israel was headed. As a result I was adopting increasingly critical positions and attracting the enmity of the Sir Alfred Shermans of the world. With the prospect of Stephen Roth soon retiring as director of the IJA, I began to focus on the possibility of being chosen to replace him. To stand any chance I needed to adopt a cautious public profile, to be seen as mature, stable and competent. I knew that I would be seen as having one serious handicap – being married to a non-Jew.

*   *   *

It had taken me more than ten years to move from raising initial, tentative questions about Zionism to a more definitive critique of its flaws, and specifically of the flaws in the socialist Zionism with which I had so fully identified. I was no longer the naïve idealist, ready to accept virtually everything I was told about Zionism. And I was now even reading certain critiques of Zionism that I judged did not go far enough.

This is how I felt about Bernard Avishai's important book, *The Tragedy of Zionism*, when I reviewed it for the *JC* on 5 December 1986. Avishai lamented the fact that Labour Zionism 'stopped short of its liberal-democratic goals'; it did not enshrine liberal democratic principles in a written constitution when the state was founded. Had it done so, 'Zionism would have been enshrined as Israel's historic prelude; having been realised, Zionism would have been superseded by Israeli law.' He did not argue that classical socialist Zionism should be revived. It was not an antidote to 'new Zionism', 'a rhetoric that frankly justified Israeli national rights in terms of Orthodox claims'. He wanted 'democratic tendencies ... [to] prevail against the anachronistic institutions which Labour Zionists once made; prevail against the new Zionist ideology of a Greater Israel.' I concluded that Avishai's comment that 'Zionism is "tragically obsolete" and provides no solutions to Israel's current problems' was probably true, but to see the attainment of liberal democracy as the ultimate aim of Labour Zionism was false. The democracy of socialist Zionism, as practised in the kibbutzim and in the youth movements, always put the interests of the collective above the individual.

Given how far I had come, it may seem strange that my interests took me in other directions over the next ten to twelve years, such that I can find no written evidence that I did any systematic thinking about Zionism during that time. But the issues I did take up – representations of the Holocaust, contemporary antisemitism, the situation of European Jewry – and my involvement in global Jewish politics contributed to a greater understanding of the nature of Jewish life worldwide and the political and ideological realities of contemporary Jewish existence. And all of this expanded the context in which my understanding of the meaning and significance of Zionism and Israel eventually developed.

7

POLITICAL ANIMAL

We [Israeli] Zionists have an [evil] inclination: that antisemitism will flourish in the West but no Jew will be hurt.

Professor Aviezer Ravitzky, 1998

From 1987 my focus on Zionism and Israel became rather oblique. I added to my knowledge in some areas but not systematically. For example, I had read some of the work of the former deputy mayor of Jerusalem, Meron Benvenisti, who was then carrying out detailed and disturbing research on growing Israeli settlement in the West Bank. But it was at a lunchtime seminar he gave at the Institute that I became fully aware of the relentless nature of the process. The cool, articulate and professional way he presented the facts was particularly impressive. We published data provided by his West Bank Data Project in the yearly *Survey of Jewish Affairs*. I was also continuing to read specialised work on Israel and the Middle East principally in connection with my role as the volume's assistant editor. I wrote an essay for the 1990 volume on 'The PLO and the "Peace Process"', which was essentially a follow-up to a *Research Report* I had written in 1988 on the significance of changes made at the nineteenth session of the Palestine National Council. I argued that the PNC decisions of November 1988 in Algiers were clear evidence of Arafat manoeuvring the Palestine Liberation Organisation towards eventual recognition of Israel and I concluded that 'Yasser Arafat had steered the PLO towards compromise, even if never going quite far enough at those times when the acceptance of a little greater risk might well have reaped rewards. What substantive international legitimacy the PLO possessed, whether justified or not, was achieved through greater stress on diplomacy and less on armed struggle.'

Yet all of my concerns about such issues were completely overshadowed by the crisis that hit the Institute in mid-1987. The WJC was threatening substantial cuts in funding, yet Stephen Roth, who never liked the new American leadership of the WJC, declined to do anything to deal with the consequences. To the senior staff members, the dangers we now faced were obvious. The only solution was for him to retire – he was already 73 – and a successor be appointed. But he was incredibly stubborn and determined to hold on as long as possible.

The four members of the IJA's executive committee, who were no lightweights, accepted the senior staff's argument that a new director had to be appointed. The committee comprised the IJA's president, Lord Goodman, Harold Wilson's lawyer and the man who Wilson sent to negotiate with Ian Smith over the future of Rhodesia; the chairman, Ellis Birk, an influential city lawyer who was a central figure in the *Mirror* newspaper group and secretly engineered the sacking of its head, Cecil King, once seen as impregnable; Sir Monty Finniston, former head of British Steel and a significant figure in the engineering industry; and William Frankel.

After much effort and unpleasantness, Roth agreed to retire. But it only came about because of my close relationship with Frankel. I persuaded him to back our plan and pressed him to get the Executive to act. Roth kept finding ways of wriggling out and William kept coming back to me in a defeatist frame of mind. I would stiffen his backbone and urge him to redouble his efforts. After repeating this cycle what seemed like numerous times, Roth finally, but with bad grace, accepted his fate.

By this time I had realised that years of indecision about my career had come to an end. While I had initially taken on the task of engineering Roth's retirement simply to protect my job and to ensure the Institute's survival, I was now determined to do all I could to secure the directorship for myself. The choice of a successor to Roth involved direct engagement with Israel Singer and the WJC leadership in New York. But they refused to cooperate and behaved as if they were willing the IJA to self-destruct. Meanwhile, after continuing to press William, the London Executive asked me, Michael May and Barry Shenker, the IJA's general manager, to submit CVs and proposals as to how we would run the Institute. No interviews were conducted. The committee members deliberated and decided to appoint Michael. By way of consolation I was made director of research.

Meanwhile, shortly before the decision was made, we learnt more about why Israel Singer had refused to participate in the process. The WJC had done a deal with the US Anti-Defamation League (ADL), the American Jewish community's principal organisation combating antisemitism, to partner the WJC in funding the IJA. In exchange, the ADL was given managerial control of the institute. The decision became common knowledge at a WJC meeting in Mexico at the beginning of November 1988. At no stage had we been informed or consulted about these negotiations. It came as a complete surprise.

Having invested so much energy in trying to shape the future of the post-Stephen Roth IJA, I was not inclined to consider leaving at that point, but I had very strong reservations as to how the IJA would now fare. By

May 1989 my worst fears had been realised and I decided that there was no future for me at the Institute. When I confirmed my acceptance of a leaving package in mid August I had no clear idea what I was going to do, except that I planned to base myself at our new Welsh home and intended to write a book provisionally titled 'Settling Accounts: The Conduct and Misconduct of Jewish Political Action in the Post-War World'. I was intending to express my real feelings about the WJC style of international Jewish political activity.

The synopsis for the book now serves as a report on what had been preoccupying me over the years since the *JQ* affair and my controversial stint as guest media columnist on the *JC*. Having focused intensely on the struggle to become director of the IJA, I was more engaged in thinking about the international political issues on the agenda of the WJC than matters affecting my views on Zionism and Israel. Nevertheless, I did intend to cover the subject in the last chapter of the book. The main chapters were to be on the Waldheim affair, the Carmelite Convent at Auschwitz and Catholic-Jewish relations, action and inaction on antisemitism, Soviet Jewry, the Jewish disappeared in Argentina and the suppression of Jewish-Palestinian rapprochement. In the synopsis I contended that: 'For years, open [diaspora Jewish] dissent from Israeli policies was completely anathema to Jewish leaders and organisations, and anyone expressing sympathy for Palestinian rights was considered at best a fool, at worst a self-hating Jew and a traitor to Jewish interests.' The situation had changed, but not very much: 'official organisational efforts are still made to prevent open fraternisation between Jews and Palestinians who support the PLO'. I planned to examine 'the close surveillance of Israelis living abroad who associate with Palestinians, [the] threatening [of] Jews who actively encourage dialogue with Palestinians and [the creation of] a climate in which the expression of dissent from Israeli policies was considered an attack on the community itself'.

At about the same time in 1989, views on Israel's future impact on Jews that I had expressed when interviewed by the author Stephen Brook were published in his book on Anglo-Jewry, *The Club: The Jews of Modern Britain*. He asked me to look ahead to the year 2000 and I predicted that there would be greater fragmentation among Jews 'because of unresolved conflicts that are bound to come out into the open eventually and because of what's happening in Israel. Israel has exerted a powerful influence here and it's been an influence for unity. It's always been possible when Israel has been under threat for appeals to be made to Jewish unity. That situation is going to deteriorate. The control over the community that the Zionist establishment has had over the years is bound to break up as things get worse in Israel.'

My thinking had also been influenced by involvement in the editing of the book of essays and papers, *Anti-Zionism and Antisemitism in the*

Contemporary World, published in 1990 (mentioned in Chapter 5). Professor Robert Wistrich was the editor and the book was published by Macmillan in association with the IJA, which partly explains my role in the project. I chased up and edited most of the papers. Back in 1981 I wrote a research report, 'The abuse of Zionism', which I updated for the volume.

In his Introduction, Wistrich observed that 'The relationship between anti-Zionism and antisemitism which forms the core of the essays in this book is in reality notoriously difficult to define in objective terms.' This was very much the conclusion I had reached after reading through all the essays. For many of the writers the nature of the relationship remained an open and unresolved question. Wistrich tended towards the view that it was very close. He concluded: 'anti-Zionism grafts itself so easily on to the much older root of classical antisemitism providing it with new sources of nourishment and revival.' I took a different view. Although I agreed that what I called 'fictive anti-Zionism' and antisemitism shared certain features, drawing a parallel between them 'does not prove that anti-Zionism and antisemitism are one and the same. It is one thing to show that they have similar characteristics; it is quite another to claim an equivalence.'

I called my revised paper 'Fictive anti-Zionism: third-world, Arab and Muslim variations', which may seem rather odd, but I was trying to highlight the fact that much of the use of the word Zionism in the international arena bore no relationship to anything that existed in the real world but was 'rather a fictive construct intended to serve the particular internal and external political purposes of those who oppose it'. In other words, when many governments and international organisations attacked Zionism it was because Zionism fulfilled the function of a cultural code and attacking it was a sign of solidarity and association with, or adherence to, a wider political ideology or movement, rather than a concrete expression of the view that the specific ideology of Zionism was wrong. I was not arguing that third world, Arab and Muslim anti-Zionism presented no dangers. I quoted examples of the use of anti-Zionism which were clearly just disguised expressions of antisemitism. But as I wrote in conclusion: 'any critical approach to anti-Zionism must seek to understand the phenomenon and the basis of understanding is differentiation. Only by separating out its different forms is it possible to assess the danger that anti-Zionism really represents.'

I was within a few weeks of leaving the Institute when the WJC and the ADL reached a firm agreement that the ADL would take control initially for one year on the basis of an annual contribution of $250,000. To my surprise the ADL asked me to remain under a new power structure giving me and Michael May entirely equal status in the organisation's hierarchy. I agreed to try this out for six to nine months, my severance arrangements with the WJC being deferred for up to nine months. 'Settling Accounts' was permanently shelved.

The new ADL arrangements were publicly announced in November 1989 but any hope that all would now proceed smoothly and amicably was soon dashed. Practically all that the ADL leadership in New York wanted from us was material on antisemitism, the more sensational the better. This would enable them to generate publicity, thereby enhancing their profile in Europe, where they had ambitions to become a major force in making public pronouncements on the threat of antisemitism, and pleasing their supporters back home. By July 1990 I had concluded that the new arrangements were not working, and asked that my severance arrangements be put into effect.

This was how matters stood when I left with my family on 12 August for a vacation in New England, house-sitting with friends in the home of the bestselling author Joe McGinniss just outside Williamstown, Massachusetts. About ten days into our stay, I had a phone call from the ADL. They had decided to withdraw from the arrangement with the WJC and cease funding the IJA in the summer of 1991. From now on, the ADL would no longer exercise managerial control. The WJC would once again be in charge. Disgusted, but not entirely surprised by the decision, I nonetheless knew that this latest crisis might present me with one last chance to take over as sole director of the Institute. By the time we returned to London, I had decided to make a final effort to achieve this. I would then be able to ensure the survival of the Institute and begin reforming and shaping it into the policy-oriented research organisation I thought it should be. I judged that I had a reasonable chance of success.

In late 1990 William Frankel took over as chairman of the London Executive Committee of the Institute and I knew that this would make all the difference. But the whole process was, once again, long and drawn out. It wasn't until May 1991 that I was finally appointed sole director. Michael May left by mutual consent. At the beginning of June a brief announcement of my appointment appeared in the *JC*.

For five years the role of Israel and Zionism in my life shrank very considerably. This was not consciously intended, but rather a consequence of deciding to try to secure the IJA directorship. I had to concentrate on the organisation's future, engage fully with the WJC and then the ADL, organise clandestinely to get William Frankel and his colleagues to follow my plans – and try to maintain a research and publications programme in what were constantly changing circumstances. In addition, following the collapse of communism in 1989 we were moving towards making antisemitism a central feature of our work. This was in small part spurred by the distorted interest in the subject by the ADL and the WJC, but more substantively by the need to chronicle and analyse the upsurge of antisemitism in the former communist countries.

My struggle to become director of the Institute during these years was like a crash-course in international Jewish politics. Later on, this experience provided part of a very significant context for a more conscious return to thinking about Israel and Zionism. And as we moved even more firmly into the world of researching and analysing antisemitism at the global level and came into direct contact with Israeli institutions and government agencies working in the area, my understanding of how Israel related to Jewish communities and how that relationship informed Israeli policy-making grew by leaps and bounds.

*   *   *

The departure of the ADL signalled the beginning of a turnaround in the IJA's fortunes. It opened the door to new funding, Lord Rothschild's agreement to be the Institute's president and the appointment of the property developer Peter Levy, one of the most thoughtful, generous and engaged philanthropists in the country, as co-chairman. One dark cloud remained: we were still answerable to the WJC. Creating a sustainable and independent institution was not going to be easy. I was determined to try.

The WJC's ten-year campaign against the President of Austria and former UN secretary general Kurt Waldheim, for hiding his Nazi past, which kept it at the forefront of international Jewish political activity, had run its course. Prompted by the surfacing of antisemitism in post-communist Europe, they now chose 'eliminating' antisemitism for their new blockbuster campaign. We were already producing information and analysis on these developments, so when the WJC decided to kick off its new programme with a major international conference on antisemitism in Brussels in July 1992, we knew the IJA had to play a significant role in it. I conceived of the idea of producing an annual worldwide, country-by-country survey of antisemitism – *Antisemitism World Report* – modelled on the annual human rights reports of bodies like Amnesty International, to be launched at the conference. Nothing like this had been done before.

A major problem we faced was the variable quality of the available data. Especially problematic was the worldwide dissemination of often distorted and inaccurate lists of 'antisemitic incidents' by the Israel Government Monitoring Forum on Antisemitism. To overcome these difficulties we developed our own international network of researchers and began working furiously to produce the report in time for the Brussels conference. As we searched for objective experts we discovered that a significant proportion of what purported to be academically-based research was tainted by political and ideological bias.

Especially troublesome was the Project for the Study of Antisemitism at Tel Aviv University – a new body, set up with the sponsorship and urging of the Forum and the Mossad, Israel's foreign intelligence service – which was planning to produce its own world antisemitism survey. In fact it was the Mossad that was responsible for gathering the data on antisemitism disseminated worldwide by the Forum.

At the Brussels conference, where our report was well received, the Israeli Forum coordinated attempts to strong-arm us into stopping production of our report and 'cooperate' with the Tel Aviv Project, and others, on a joint venture. Persuasion turned to threat when we were told that unless we agreed, Tel Aviv would immediately start producing its own annual report. Not wanting to be accused of Zionist bias and deeply suspicious of working with the Forum, we declined. The Forum was seeking to establish Israeli hegemony over antisemitism monitoring undertaken by Jewish groups and individuals worldwide. It was also establishing networks of young Jews tasked with supplying it with country-specific data, which was then crudely collated and repackaged for worldwide dissemination. Its aim was to sensitise those young Jews to the danger of antisemitism and thereby encourage *aliya*.

So, in short, the Israeli government's civil arm devoted to monitoring and dealing with the problem of antisemitism, working hand-in-hand with the Mossad, was acting as a Zionist recruiting tool of the crudest kind.

Many other Jewish bodies sympathised with our critique of the plans and Zionist assumptions of the Forum and the Tel Aviv Project, but over the next seven or eight years we were subjected to concerted efforts to undermine our work. The more we took an independent line on antisemitism, the more these Israeli institutions tried to isolate and bully us. I decided to alert our trustees to this problem and seek their advice on the policy we should follow. On 15 March 1994, I explained that much of the work of Tel Aviv and the Mossad was 'highly alarmist and exaggerated, and is directed at vulnerable communities and young people'. What was important was 'a rigorous and objective approach [that] will command the respect of governments, international organisations and so on ... It [is] entirely wrong for [Israel] to be attempting to dominate this work, since [the country's] interests as a state are bound to diverge at times from the interests of Jewish communities.' I tried to persuade the Israelis to allow us to operate without interference, but was given short shrift by the Mossad representative at the Israel embassy in London and by the Israel ambassador himself.

After relatively little engagement with Israel and Zionism for five years, I had now encountered a particularly ugly face of Israel's attitude to diaspora Jews and the issue of antisemitism and found myself at loggerheads not only with the Israeli government agency dealing with antisemitism but also with the Mossad. The direction in which I then took the Institute had further implications for our role in working on contemporary antisemitism and therefore also for our relationship with the Israeli authorities – and consequently for my thinking on Israel.

I discovered that the WJC leadership wanted to close down the IJA in London and re-establish it as an office within their Madison Avenue headquarters. The only way to forestall this was to make the IJA completely independent. When William Frankel suggested we link up with the American Jewish Committee instead, a body with which he had close connections, I realised that this could be the path to eventual complete independence and a chance to realise my secret aim of turning the IJA into a fully-fledged policy think tank. There was mutual loathing between the AJC and the WJC, so when we declared independence in 1994 Israel Singer was apoplectic. A messy divorce was finally arranged in summer 1995 at a summit between Lord Rothschild and Edgar Bronfman where it was agreed that the name 'Institute of Jewish Affairs' would be consigned to history. I persuaded the Institute's trustees to accept my policy think tank plan and the Institute for Jewish Policy Research (JPR) was successfully launched in summer 1996. The partnership with the AJC ran from 1994 to 1999 and although it soured badly towards the end, it did indeed lead to complete independence. JPR had become financially self-sustaining and answerable to no one.

*   *   *

I began to speak out about my concerns at the growing barriers to maintaining dispassionate objectivity in the study of antisemitism, choosing to do so first in a lecture I gave at Chatham House on 30 November 1998, entitled 'Antisemitism at the End of the Twentieth Century: The New Context of an Old Prejudice'. I subsequently reworked it into an academic paper for the opening panel of a major conference in Israel in June 1999 organised by the Sassoon International Centre for the Study of Antisemitism at the Hebrew University. My message was frank:

> We see [the exploitation of antisemitism for ideological ends] also where the study and monitoring of antisemitism is too closely bound up with the Zionist imperative, and as a result is so easily muddied. Clearly, if Jewish perceptions of antisemitism in the Diaspora are full of foreboding and fear, this may lead to increased immigration to Israel ...
>
> The danger is that in recent years more Israeli institutions have taken up the study of contemporary antisemitism and their influence in the field has grown. In most areas of study where objectivity is the norm and peer review

succeeds in maintaining standards, the fact that Israeli institutions might be a dominant force would have absolutely no bearing on the quality and validity of the work produced. But because these safeguards do not exist in the study of contemporary antisemitism, Zionist ideological assumptions can easily colour the work of these institutions. [This] stricture would especially apply to any institution that has close links with or is supported by the Israeli government and international Jewish political organisations which combine an ideologically determined approach with an avowedly Zionist political orientation.

I felt able to speak so openly on the influence of the Zionist imperative on the study of antisemitism because I was considering leaving JPR and therefore felt less inhibited about making controversial public statements. I needed a new challenge and wanted the freedom to think through the many half-formed ideas and questions about antisemitism, Israel and Zionism that had been preoccupying me over so many years, but particularly since I had become director of the Institute. I had developed a strong critique of Zionism, which had not changed very much over the previous decade. I had hopes that in whatever job I might do next I would have greater freedom to write and speak publicly about these issues.

It was one thing to want to move on; quite another to find something I wanted to do. But in the end, like buses, you wait for ages for a suitable job and then, two came along at once. I applied for the post of president of the Oxford Centre for Hebrew and Jewish Studies and reached the final shortlist of two. Meanwhile, a new London-based position with the Rothschild family's Yad Hanadiv foundation was mentioned to me by one of its trustees. The job involved setting up a programme of charitable grant-making devoted to supporting Jewish life in Europe. Three days before I was due to be interviewed for the Oxford post, Jacob Rothschild offered me the Yad Hanadiv position and I accepted.

8

DARKENING SKIES IN ISRAEL AND EUROPE

What about the crimes and atrocities themselves? And I don't just mean Sabra and Chatila ... colonization through the settlement policy of large parts of occupied Palestinian territory that is unlawful and oppressive; and the building of security barriers that effectively imprison whole communities, which is also unlawful and oppressive. The frequent torture of Arab terrorist suspects, first with the complaisance of the High Court, and then in circumvention of its landmark 1998 ruling – is unlawful and oppressive.

Sir Nigel Rodley, 2003

There is a state of war against the Jews in the world.

Roger Cukierman, 2002

After I left JPR in December 1999, suppressed thoughts on Israel and Zionism soon came to the surface and I became more engaged with the realities of the Israel-Palestine situation. It may seem strange that this occurred as I was setting up a grant-making programme for Lord Rothschild to support Jewish life in Europe. But four factors explain why. I came into closer contact with Israel through my new post; I was focusing intensively on the revival of European Jewish communities and the work of Jewish academics, writers, filmmakers and journalists who were both creating and responding to the conditions in the new Europe, and many of them had complex, insightful and challenging views on Israel; barely nine months into my tenure, the second intifada erupted; and I no longer felt vulnerable to Jewish communal pressure.

Initially, the programme was to be a subsidiary of Yad Hanadiv, the $1 billion Geneva-based foundation run out of a large, Bauhaus-style house in Rehavia, West Jerusalem, which focused on grant-making in Israel. Founded in 1958, Yad Hanadiv was named in memory of Baron Edmond de Rothschild who supported the Jewish revival and settlement in Palestine in the second half of the nineteenth century. Yad Hanadiv means 'memorial of the benefactor'. The foundation was controlled by the British Rothschild family, under the leadership of Lord Rothschild, who was chairman of the advisory committee.

Widely known in Israel as *Keren Rotchild* (Rothschild Fund), its grant-giving style was discreet. Nevertheless, it has had a major influence in certain key areas of Israeli life. Yad Hanadiv's most ambitious project of recent years was to propose, finance and oversee the construction of the new Israeli Supreme Court, inaugurated in 1992, which cost probably in excess of $35 million.

My task was challenging and exciting, but how could I reconcile working for an organisation with such avowedly Zionist connections with my increasingly critical views on Israel and Zionism? I no longer regarded myself as a Zionist. If asked I would have described myself as a non- or post-Zionist. I thought Israel should repeal its Law of Return and introduce a fair and liberal immigration policy. I still had faith in the 1993 Oslo Accords and the prospect of a two-state solution, which I thought was very close despite the turn to violence. I opposed the building of more settlements in the occupied territories and wanted Israel to withdraw to the 1967 borders, with land swaps mutually agreed with the Palestinians. I had concluded that the Zionist and Israeli notion of a special bond between Israel and the diaspora was a myth. Israel would always put its national interests above those of diaspora Jews. And sometimes it deemed that its national interests were best served by exaggerating levels of antisemitism, to the detriment of Jewish life. The sooner Jews worldwide and the State of Israel recognised that it was perfectly natural that Israel should go its own way, the better for all concerned.

With this cluster of views, surely working for an organisation devoted to supporting the aims of Zionism and the state of Israel would be an uncomfortable experience. But at the time I did not think so. I still had much to learn about how Yad Hanadiv operated and what it supported. Nevertheless, I was not responsible for the Israel-based philanthropy. Jacob had decided to devote serious financial resources to supporting Jewish life in Europe, a cause that I passionately believed in. I was being given a unique opportunity to influence how that money should be spent. I took it on trust that Yad Hanadiv was devoting some funds to helping Israel's Arab citizens and to Israeli-Palestinian reconciliation. I was ready to put my reservations about Zionism aside in order to seize the opportunity to give a vital boost to the European Jewish revival.

After taking up the post, I went to Israel in January 2000 to learn more about the Yad Hanadiv operation and to meet people who might help me as I prepared proposals for the European programmes that the foundation should adopt. I visited the new Supreme Court building and was given an individual tour. There was barely any sign that it was a Yad Hanadiv-funded project. I was taken to Ramat Hanadiv, situated at the southern end of Mt Carmel between the towns of Zichron Yaakov and Binyamina, the beautiful nature park and mausoleum of Baron Edmond de Rothschild and his wife, which was maintained and financed by the foundation. I left Israel that day, 13 January 2000, and wrote in my diary: 'I feel more conscious than ever of my good fortune. You enter this historical stream, with all its resonances in Israel and Britain. You have this security as long as you can perform your job well. You're in a milieu in which excellence, taste, quality prevail – it lifts your horizons. You have the opportunity to do something creative, exciting – you can think, dream, turning the fruits of both into reality.' Yes, I was swept up in what William Frankel called the 'mystique' that surrounded the Rothschild family and all its works, and it was too good to last. I was already on a steep learning curve about the complexities of the Rothschild set-up.

A UK-based grant-making foundation, Hanadiv Charitable Foundation, with its own endowment fund of approximately £60 million, was established for the European work. I was appointed its chief executive. The director of Yad Hanadiv, Ari Weiss, held overall responsibility for all the grant-making and he and I were to be in close contact. More or less the same trustees served on the Boards of both foundations: James Wolfensohn, president of the World Bank; Emma Rothschild, Jacob's sister, an economic historian and Fellow of King's College, Cambridge; Dr Lisbet Rausing, an academic and philanthropist; Dr David Landau, chairman of a venture capital fund; Beatrice Rosenberg, Jacob's cousin from Paris; Michael Kay, the family lawyer; and Sir Ronald Cohen, founder of the private equity industry in Europe, who became a trustee in 2003. I sat in on the Israel grant-making meetings. And since Ari Weiss rarely came to London, Jacob, from the earliest days of my employment, tried to involve me directly in Israeli projects.

I first met Ari in December 1999 at Trinity College Cambridge, in the apartments of the Master of Trinity, the eminent Indian economist and philosopher Amartya Sen, who was married to Emma Rothschild. We got on well. An orthodox Jew, Ari was born in America, educated at Yale, and served as chief aide to the Speaker of the House and Democratic Majority Leader, Tip O'Neill. He emigrated to Israel in 1985 and became director of Yad Hanadiv in 1999. He was also a close friend of and adviser to Natan Sharansky, Israel's interior minister and former Soviet Jewish refusenik and prisoner, and accompanied him to the Wye Valley talks with the Palestinians in America in 1998.

My office was in the old Dairy at Waddesdon Manor in Buckinghamshire, the former Rothschild family country mansion, owned by the National Trust since 1957, an hour's drive north-west of London. But the contrast with my old office in Wimpole Street, central London, was difficult to get used to. I began with no framework of projects or employees and was entirely alone almost all of the time I spent at Waddesdon, where the phone hardly rang and practically no one interrupted me. After almost 21 years in the one organisation, it would have been surprising and disappointing if such a fundamental change had not produced some sense of disorientation.

I first experienced tension between my views on Israel and Zionism and my job when we were presented with a request to give a large donation to the new Birthright-Israel programme, designed to send large numbers of young American Jews on free ten-day trips to Israel to awaken their Jewish identity. This was a scheme dreamt up by American Jewish philanthropists and set up as a partnership with the Israeli government; $250 million was required to fund the project over a five-year period. Eventually, the scheme was to be extended to Europe. Meanwhile, Jewish philanthropists everywhere were being approached to contribute.

My instinct was to advise Jacob to have nothing to do with it. Fortunately, he was not keen, but I sensed that his personal relationship with some of the key funders probably made it difficult for him to refuse to support the initiative altogether. I recorded my initial thoughts in January 2000: 'I think Hanadiv should not get swept up in this process. It's the gung-ho school of Jewish philanthropic action that's in the lead here, I would not have thought that Hanadiv should be part of that.' There was nothing new in the idea that trips to Israel for young people had an inspirational value. But the Jewish world and Israel had changed radically and I was extremely doubtful about supporting this method of strengthening Jewish identity. I feared that the participants would be presented with a sanitised view of a country facing deep, unresolved divisions, run by a government ruling oppressively over 3 million Palestinians denied their right to self-determination. Maintain Jewish identity, yes, but use diverse means not centred so exclusively on Israel.

Nevertheless, I had to come up with something practical that would allow Jacob to make a contribution, but not by funding the trips directly. Ari and I recommended that the foundation fund an internet-based, post-trip educational programme for those young Jews who wanted to explore their Jewishness on return from Israel. The trustees agreed. After the meeting, I looked more closely at the Birthright organisation's planning material and wrote to Ari: 'the whole programme of Birthright is based on an image of [an] Israel that no longer exists. How can it fulfil this function [of ensuring Jewish continuity] when the strong idealistic base on which it was founded has been so severely eroded, when Israel is, quite naturally, increasingly about doing the things any normal state does?' In the end, it became apparent that e-learning was not what it was cut out to be and eventually the grant was cancelled. I was relieved.

Fortunately, some of the other projects I had to deal with that were directly linked to Israel were more promising. Various creative educational-ists in liberal-minded colleges and institutes in Israel were developing ways of improving Jewish literacy among secular Jews interested in increasing their Jewish knowledge. They were all keen to extend their educational work to Jews in Europe. Practically all of them had critical perspectives on what was happening to civil society in Israel, on the erosion of the values of tolerance, equality and fairness and on the way the government and other official agencies related to Israel's Arab population and the Palestinians in the occupied territories.

I was especially interested in what Yad Hanadiv was doing in the area of Israeli-Palestinian dialogue. The foundation had been modestly active on various levels, but after the outbreak of the second intifada in September 2000, much of the foundation's work in this field came to an end. The ongoing violence and restriction of movement made it difficult to hold meetings. But in addition, many Palestinians were increasingly unwilling to engage in dialogue at a time when they felt that they were under siege. While the overall situation in Israel, the conflict with the Palestinians and the problematic politics of the Middle East almost always framed discussions at every foundation meeting, trustees urging more action seemed to have little direct influence on the direction of the foundation's philanthropy.

When the Palestinians began their second uprising against Israeli occupation, I was mentally more attuned to, and so much better informed about, developments in Israel-Palestine than I had been a year earlier and was profoundly disturbed by the possible consequences. Until then I was still convinced that the conflict would soon be resolved within the framework of the admittedly somewhat battered Oslo Accords. The Israelis and Palestinians seemed like two boxers who had fought each other many times and were on the verge of agreeing to hang up their gloves, but they could not resist slugging it out one last time. Peace was inevitable; the violence was a sideshow.

I was soon disabused of this comforting theory. I swung between anger that the Palestinians had taken up the violent option again when a settlement, which appeared to promise them so much, was within their grasp, and anger that the Israeli response to Palestinian violence was completely dispropor-tionate. Especially depressing was the apparent collapse, bewilderment and paralysis of the peace camp. Desperate to make sense of what was happening, I read constantly, especially material from Israel which shed light on the real situation of the Palestinians, something I had not seriously engaged with in the past. I recorded in my diary: 'I remember doing a radio interview jointly with ... Rana Kabbani [the Syrian-born writer] at the time of the Oslo agreement. She argued that the proposed return of territory to the Palestinians would result in the creation of a series of Bantustans [racially segregated, unconnected enclaves with limited self-government] and not a viable state. I said this was not so and she was being churlish for not focusing on the positive benefits of peace. I now think she was right about the Bantustans. I was wrong.' Critical of Zionism as I was, I had continued to believe that Israel's leaders would behave honourably when it came to exchanging 'land for peace'. The evidence appeared to undermine that belief.

Jewish opinion was becoming increasingly polarised over who was responsible for the outbreak of violence and the collapse of peace negotiations, but it was largely united in shock and incomprehension at the dramatic rise in the number of suicide bombings in Israel during 2001. By the time I arrived in Ashkelon for a conference in October, there had been 34 attacks and 85 people had died. Being only a few kilometres up the coast north of Gaza, it's perhaps not surprising that Ashkelon felt like a ghost town.

I was giving a paper on the implications of the Shoah for post-Holocaust Jewish unity. Speaking before me, the Israeli philosopher Eliezer Schweid insisted that Jews had finally returned to a normal existence after the Holocaust and that, despite the current pessimism, 'we do not need to change our view that a return to normality took place'. But the price of physical survival was solidarity, Schweid argued. And the most serious problem we faced was that there was no solidarity, no common Jewish movement, no centre. I took issue with this in my paper. 'The fact is that the call for unity today is invariably politically motivated: unity, as long as you sign up to someone else's political or religious creed. As a columnist [Jo-Ann Mort] in the *Jerusalem Report* wrote [23 April 2001]: "in reality, Jewish leaders embrace the slogan of unity to mask differences that are best left clear and distinct ... At its worst, faux unity beckons us to be blind toward reprehensible acts committed by Jews, even as we condemn those committed by non-Jews."'

Thousands of miles away, another event had just taken place which was used to strengthen the case for 'faux unity': the UN Anti-Racism conference in Durban. Virulently anti-Israel rhetoric and naked antisemitism expressed by some NGOs caused consternation among Jewish groups and was seen as evidence of a mounting wave of global Jew-hatred. And then soon after I returned to the UK from Israel, Al Qaida terrorists struck the World Trade Center towers in New York with two hijacked passenger jets. Although it was quite clearly an attack on the United States, its link to Jews, both real and imagined, soon surfaced. Al Qaida propaganda railed against Israel and Jews. Those who argued that a resurgence of antisemitism was taking place saw this as further proof.

I was in New York less than a month after 9/11. There was an air of forced normality, of a city trying to hold itself together especially as the Christmas season was fast approaching. But every New Yorker I spoke to was, underneath, bruised and subdued, and many were confused. At the meeting I was attending, a wise and sensitive witness to the tragedy, Geoffrey Solomon, head of the Charles and Andrea Bronfman Philanthropies, spoke movingly about it. He said 9/11 had a profound impact on 'those of us dedicated to service'. Forced to leave his Ground Zero area apartment for seven weeks, he was only allowed back for ten minutes to remove essential items. He felt the experience gave him a personal connection with the tragic history of the Jewish people. On the national level, there was a strong sense of a country at war. The patriotic atmosphere was very pervasive. But it had also led to the issue of dual loyalty being raised – for Muslims, rather than Jews. But nonetheless, Geoffrey said, it left some in the Jewish community feeling uncomfortable.

*   *   *

By early 2002, I was still acutely conscious of the atmosphere of crisis which the second intifada, the Durban anti-racism conference, 9/11 and the perceived upsurge in antisemitism worldwide had engendered. Yet I was beginning to understand more clearly how relations between Israel and the Palestinians were deteriorating and how the crisis atmosphere was affecting Jewish life, especially in Europe.

In March, some experts on politics in Israel and the Middle East addressed a meeting of the Westbury Group of international Jewish grant-making foundations (named after the London hotel where the first meeting took place), a networking initiative I helped to create. They painted a fairly bleak picture of a country withdrawing into itself and seemingly caring little about harmful gaps opening up between groups of its own citizens. With no international authority keeping them on track, negotiations between the Israelis and the Palestinians were going nowhere. The Israeli authorities were employing harsher measures against Palestinian demonstrators, including the use of sniper rifles and a treacherous variety of rubber bullet, and soldiers suspected of violating rules on policing of demonstrations were not being investigated. Promises of substantial additional resources for Arab-Israeli communities, made in the wake of the killing of twelve Arab citizens in the October 2000 demonstrations, had not been kept. Meanwhile, the Israeli political right's rhetoric against Arabs had worsened. The settlements in the occupied territories were a drain on the economy and undermined social solidarity in Israel; protecting them and maintaining roadblocks led to injuries and humiliation for hundreds of thousands of Palestinians. And rather than confront these problems, the Israeli authorities were increasingly fretting over demographic projections that from being 53 per cent of the population of Israel and the occupied territories in 2002, Jews would be only 43–48 per cent by 2020. One expert drew the most ethnocentric implications from these statistics: 'Anyone who wants to live in Israel as a democratic state with a Jewish majority must bring an end to the occupation.'

For me, the major question prompted by this picture was why Yad Hanadiv, with its huge resources, was not doing more to help organisations in Israel that were trying to reverse these negative political and social trends. At the July Board Meeting at Waddesdon Manor, Jacob himself posed the question of what the foundation could do to help advance the quest for peace. For the president of the World Bank, Jim Wolfensohn, this was first an economic matter. Hanadiv could act as an honest broker; giving some support to get people together on this would be very important and useful. But neither Ari nor Jacob seemed very enthusiastic. Given the urgency of the situation, I found these attitudes deeply depressing.

Meanwhile, I was becoming increasingly exasperated in the light of evidence that diaspora Jewish and Israeli leaders were drawing the wrong conclusions about how to respond to the post-2000 challenges. The effect of Israel's response on Jews was all too clear at a meeting of the European Council of Jewish Communities (ECJC), a body facilitating cooperation on welfare, education and culture, in Prague in November 2002. Most of the talk was of threats to Jews, solidarity with Israel and how 'not to lose the propaganda war in Europe'. Roger Cukierman, head of the French Jewish community's main representative body CRIF, said 'there is a state of war against the Jews in the world'. 'Europe is no longer an open society in which we can bring forward Jewish values', proclaimed Cobi Benatoff, ECJC president. In a belligerent presentation, David Harris, the increasingly hawkish director of the AJC, a cheerleader for George W. Bush-style interventionism in the Middle East, lectured European Jews on why they should adopt the priorities of his organisation. Of the ten challenges that the AJC was dealing with, he told us, the first three stressed shoring up support for Israel, three more focused on antisemitism and four were about Islamic fundamentalism and the Arab world. This intense preoccupation with perceived threats to Israel and Jews worldwide on the part of heads of major organisations, couched in Holocaust-inflected language, stood in marked contrast to the desire to explore how Jews could preserve the new openness in Europe, maintain the resurgence of a flourishing Jewish life and chart a new way of fully participating in the European project, as expressed by Jewish activists, academics and intellectuals in panel discussions at the meeting.

Back in Israel later that month, I heard the same negativism about Europe and warnings about threats to the Jewish people. But this time it was at an international conference considering the current state of world Jewish demographic studies. The event also marked the launch of a new think tank, the Jewish People Policy Planning Institute (JPPPI), sponsored by the Jewish Agency for Israel (JAFI).

JAFI was founded in 1929 as the Jewish Agency for Palestine. In 2002 it was the largest Jewish organisation in the world, with a budget of close to $500 million and still had the aim of instilling in Jews a desire to emigrate to Israel. But even many Zionists believed that there was no longer any need for the organisation and that it should be formally abolished. The setting up of the JPPPI was part of JAFI's attempt to carve out new areas of activity for itself to ensure its survival.

It became obvious that we were being mobilised to support these ambitions when all participants attended a lunch session on 2 December, which constituted the formal launch of the JPPPI. The event was replete with video cameras, journalists, dignitaries and bureaucrats. Dennis Ross, the former Middle East peace negotiator in the Clinton administration and chairman of the JPPPI, was the main speaker. He was flanked by the chairman of JAFI, Sallai Meridor, the Sharon government's minister for the diaspora, Natan Sharansky, and the senior research fellow of the JPPPI, Professor Sergio DellaPergola.

The session was an unabashed exposition of how the JPPPI's work aimed to ensure the achievement of the aims of Zionism. Its fundamental concern was the decline in Jewish populations around the world and the impact this would have on numbers immigrating to Israel. Part of the answer, Meridor said, was to reduce the cost of Jewish education so that more people could take advantage of it. His aim was to ensure an *aliya* of 50,000 Jews every year. Sharansky's assumption was that all Jews were sitting on suitcases waiting to return to their homeland. He kept referring to 'those that don't yet sit in Zion' and how 'Israel has to continue to be a magnet and a shelter'. Dennis Ross gave a patronising and simplistic speech in which he spelt out, in words of one syllable, the link between research and policy-making. The entire event was insulting to the academic participants who were being used as cheerleaders for the ambitions of JAFI. And the more I thought about the core of the name of the new think tank – 'People Policy Planning' – the more it smacked of a faintly disgusting endorsement of eugenics as a tool of Israeli government policy.

I had expected that my greater sense of realism about Zionism and the significance of Israel for diaspora Jews would be echoed among thinking Israelis, but such people still seemed few and far between. A long and tendentious article in *Ha'aretz* on 28 December 2001 by the prominent Israeli journalist Ari Shavit, entitled 'Our good mother Medea', argued that Europe, like Medea, was continually devouring her Jewish children and that Jewish life in Europe was rapidly coming to an end. The only conclusion to be drawn was that Zionism remained the sole path to a sustainable Jewish future. Ari Weiss, who knew Shavit well and wanted to offer him a different view, asked me to write a response, which he would pass on to Shavit. I was so incensed that I wrote a seven-page reply. 'I was under the impression', I said, 'that in recent years intelligent Israelis had begun to develop a more realistic and balanced approach to Jews living in other parts of the world, an approach which rejects both the old charity-based paternalism of the Diaspora and knee-jerk Israeli Zionist triumphalism.' In a tone of controlled anger I argued: 'what Shavit presents is a completely unreconstructed, Diaspora-negating, classic Israeli Zionist argument'.

My answer to Shavit was coloured by having already worked for two years to get the new European grant-making foundation up and running. I had travelled extensively around Europe and witnessed the amazing revival of Jewish life that we were encouraging in Russia, Ukraine, Belarus, Poland, the Czech Republic, Slovakia, Bulgaria and elsewhere. Seeing authentic progress for myself, it angered me that Israel, acting through such institutions as JAFI in the narrow interests of Zionist ideology and state policy, was working for the end of Jewish life in Eastern Europe by encouraging Jews to shut up shop and emigrate.

Worldwide, Jews faced two fundamentally different ways of living in the modern world. The first meant embracing pluralism, universalism, diversity, multiple identities, and drawing strength from the encounter between Jewish culture and values and the wider world. The second was grounded in guarding Jewish exclusivity, rejecting multiculturalism, stressing the centrality of Israel and acknowledging Zionism as the primary political ideology uniting the Jewish people. This was the option chosen by JAFI, the JPPPI and the Israeli government.

I discovered how one Jewish community was facing this choice when I was in Rome in February 2003 and met Giorgio Gomel, head of international relations at the Bank of Italy and a member of the Board of the Jewish Community of Rome. The right-wing government included former fascists who were proclaiming their new-found love for Jews and Israel. This had placed Italian Jews in a difficult position. The public relations officer of the community had told a newspaper that he'd rather vote for Gianfranco Fini, the head of the former neo-fascist party, than a Green, anti-Israel candidate. 'This caused uproar in the community,' Giorgio said, 'although there are very many Jews who are happy about government support for Israel and some even swallow Fini's new line.' He praised Amos Luzzatto, chairman of the Union of Italian Jewish Communities, for his leadership because he refused to come out in support of Fini. All this was new to me. But it seemed obvious that far-right support for Israel would make the difference between the two futures starker than ever.

*   *   *

Of course, I was not alone in my confusion, anxiety and anger. Many of my friends and acquaintances had similar feelings and it wasn't long before we sought out each other's company to share concerns and try to develop a better understanding of what was going on. The venue for our informal discussions, which began early in 2002, was the home of June Jacobs, a Jewish feminist activist dedicated to an open, pluralist vision of Jewish life, in which she played a full and central part. For many years she had been a leading figure in national and international groups working for Middle East peace, human rights and the equality of women. At June's we could openly express our common, dissimilar and even opposing views in an atmosphere of mutual respect and support. We came to these discussions without labels. We were all critical of Israeli government policies and the full gamut of views on Zionism was expressed. What brought and held us together was our belief in the primacy of human rights values, no matter, for example, whether we were discussing anti-Muslim racism or the impact of Israeli government policies on Jews in the UK.

In June 2002 we began to consider seriously the possibility of turning our group and its informal discussions into an organisation. In a discussion paper I argued that it was harder than ever for those who placed the need for peace, reconciliation, justice and human rights above ethnic attachment and loyalty to create a space in which their views were heard. And yet renewed interest in Jewish culture as well as hope that the Oslo accords were about to bring peace had pushed the Israel-firsters and those who believe 'Jews are a people who always dwell alone' into the background. But with the outbreak of the second intifada and the perceived resurgence of antisemitism, defensive Jewish leaders came to the fore once again demanding loyalty, solidarity and improved propaganda for Israel. The abuse directed at those who rejected this made it all the more important to reassert the moral and ethical tradition which both informed the development of human rights values and placed the pursuit of justice at the centre of Jewish values. What brought together the Israel-Palestine issue and the issue of racial justice in British society was our concern that no society could be fair or just where the 'other' is demonised and denied his or her humanity and human rights. I concluded: 'What we can do as Jews is bring serious and sustained analysis and discussion to bear on these issues, make the results of that public and thereby ... significantly expand the space for alternative voices.' This would not prevent us from being maligned by other Jews, but it would make it easier to reach and hold to critical conclusions in the knowledge that we were part of a larger, liberal-minded sector of Jewish opinion. And it might have an impact on the balance of opinion in the wider Jewish community.

It took more than a year, but on 2 October 2003 we launched the Jewish Forum for Justice and Human Rights (JFJHR) in the presence of an invited audience of about 150 people at the Commonwealth Club near Trafalgar Square. Three of us spoke. Sir Nigel Rodley, the internationally respected professor of law at the University of Essex and the elected UK member of the UN Human Rights Committee, gave the keynote. Anne Karpf, the author and journalist, introduced him. I spoke of how Jewish leaders were now playing on Jewish fears of antisemitism, anti-Zionism and the alleged failures of multiculturalism, thereby creating

> a perception that Jews as a whole are unwilling to face up to the fact of human rights abuses by Israel in the occupied Palestinian territories, that Jews are turning their faces away from those seeking refuge from oppression in this and other countries, that Jews pay lip service to the fight against racism but seem to have eyes only for antisemitism ... [And there is] a genuine danger that, in the minds of too many people, Jews would become permanently associated with the abuse of human rights and not with the moral and ethical tradition which has both informed the development of human rights values and places the pursuit of justice at the centre of Jewish values.

In a strong and very personal speech, Nigel Rodley said: 'I have no doubt about the right to existence of the state of Israel, [but] I have serious misgivings about some Israeli policies and the apparent reluctance in the Jewish Diaspora to challenge them.' He spoke of Israel's 'crimes and atrocities', namely the

> colonisation through the settlement policy of large parts of occupied Palestinian territory that is unlawful and oppressive; and the building of security barriers that effectively imprison whole communities, which is also unlawful and oppressive. The frequent torture of Arab terrorist suspects, first with the complaisance of the High Court, and then in circumvention of its landmark 1998 ruling – is unlawful and oppressive.
>
> What have the mainstream Jewish organisations had to say about these practices? Not a lot, as far as I know, other than from time to time defending the government. Such a posture amounts at least to collusion in the notion that *all* Jews support the practices – even when many *Israelis* do not – and further, it makes the attempts of Jews to challenge the practices seem like disloyalty verging on treason.

Most of us shared similar criticisms of the Israeli government and the Zionist movement, and for some those criticisms stemmed in part from more fundamental doubts about the political ideology that brought the state into being. But others had no such doubts. These differences were, understandably, suppressed as we worked together to achieve the aims of the JFJHR, but they were never far beneath the surface.

9

SHEDDING ILLUSIONS

[E]nding the occupation and establishing a Palestinian state in the West Bank and Gaza Strip only realises one demand of the Arabs within Israel. Their second demand is total equality. They demand an end to the discrimination inherent in a state 'solely for Jews,' and demand that Israel become a state for all of its citizens, both Arab and Jewish.

Dr Adel Manna, 2002

A nationalist development can have two possible consequences. Either a healthy reaction will set in that will overcome the danger heralded by nationalism, and also nationalism itself, which has now fulfilled its purpose; or nationalism will establish itself as the permanent principle; in other words, it will exceed its function, pass beyond its proper bounds, and – with overemphasized consciousness – displace the spontaneous life of the nation. Unless some force arises to oppose this process, it may well be the beginning of the downfall of the people, a downfall dyed in the colours of nationalism.

Martin Buber, 1921

My frustration with the Israel grant-making programme of Yad Hanadiv was tempered somewhat by an ethos which encouraged high-level debate, enquiry, investigation and discussion to assess the impact of what we were doing and inform new ideas and initiatives. I was therefore very comfortable accepting invitations to speak at conferences and seminars on issues related to the grant programmes we were developing for Europe, as I saw this as another way of giving effect to that ethos. But the trustees also wanted to feel that Rothschild grant-making was giving a lead, so I used these opportunities as a means of attempting to influence the direction of Jewish organisational life – encouraging pluralism, advocating engagement with other minority groups in activity to strengthen civil society, supporting communities and groups no matter how numerically small they were and arguing that Jews should not be deflected from furthering Jewish renewal by fears of antisemitism.

Knowing that the trustees would be sympathetic to proposals to bring people together to explore questions relating to our grant-making, I was able to renew a working relationship I had with my friend Diana Pinto, the Paris-based intellectual historian who was one of very few people thinking freely and creatively about the condition of Jews in the new Europe. Born in Italy, educated at Harvard and living in Paris, Diana was for many years a consultant on civil society to the Council of Europe. She had chosen to spend much of her time, since the early 1990s, providing the rationale, through her writing and speaking, as to why Jews in the new post-1989 Europe had great opportunities to become fully part of the political, cultural and intellectual mainstream.

Diana was very keen to promote deep discussion among Jewish intellectuals on the position of Jews in Europe and their contributions to building European civil society in the light of the numerous problems that were now facing both the European project and Jewish communities, problems that had significantly fractured the optimism that characterised the 1990s. On her initiative, together we drew up a plan for what Diana chose to call a 'round-table' – to emphasise the equality of status and contribution of all who were invited to attend – that would explore these issues. I put the proposal to the trustees and they agreed to fund it.

It was Diana's idea to hold the round table at Chateau Canisy in the Normandy countryside, and a more appropriate spot it would have been difficult to find. There were no city distractions to draw people away. The extensive grounds reinforced the feeling of seclusion and offered ample opportunity for contemplative or merely recreational walks. Le Comte Denis de Kergolay, whose family has owned the Chateau for more than 1,000 years, ran the place as a retreat for groups and organisations with whose ethos he sympathised. If this was hardly what one might have expected from a Comte of such lineage, it was easier to understand knowing that, in his youth, Joan Baez was his girlfriend.

Twenty-five people from across Europe – academics, writers, filmmakers, entrepreneurs, educationalists, political activists, public intellectuals – converged on the Chateau in March 2003 in the shadow of the commencement of the Iraq war and conscious of the immense problems facing the new Europe. Although neither Israel nor Zionism were on the agenda as discrete topics, Israel figured in a number of the sessions, given its influence on Jewish identity and the impact of Israeli actions on Europe's Jews.

In her opening remarks, Diana Pinto told the participants: 'You are chosen for your diversity, not because you agree with us. From the point of view of Jewish identity, this is a motley group. A creative "mess" sociologically. We are on a different planet now. Haven't we come a long way in three years? Where do we stand? Antisemitism has returned. Israel is the Jew among the nations. Europe is decadent – but is this a perfectly accurate picture?'

Following Diana I asked: 'Has Israel become a liability for Jews rather than a reinforcement of positive Jewish identity?' This went to the heart of the question of the relevance of Zionism, and many of the participants made it clear that it was a central question for them too. Professor Susan Neiman, director of the Einstein Forum in Potsdam, seized on it and spoke of how the notion of Israel as a possible liability was not being discussed at all in the United States and how we, as a group that transcended national boundaries, could play a role in encouraging critical discussion of Israel in Europe.

The tension between working for a viable European Jewish future and being bound by a Zionist ethos that permeated Jewish leadership at all levels was best encapsulated in remarks made by Göran Rosenberg, one of Sweden's leading columnists, authors and broadcasters. In speaking of what constituted his 'Jewish voice', he referred to 'inward-bound values' and 'outward-bound values'. The former were defensive, they stressed memory, 'never again'. They were about 'the unopposed adherence to Zionist values. But I refuse to be bound by those', he said. The latter values were about 'pluralism and diversity; religion that explains the world. Jews have thrived in more pluralistic societies ... The antithesis to these outward values is homogeneity – the nation state is not a good Jewish idea.' Göran was a radical critic of Israel and the Zionist narrative, and cared passionately about the possibility of a thriving cosmopolitan Jewish presence in Europe.

Professor Dominique Moïsi, a leading French political commentator and expert on international affairs, spoke of the 'alienation of the Israeli cause in Europe, a process of self-isolation. This was not anti-Zionism exactly, nor was it antisemitism. Israel had lost its closest, universalist, humanist friends in Europe. This is the era of suspicion. Memory of the Holocaust is fading. Israel is [seen as] the matrix of all international relations.' This was why Europeans, Jews and Americans had to find an answer to the conflict: '[the neoconservatives] who claim to represent us in the US and Israel don't'.

The Iraq war, which began on 20 March, overshadowed discussions and seeped into them in a very significant way. Göran Rosenberg said: 'There has been an Israeli motif in this business of the war – but I have argued that what has changed in the world in a dramatic way is the American policy. I can see an alliance of darkest forces in Israel and the US administration which say "We need to change the world until it suits us". This is a kind of hubris. The Israeli view is "We can only survive in the sea of Islam with the help of the Americans."' This Israel, argued Professor Lars Dencik, a social psychologist at Roskilde University in Denmark, which saw itself isolated and under siege, presented itself as a more attractive focus of identification for European Jews who were lapsing into victimhood again. The misrepresentation of antisemitism was partly responsible for this. In fact Israel had a much greater impact on our lives than antisemitism. What the public now saw as Judaism 'has been colonised by Israel. To combat this we need an oppositional force'. One participant then signalled his agreement to this when he said: 'Israel was partly an answer to antisemitism; today it's part of the problem'.

Anna Foa, professor of modern history at the University of Rome La Sapienza, described the burden carried and the challenge faced by Europe's Jews today: 'We are a new reality in relation to Israel and the US – *we* have to cope with *this* European past. We're not speaking about something which is dead. We didn't break with the past as Jews in Israel and the US did. Antisemitism is very disturbing for us but Israel is a more important issue.'

These critical comments on Israel were made from positions of strong sympathy for the country but highlighted the very problem of Israel as a 'liability' for Europe's Jews. While no one used the word 'liability', most people believed that Israel had a major impact on the way Jews could live in Europe and that it was an issue that had to be squarely faced.

*　*　*

From personal experience of living in Israel and from reading, I knew – but not in any detail – that Arab-Israelis, who now called themselves Palestinians, were second-class citizens, facing discrimination in many areas of Israeli life. The extent of my knowledge changed radically when a meeting of the Westbury Group of international Jewish foundations that I chaired in November 2003 in Israel devoted a significant part of a very full programme to the situation of Israel's Palestinian population, as explained by Palestinian-Israeli experts.

The first speaker, Dr Adel Manna, a highly respected educationalist, gave a compelling overview of the situation. Completely rooted in facts and thorough research, Dr Manna's account was that of someone who had wanted to work with the Israelis and create a successful future for the Arab community that remained after the 1948 war, but who had become deeply disillusioned. He remained very measured throughout, but he could barely suppress the pain, frustration and despair he had experienced.

Dr Manna's single most disturbing message was that the structural discrimination against the Palestinian community, which began with the establishment of the state, was still continuing in 2003. After June 1948 Israel built 700 new settlements, but almost no Arab villages were built. The aim was simply to limit space for the Arabs. Between 1948 and 2003 there was a seven-fold growth in the Arab population on less than half the land they held in 1948. Not included in that was the land expropriated by the state from the 400 villages that were destroyed. The lack of land and water meant that fewer men could be employed in agriculture. Proletarianisation occurred, but without industrialisation in the villages. Men had to commute to find work in townships, but the women couldn't, so they remained a relatively low percentage of the labour force. The gaps between Arabs and Jews had not narrowed. Poverty in 2003 was double the median of the general population. Among 30 localities in Israel with very high unemployment, 25 were Arab.

Arabs were excluded from the collectivity because Israel defined itself as a Jewish state, Dr Manna said. 'Being Israeli per se is not possible because Israel is not the state of all its citizens. You are either Jew or Arab, you cannot just be Israeli.' He said 'Arabs in Israel continue to live under siege and in distress … Israeli leaders say "Be patient, things will change when peace comes." I say peace will only come when Israel makes peace with its citizens. If you can't give them equal rights, how can you integrate into the region?'

The other grant-making foundation representatives in the room did not seek to deny the accuracy of his statistics but I could see that his conclusions made them feel very uncomfortable. I saw myself as deeply concerned and well-informed about the Israel-Palestine conflict, and yet not knowing the facts as set out by Dr Manna in his talk suddenly seemed vaguely fraudulent. It made me realise how much my awareness had been formed by chance encounters rather than systematic enquiry. A key reason for this glaring gap in my knowledge was a residual resistance to empathise with the plight of the 'other', to see things from the Palestinian or the Palestinian-Israeli point of view. Because Zionism was largely built round a series of myths, any questioning of its fundamentals could engender serious doubt about its validity. I had been asking such questions for a number of years, but fear that accepting the Palestinian narrative meant a complete negation of the Zionist narrative was clearly holding me back. Listening to Dr Manna, however, I became aware that this was not a zero-sum game; that whatever conclusions one might come to about the rights and wrongs of Zionism, it had produced a new reality which was not going to go away. And that achieving justice for and promoting the human rights of the Palestinians could not be done on the basis of the infringement of the human rights of Israeli Jews, no matter what mistakes had been made in the past. Much had to be put right and significant changes in the Israeli mindset had to occur, but that would only come about by acknowledging and allowing for the expression of the national aspirations of both peoples.

There then followed a very contrasting talk by Dr As'ad Ghanem, a political scientist at Haifa University. Far lighter on facts and far more focused on the politics, Dr Ghanem made no attempt to hide his anger, although he too was very measured. As head of Sikkuy, the Association for the Advancement of Civil Equality in Israel, he had given testimony to the Or Commission investigating the killing of twelve Arab citizens of Israel and one Palestinian by Israeli police in 2000. But he had decided that he could not fight for equality without actually doing something. So he moved from Sikkuy to the Ibn Khaldun Arab Association for Research and Development, a Palestinian Arab non-profit organisation founded in 2002. The state regime was the main problem, Dr Ghanem said. Israel was not acting as a democracy. 'There are 600 Jewish localities where I cannot legally live. This is a basic element of the Israeli regime. Israel being a Jewish state means I can't live or work in some areas. Jewish, non-Israeli institutions are part of the body-politic. There is no equality – even my vote doesn't have the same meaning. Forty per cent of Arabs did not participate in the last election.' Dr Ghanem continued: 'Arabs must take responsibility for themselves. But they need the help of the majority, and also of Jews outside Israel because of the role Jews have played in creating and maintaining the state structure.'

Listening to Dr Manna and Dr Ghanem, and a third speaker, Dr Ghanem Yacoubi, who described the educational disadvantages faced by the Arab sector, was not, and should not have been, a comfortable experience. Many of the foundations represented had been active in various projects designed to improve conditions for Palestinian-Israelis, especially in the areas of welfare, young people and women. But it was impossible not to be aware that we were part of the problem. Although my work was focused on Europe, nevertheless, at this meeting I was seen as representing Yad Hanadiv and therefore felt a sense of responsibility for what the foundation could have done but hadn't. Why should fulfilling the aims of Zionism prevent a sensibly and ethically run foundation from devoting a considerable part of its resources to ensuring that Palestinian-Israelis ceased to be second-class citizens and felt that they belonged, that the state was theirs too? How could Israel afford to continue to alienate one-sixth of its population and hope to have social peace and security?

While there was much sympathy expressed for the plight of Palestinian-Israelis during the discussion, the foundation representatives bristled at the mention of Israel becoming a state for all its citizens. The gap between the level of sympathy and understanding among liberal Zionist Jews and what Palestinian-Israelis regarded as their minimum needs and rights was considerable. And it was even more evident when a prominent Israeli, well-known for his pragmatic approach to the country's needs and with a track record of opening up higher education to more Arab students, presented his view of the situation.

Professor Avishay Braverman, the dynamic president of Ben-Gurion University of the Negev, soon to leave his position and become a Labour Party politician, began by 'expressing his concern for the survival of the Zionist state', not because of the political, social and ethnic identity problems within the country, but because it was becoming more difficult for Israel to be accepted by the southern part of Europe and 'because Europe would be one-third Muslim in 30–40 years'. It seemed incredible to me that someone of Braverman's much-vaunted intelligence could care more about being accepted in southern Europe as the way to ensure the survival of the Zionist state than ensuring the survival of Israel by creating a society in which all felt a sense of belonging.

*   *   *

When Diana Pinto and I began to talk about organising a second round-table at Canisy at the end of January 2004, it seemed obvious that it should focus in great part on Israel, since the first and very successful Canisy did not discuss Israel as a specific topic. Once again, the trustees of the foundation agreed to fund the event. But exploring the connection between Europe and Israel and European Jews and Israel was undoubtedly going to be more difficult because of the differences over Israel that existed even among those whose criticisms of the country's policies would seem to imply that they were of one mind.

Many of the people from the first Canisy round-table were there. Professor Michael Brenner, Göran Rosenberg, Professor Ana Foa, Professor Susan Neiman, Professor Dominique Moïsi, Professor Jonathan Webber and others. But there were also new participants: Professor Jacqueline Rose, from the English Department of Queen Mary, University of London; André Glucksmann, a philosopher from Paris, and Professor Micha Brumlik, from the University of Frankfurt's education department. However, since it would have been wrong to talk about Israel without Jewish Israelis present, also attending were: Gideon Levy, the *Ha'aretz* journalist known for his trenchant critique of the occupation; Professor Fania Oz-Salzberger, a writer and historian at Haifa University; Daniel Ben-Simon, another *Ha'aretz* journalist with a special interest in writing about the Jewish diaspora; Daphna Agnon-Golan, director of the Minerva Centre for Human Rights at the Hebrew University Jerusalem; Professor Eva Illouz, a sociologist also at the Hebrew University, and Avner Azulay, managing director of a philanthropic foundation and a former colonel in military intelligence.

Two of the Israelis were particularly outspoken critics of Israel's current path: Levy, whose powerful articles had made him a hero to some and a traitor to others; and Golan, whose involvement with human rights groups and women's groups made her one of the most prominent feminist voices against the occupation. She and Oz-Salzberger brought an extra symbolic weight to the discussions because of their family connections to iconic Israeli figures. Oz-Salzberger's father was Israel's leading living novelist, Amos Oz. Agnon-Golan's grandfather was the Nobel Prize laureate for literature in 1966, the late S.Y. Agnon.

To have emerged enriched from such an intense weekend of discussions with a group of people both expressing support for Israel's existence and contributing to a searching and troubling critique of Zionism may sound Panglossian. But to think this is to be unaware of the way many thoughtful Jews were grappling with the contradictions of reconciling the legitimate historical longing for Jewish emancipation with the messy reality of national self-determination produced by the Zionist movement. And although the focus was on Israel, Europe remained the bedrock for the discussions. Everyone used Europe – an ideal and a source of tragedy and pain, both in the past and the present – as a reference point for thinking about Israel and this was a source of considerable creative tension, a tension so palpable that at one moment it looked as if verbal argument would turn physical.

As a settler state, Israel, with its nationalist ideology of extreme exclusiveness, arrived very late in the day, Giorgio Gomel reminded us, just as colonial states were being dismantled and indigenous national liberation movements were securing independence for their countries. In the prototypical nineteenth-century nation state, there was a close overlap between nation and state; the nation was embodied in the state, which relied on the indivisible unity and totality of the nation. The Israeli model was very different, Eva Illouz explained. Since its inception there was a disjunction between the nation – the Jewish people – and the state, which was supposed to grant equal status and rights to its minority through citizenship. There was a structural discrepancy between the national identity of the country – its Jewish culture and religion – and its capacity to function as a universal state. Can a state that embodies a particular people and culture, she asked, also be a state that grants equal rights to all citizens? For Jews in Europe, this question was especially difficult, Göran Rosenberg argued, since we support both the supranational character of the EU and multicultural states that give equal rights to all, no matter what their colour, creed or ethnicity. How could we advocate one social vision here in Europe and support the Zionist vision of Jewish exclusivity in Israel, especially when, de facto, Israel itself was a pluralist country?

Since Zionism did not recognise the existence of a Palestinian people, the Zionist leaders could not tell the truth about the hundreds of thousands of Palestinians who were forced out of their homes in order to make it possible to establish as exclusively Jewish a state as possible, Daphna Golan said. Neither young Israelis nor young Zionist Jews outside of Israel were told the real reasons why the Palestinians were angry. Eventually, the Zionist narrative broke down when the politicians decided it was permissible to talk to Palestinians as Palestinians and then eventually to negotiate with them over two states. But this did not do very much to alter the demonised view of Palestinians which so many Israelis had and which was legitimised by people like the historian Benny Morris, who now said that the ethnic cleansing he had revealed as a left-wing historian was justified because the Arabs were 'barbarians'.

Since Zionism was a reaction to antisemitism, it was not surprising that the Holocaust was seen as the ultimate justification for the establishment of a Jewish state. But, Golan insisted, while it was right that the world, including the Palestinians, should know about the Shoah, that did not mean that everything was permissible in the name of having a Jewish state. She asked: 'Did the Jews envisage the country being run by generals? The Holocaust does not allow us Israelis to imprison, arrest, deport, enslave and oppress another people.' While the lesson drawn was 'Because it happened to us we will make sure it never happens again', this could lead to the militarisation of suffering. One of the things that drove this determination was the sense of shame felt about the Holocaust, which was linked to the internal violence the state enacted against itself and against the people it found itself in opposition to, argued Jacqueline Rose. The imperative of Zionism made it difficult to confront the question of how far a nation state could think about what it was doing without damaging itself internally to the point of no return. But it was a question of justice and unavoidable.

If our history had to be understood by all, Jewish Israelis had to listen to the history of the Palestinians, said Daphna Golan. Just as we needed to hear the voices of Jews who dreamed about going to live in Israel, so too we needed to hear the voices and acknowledge the pain of the Palestinians who still dreamt about their homeland. Which also meant talking about the right of return and not declaring it taboo.

Fania Oz-Salzberger said Zionist particularism posed a formidable challenge to critical Zionists who stressed universal values and human rights. Looking around Israel it was a troubling fact that there was a complete absence of any moral voice on these wider human issues expressed by anyone in the orthodox world, with the honourable exception of Meimad. 'None of the established religious parties say anything. It's the institutes dedicated to secular Judaism which are flourishing and exploring a general Jewish cultural and moral voice,' she said, 'which is both cosmopolitan and addressed specifically to the Israel-Palestine conflict.'

Immediate withdrawal from the occupied territories was in the best interests of the future of Israel. Some might think this was naive, without knowing what would come after. But, Gideon Levy said, this was irrelevant. 'It has to be done, come what may. There is no other option if Israel wants to be accepted into the region.' But there lay the rub and up popped the question of Europe. Danny Ben-Simon told this story: 'Shimon Peres, then foreign minister, had a meeting with the Egyptian president, Hosni Mubarak, in 1995, one year before darkness fell [the assassination of Yitzhak Rabin, Israel's prime minister]. Mubarak asked him: "How would you like to see Israel?" He said "At peace with the Arabs". But what kind of Israel would you like to see? "At peace with the Arabs, we would help you with high-tech, make you modern etc." "But Shimon," Mubarak said, "in 25–30 years, will you be part of us?" Peres replied: "Of course not. We are Europeans. We will be part of Europe." Mubarak said: "Shimon, even if we have peace we cannot live like this."' And large numbers of Israelis were turning increasingly to Europe, taking out EU passports on the basis of their parents' countries of origin. But, Ben Simon said: 'Israel without peace and without integration in the Middle East will not exist.'

Zionism aimed to complete the story of the Jewish people, but the Canisy discussions seemed to show that reality had gotten the better of this ambition. Göran Rosenberg saw this as a much deeper problem than just mistakes made by Israelis over the decades of Israel's existence. There could be a tragic end to history, he said, and it was the Europeans who knew it and who therefore rejected 'the notion of a final good society', whereas George Bush and Ariel Sharon believed that Western man was charged with a higher mission to reach that end, with little concern about the means needed to achieve it. But anyone who knew Zionism knew that there was a strong link between Zionism and messianism. For Jews, the fulfilment of Zionism was a central building block in the creation of a truly harmonious world order. But, Rosenberg argued, 'there is no end to history, no solution by fiat to future conflicts between human beings'.

A common theme for the Israelis was the extent to which European Jews could support Israelis struggling to get their government to respect human rights and to achieve justice for the Palestinians. For Gideon Levy it seemed to begin with what Israeli Jews and diaspora Jews had in common: 'Speaking as an Israeli, I wonder why I feel so close to those present. Is it because of shared values? Even in Israel there are few Jews I feel close to. Is it because of shared Jewish values? If so, where does the support in Israel for transfer [of Palestinians out of biblical Palestine] come in? I always understood this to be inimical to Jewish values.' Daphna Golan made a simple plea: 'I came to ask you for advice, help, support. Is this the Israel you dreamed about and yearned for?' But Ben-Simon expressed scepticism: 'of course we hate anybody who dares do something to help us out of this mess; and all the suggestions by Europe and anyone else were killed by Sharon. I don't think you European Jews can help; most American Jews are in the pocket of the prime minister … The head of the French, the English Jewish communities, they have become soldiers of Sharon. It's a shame; they have lost their dignity. To take a picture of themselves near Sharon or a tank gives them something more than let's say to have some influence.'

Michael Brenner argued that European Jews need to speak out: 'Most [Jews] in Europe would feel that what the Israeli government is doing is right. But this is not the advice we should be giving Israel. We all know that Jews in Europe play a minor role, but we have to start thinking that we do have to say something, and we can't expect it from Jewish organisations.' Levy was much more emphatic: 'Politically, Israel needs European Jewry desperately. It is incapable of helping itself ... European Jews need to say what they believe – the truth as they see it.' Rhetorically he asked: 'what does it mean to be pro- or anti-Israel? Who is the sincere friend of Israel? The loving critic or the unthinking patriot?'

'European Jews can also contribute a great deal in helping Israelis, as a whole, recognise and understand the legitimacy and authority of international organisations', Eva Illouz argued, 'and even perhaps start to think of supranational solutions to the conflict, such as, for example, a framework like the EU itself for Israelis and Palestinians which could perhaps coordinate and integrate the two states.' Fania Oz-Salzberger advocated a different kind of engagement: 'Identity is not about identification. I'd like Israel to be part of your identity but in a much more diverse and differentiated way. Become more subtly interested in what is going on in the Israeli public sphere now and latch on to the parts of Israeli civil society you feel you can identify with and support ... and state loudly your critique of what you dislike. Stop identifying with the official Israeli government – we must say this to the official Jewish organisations – because so many Israelis don't identify with it.' In my remarks, I linked this view to the fundamental need for a new approach to relations between Jews in Europe and Israel: 'We have to bury the idea of an eternal, spiritual, mystical relationship between the Diaspora and Israel ... Israel is going to go its own separate way as a state, and the longer we perpetuate the notion that there is an eternal spiritual bond, it will be bad for us and bad for Israel. We can, however, in a post-spiritual bond world, engage with groups in Israel on things we care about: civil society issues, racism, minorities, values. But we can only do that if we here in Europe fully engage in our own societies on these issues too.'

One of the most striking things about these discussions was the fact that the most searching critique largely came from the Israelis and not the Europeans. While virtually all of the European Jews were considerably left of centre on Israel and much else, most spoke out of a need to demonstrate a high degree of protectiveness of Israel, seeing it in the predicament of being under threat from local enemies and enemies in Europe that would not simply disappear on Israel leaving the occupied territories and recognising Palestinian rights.

Most of the Israelis, on the other hand, seemed to see the damage Israel was inflicting upon itself as more serious than any external threats. And so there was this curious situation in which the European Jews were telling their Israeli counterparts: 'You are going too far, you are going too fast, you are naive.' As Diana Pinto later summarised it, some of the European Jews said that Israelis 'had not mentioned Palestinian terrorists and suicide bombings even once. And that they were destroying their own powerful civil society arguments by exaggerating some of the critiques. A fierce debate then ensued because the Israelis considered that their positions, based on real life and actual experiences, were not trusted and that they were being spoken to by ideologues who were "lecturing" to them on the meaning of "too far", as though they were naive idealists without stakes in Israel's survival and security. A significant number of European Jews were basically "defending" Israel against its home-made critics.' An Israeli participant was told 'Ultra self-criticism is ultra-egoism.' Some of the Israelis resented this as patronising or worse.

What the Israelis and Europeans had in common was an existential connection to the problems being considered. What was happening in Israel and to Israel, and what Israel was doing, had a direct impact on the lives of all concerned. These weren't abstract discussions. As Gideon Levy said: 'In any event, we are fated to be together. The behaviour of the soldier at the checkpoint harms the Palestinians, the Israelis and European Jews. The "selection" in Jenin harms you directly. An unjust Israel harms you so we have a responsibility towards each other.'

An especially sharp exchange occurred over the direction of Israeli politics and society and the degradation of democracy. Danny Ben-Simon set the tone when he said: 'Israel has been taken over by a military junta.' In a later session Gideon Levy made a comparison between Israel and late Weimar Germany: 'Sebastian Haffner's book *Defying Hitler* would have resonance for every honest Israeli because Israel is in a 1930s situation. Not the Shoah, but the Shoah arose out of certain circumstances which were not the Shoah to begin with.' Taking up the point, Jonathan Webber said: 'To get Jews to recognise that Israel is in a 1930s stage is too much of a paradigm shift, even though there is quite a lot of evidence in support of this.' Kostek Gebert, a leading columnist on *Gazeta Wyborcza* and a key figure in the Jewish revival in Poland, radically disagreed: 'If Israel is like Nazi Germany in the 1930s, it justifies going to war against her. Kosovo was taken for less. There are any number of unjust societies, but to compare Israel with Germany is to say that Israel is preparing genocide. I cannot have a dialogue with Israelis who say this because I am not prepared to support a state of war against Israel. This exaggeration is counterproductive and unreal.'

A third Israeli came partially to the aid of the two who argued that Israel was in a pre-fascist or proto-fascist situation. Avner Azulay said: 'There are fascistic elements in Israel and in the government, willing to undermine democracy and the rule of law. The settlers are responsible for this too, behaving worse than the soldiers. The soldiers are being forced into it. All civil rights and democracy education has been abandoned by the Education Ministry because of money. But it is still not the 1930s.' Levy then clarified his earlier remark: 'In saying that Israelis should be able to see that Israel was like Germany in the 1930s I did not mean to imply that Israel is Nazi, or in any way like the Nazi state. I never said that and I never meant that. A situation was developing which could *lead* to genocide.' But another European voice expressed strong support for Levy's view. Micha Brumlik argued: 'If what's meant is 1932, it's right: a deteriorating economic situation; a weakening democratic system which worked on the surface but which was deeply wounded in its structure, a democracy without democrats; a situation which was equal to political anarchy and social anomie and for years a proto-fascist right-wing government – which is exactly what we have today in Israel.'

By any measure this was a remarkable exchange, all the more so because it took place *between* Zionists. I could understand the sensitivity of Brenner, Moïsi and Gebert, but I felt that they were being swayed by the thought of having to face such an argument were it to be made by critical European leftists. Whereas there was something compelling about the testimony of the Israelis. There was no reason for them to make this comparison if they didn't believe in its validity. Shocking though their judgement was, I quietly felt that they must be right.

For me, the second Canisy discussions were transformative. I could never again think in the same way about the Israel-Palestine conflict. I saw that a profound metamorphosis in thinking was required for there to be the reconciliation of historically significant proportions between Palestinians and Israelis so essential to a just resolution of the conflict. But when Ari Weiss heard about the nature of the discussions he was less than impressed. They were far too critical of Israel for his liking. Shortly before the round-table commenced he made known to Diana that he was not happy with the composition of the Israeli group. While neither Diana nor I felt that we were bringing over some anti-Zionist cabal that would trash Israel, we made a last-minute effort to take Ari's concerns into account. However, this was difficult because the event was more or less upon us. But, as it turned out, Israel did not lack friends at the discussions and even the severest Israeli critics, Gideon Levy and Daphna Golan, spoke from a deep sense of Israeli patriotism. They were critical but had no wish to see the State of Israel dismantled. On the contrary, they wanted to see the state survive and thrive on the basis of liberal-Zionist values. By the end of the weekend, Diana and I felt that a broad range of views on Israel had emerged.

A few weeks later, Diana wrote an article for the *International Herald Tribune*, 'A reconciliation between distant cousins' (20 February 2004), discussing some of the themes of the round-table. At the heart of her piece were these two paragraphs:

> Fully aware of the new dangers that were besieging the Jewish – and Western – world and caring deeply about Israel's future, [the participants] refused to succumb to the current Jewish spiral of anguished accusations and historical pessimism. In their eyes, the Jewish world as well as the state of Israel were capable of determining their own fate, and not victims at the mercy of forces bent on their destruction.
>
> The Europeans shared with their Israeli colleagues a commitment to democratic pluralism, human rights, the imperatives of social justice and the ideal of reconciliation. They all supported a state of Israel anchored in these principles, a state that would respect the rights of all its minorities.

Diana sent a draft to Ari Weiss, who only responded to her after it was published (with some editorial changes), strongly objecting to practically everything in it. He expressed his deep disquiet with what had been discussed at Canisy and bitterly criticised Diana, and, by implication, me (he cc'd his email to me).

Ari took exception to the whole idea of the article, doubting whether it was appropriate to bring the substance of the discussions to public attention. He dismissed the notion that universal values and Jewish concerns needed reconciling. He interpreted the article as virtually condoning unfair criticism of Israel and accused Diana of being dismissive of Israel. He rejected any criticism that Israel was not respecting the rights of its minorities. He blamed the problems limiting Palestinian-Israeli dialogue on the Palestinians' lack of will to accept that Jews might have a legitimate claim to a state. Diana had written that Israelis, 'anguished by their country's political direction', were 'asking support from Europe's more critical and more independent Jews', but he dismissed this as not credible. Referring to the fact that some of the participants visited a German military cemetery and Diana had written that this promoted a 'better understanding of "Europe's complexities"', Ari accused her of failing to demonstrate that she had the same sensitivity to the reality of what was going on in Israel and the Middle East. He concluded that neither the issues under discussion nor the people invited were appropriate.

The tone of his email was, by turns, petulant, supercilious, insulting and illiberal. It was not a balanced reading of what Diana had written. He positioned himself as the 'good Jew', while at the same time wallowing in an anguished indecisiveness.

Ari's reactions epitomised everything that was wrong with Yad Hanadiv's approach to Israel's problems and showed his failure to understand the concerns of European Jews. He seemed to be trapped in a mindset that could only see the Canisy discussions as a forum that legitimised Jewish 'Israel-bashing', although they were nothing of the kind. His words seemed to reflect a blinkered, fearful, aggressive Zionism that justified Israel's current positions on the grounds of 'Who are you to lecture to us?'

His response to Diana convinced me that he would never lead Yad Hanadiv towards an engagement with Palestinians in Israel or the occupied territories that would result in true reconciliation. And he would never fully support me in my efforts to persuade the trustees of the value of the European work. I think it was this experience that led me to conclude that my time with the Rothschilds would need to be brought to an end sooner rather than later.

* * *

In the many talks, lectures and panel presentations I gave during 2003–05, I constantly returned to the question of the damaging effect Israel's policies were having on European Jews and on Jews worldwide. 'We are fooling ourselves if we do not see how the policies of the Israeli government are fuelling anti-Jewish hostility', I told the World Union of Progressive Judaism's European Region Conference in my keynote lecture in March 2004. 'And if the public positions adopted by so-called representative Jewish bodies in Europe offer nothing but unqualified solidarity, we can hardly throw up our hands in shock horror when Jews and Israel are publicly seen as one and the same.'

Not only did I feel that Israel held some responsibility for the state of antisemitism, but I was already convinced that Israel was largely the agent of its own misfortunes, a view seen by the Israeli government and staunch pro-Israel groups as singling Israel out for special opprobrium and therefore fuelling anti-Zionism. But the folly of this response was laid bare at a conference in July in Jerusalem on the impact on the Jewish people of globalisation and the clash between civilisations, religions and people, at which I delivered a paper on a panel together with Professor Aviezer Ravitzky.

Ravitzky was one of Israel's leading orthodox religious intellectuals, an expert on Jewish theology and philosophy and a Zionist. I was rather hoping that, as a frank and fearless thinker, who I had heard in 1998 acknowledging that antisemitism can serve the interests of Zionism (see the quotation following the title of Chapter 7), he would say something that would complement the controversial remarks I was about to make. And he didn't disappoint. Ravitzky was deeply worried about Israel and Jews taking sides in the debate over the 'Clash of Civilisations'. In the early days of the state, Israel was seen as more neutral. Assimilation in any one camp was avoided. But now Israel was constantly being urged to line up with the United States and this was a 'dangerous development which threatens our future'. The Middle East conflict was already increasingly seen as a clash between monotheistic religions, one that could be 'total, acute and to the death. To overlay this struggle with a global dimension would pose a radical threat to us all.'

'Are we to view all of these developments as ordained by fate?' Ravitzky asked. No, they are largely the result of objective factors which the Israeli state and Jews generally can influence. 'We must make every effort to separate the Middle East conflict from the global conflict. The struggle with the Palestinians must be local, regional and political', he said. 'But when we liken Arafat to Bin Laden we are doing the opposite.' We must not do anything that reinforces our destructive image. 'The support of the Christian Right in America is dangerous. We must not condone this alliance.' Finally, he said: 'we must protest the attempt to impose on the world the regime of the West. Jewish historical memory says that we must avoid particularist imposition.' It is precisely the Jews who have to fight against the demonisation of Islam – who better than the Jews to do this? The subtext of his remarks, as he acknowledged during questions, was that Israeli policy was fanning the flames of antisemitism.

Although my subject was Jewish culture in the era of globalisation, I had to address the question of the degree to which globalisation was leading to an intensification of antisemitism and how far anti-Jewish hostility affected the revival of Jewish culture in Europe. I was sceptical on both counts, but sure that whatever new hostility was being generated had much to do with Israel's behaviour on the world stage, the same point Ravitzky was making. Like him, I believed that Jews and Israel could meet the challenges posed by globalisation and not take sides in any clash of civilisations. But I actually saw certain advantages for the continuation of cultural renewal in a more globalised world. I argued that the dominant Jewish response to the consequences of globalisation 'is a retreat into defensive particularism … [M]uch of this, in my view, stems from the policies of the government of the state of Israel acting as if it were under a state of siege, exporting its internal crisis by shamelessly exploiting the vulnerability of Jewish communities, especially in Europe.' Globalisation was a fact, though by no means as new as many commentators made out, yet it was being turned into a destructive ideology, as both Ravitzky and I argued. Ravitzky was the kind of Zionist who could see that certain Israeli and Jewish interpretations of this ideological globalisation constituted a trap for the Jewish people. Falling into it played into the hands of those promoting a right-wing, aggressive-defensive, neoconservative agenda, which was antithetical to Jewish values.

Another positive manifestation of globalisation I identified was the development of the EU, 'the symbolic embodiment and the practical realisation of that post-war determination to create a Europe in which the Holocaust could never happen again, Nazism and fascism could never return, the universal principles of human rights would prevail.' To make the most of the EU, Jews needed to fully realise that they were now the *subjects* of history and not the *objects*. One of the reasons why Jews had become so fully the subjects of history was undoubtedly the creation of the State of Israel, which marked the emergence of Jews from a sense of powerlessness. 'It has transformed our relationship with the world – whether we wanted it to or not', I argued, 'first, because it played a crucial role in the construction of Jewish identity in the post-war world; and second, because a sovereign state and government claimed to speak for and take action on behalf of the Jewish people as a whole.' But it was always naive to believe that Israel would never take decisions and follow policies that had a direct negative effect on Jewish communities in Europe (and elsewhere), thereby contributing to the incidence of antisemitism. It was not hard to understand the historical, psychological and emotional reasons why Jews should want a specifically *Jewish* state, but there was a contradiction between Jewish support for an ethno-religious homogeneous state with a Jewish majority guaranteed in perpetuity, and Jewish support for a fully democratic, multicultural Europe promoting equal rights for all minorities and citizenship status for all.

Whether I was succeeding in influencing opinion with these arguments I can't say. And I don't know whether I was any more successful when I addressed the question 'Israel-Palestine uncensored: what future for the two peoples?' as a panellist at a JFJHR public meeting in March 2005. We found that we were preaching almost exclusively to the converted at such events rather than achieving our aim 'to reach Jews who might otherwise feel isolated and remain silent'. Nevertheless, those of us who spoke at these meetings treated them as occasions to speak freely and frankly. And in some respects the views I expressed that night were the closest I had come to an overall summation of my thinking on Zionism and Israel. 'My preferred option', I argued,

> is for the eventual evolution of one Israel-Palestine state – possibly in a federal or confederal structure – a state of all its citizens, in which Palestinian and Jewish nationalisms are superseded by a civic patriotism based on the recognition of the legitimacy of the historical narratives of two peoples – Jews and Palestinians – and the reality of the presence of living communities of those peoples in the state. The law of return, which exclusively favours Jewish immigration, would

be repealed and the issue of Palestinian refugees would be dealt with on the basis of a recognition of the right of return. Written into the revised constitution of the state would be safeguards for the continued cultural and religious distinctiveness of all national, cultural and faith groups, but also principles designed to guide the state towards social and civic cohesiveness. Groups – such as Haredim and Islamic fundamentalists – who wish to maintain separateness, will have the right to do so, but they will also have to abide by certain human rights based laws and values which are common to all, and these will carry with them certain duties and obligations.

Jewish and Palestinian nationalisms, like all nationalisms, I maintained, were flawed and could lead to the denial of human rights and racism. Zionism was an understandable answer to the failure of emancipation and the rise of antisemitism, but was based on at least three myths: 'a land without a people for a people without a land'; the biblical claim to the land; 'real' Zionism was humanistic and progressive. Zionism successfully created a Jewish state and Israel was a central factor in Jewish identity for most Jews, but the ideology aimed to achieve more. Did it? I tried to show that Zionism fell far short of achieving its ambitions.

Zionists may well be bullish; it was the answer to all contemporary Jewish problems, they still claimed. But I reasoned that some Zionists actually manifested deep ambivalence about what it had achieved: they loudly claimed that the state was susceptible to destruction, antisemitism rampaged worldwide, international delegitimisation continued apace, millions hated Israel – hardly proof of success.

But Zionism failed to eliminate antisemitism and now Israel provoked it. It hadn't provided Jews in Israel or elsewhere with security. The Jewishness of Israelis was in doubt. The 'new Jew' Zionism aimed to create was no longer the kibbutznik but the 'Rambo Jew' or the 'black-hatted Jew'. Securing a Jewish majority in perpetuity was in doubt. The secular ethos Ben-Gurion wanted for the state had been trumped by religious orthodoxy.

Zionism predicated that the state would be different, acting on a higher moral plane: a 'light unto the nations'; the experience of the Holocaust would make it evil's absolute opposite; the socialist ideals of the kibbutz were synonymous with the ethos and ideals of the state. But Israel acted like any other state, I insisted. Experiencing evil and extreme adversity hadn't prevented the victims from perpetrating acts of evil themselves. And the idea that the state's values were those of the kibbutz was redundant.

Zionism and state policy increasingly conflicted with human rights principles and universal values. Born out of the new universal human rights system and seen as progressive, Israel then followed a narrow nationalist and ethnocentric path. Initially, that ethnocentrism was hidden. But for right-wing and religious Zionists universalism was seen as a weakness. To determine your own history, you must compromise your own ethics. Post-1967 Zionist messianism ripped the mask off ethnocentricity: 'Our destiny is all the land. It's the fulfilment of God's promise', such Zionists argued. And when Palestinians took extreme and evil measures to resist, Israel said the world hated us anyway so we'll respond however we liked. Being the ultimate victims seemed to imply that Jews could not abuse human rights. And anyway, protecting the national project superseded human rights. If the Palestinians accepted the Zionist project there would be no need for violence. This was the logic of twenty-first-century Zionism and Israeli state policy, I argued.

After the conclusion of the Oslo Accords in 1993, post-Zionism promised a new future, but it was a false dawn because Israel would not go far enough. I concluded:

> I am convinced that [peace and reconciliation] will only come when Israel realises that the ethnocentric path, the path of ethno-religious homogeneity, which can only be followed at the expense of human rights and universal values, is the wrong one. It's a realization that the Palestinians must reach too, but it's not something that can be achieved simultaneously or negotiated to occur at the same time ... Israel must begin its own journey beyond Zionism. There is nothing to wait for.

I had reached these conclusions over a long period of time and they seemed to me fair and logical, but I could understand that others might have been shocked to hear such thoughts from someone who, in many respects, was seen to be at the heart of the establishment of the Jewish community. After all, I was employed by Lord Rothschild, whose grandfather was the recipient of the letter from Lord Balfour, which came to be known as the Balfour Declaration, the document that expressed the British government's support for 'the establishment in Palestine of a national home for the Jewish people'. Jacob was deeply conscious of the Zionist tradition of which his family was such an integral part. That someone who argued for the retiring of Zionism as the state's guiding ideology could be in such a position seemed, even to me, highly implausible.

*   *   *

My view that European Jews needed to understand that Israel's interests did not coincide with theirs was shared by Avner Azulay, managing director of the Marc Rich Foundation. We had been active together in the Westbury Group and were constantly discussing ways to further common objectives.

My principal interest was in the European Jewish revival and his was in influencing Israel to change its policies. And we were both aware that a strong and assertive European Jewish community could be an effective tool in helping to bring the Israeli political leadership to its senses. Together, we devised an initiative that would focus on achieving these twin aims. Our plan was to set up a new Europe-based think tank, which would influence European Jewish and Israeli leaders, policy-makers and opinion-formers through the development and dissemination of new policy ideas on the Jewish future in Europe and on Israel's relationship with European Jews and Europe.

At the same time, having remained in close touch with developments at the Institute for Jewish Policy Research, I was hearing of serious problems there. JPR's trustees had decided on a new programme focusing on European Jewry, but the director, Barry Kosmin, was unhappy with this development. The idea came to me that the promise of a substantial, multi-year grant, equal to the annual income – approximately $350,000 – that JPR was receiving from its endowment fund, would be enough to convince the trustees to persuade Barry Kosmin to resign and engage a new director to implement the new European programme. Avner accepted my argument that if the Rich Foundation promised these funds for the purpose of revitalising JPR, an institution with a high public profile and a record of very good-quality policy research, the trustees would accept our desire that it pursue the joint aims of European Jewish revival and a reorientation of Israeli government policy. Avner readily agreed to the scheme. I discussed the plan initially with JPR trustees Lord Simon and Lady Carole Haskel (Simon was a Labour Peer with very close connections to Gordon Brown). They discussed it with JPR's chairman, Peter Levy, who also gave his support.

In spring 2005, a lunch was arranged at Claridges to discuss the plan with Marc Rich, Marc's friend and sometime adviser Michael Steinhart (the former US hedge-fund giant), Avner Azulay, Peter Levy, Simon Haskel, and myself. Avner and I outlined the proposal. Marc Rich listened carefully, but seemed to be mainly interested in what Steinhart had to say. Voluble and opinionated, Steinhart was not very sympathetic, but neither was he negative. This did not surprise me as I knew that he understood practically nothing about the needs of European Jewry. Nevertheless, there was an amicable atmosphere and Avner confirmed to me afterwards that Marc Rich was ready to go ahead if a deal could be done.

The JPR people then began to reconsider. They were worried about taking money from someone who had been a fugitive from justice in the US. Some charitable bodies refused to accept his money, but JPR and many other perfectly respectable organisations had done so in the past, so the attitude of the JPR leadership seemed to me contradictory. Why single out Marc Rich as if there would not be question marks hanging over the provenance of the funds of most philanthropists? The Rich Foundation was a generous supporter of numerous worthwhile causes, both large and small.

In the end, it was never formally or properly discussed by the JPR Board. Only an inner circle considered it and rejection was eventually put to the Board as a fait accompli. Nevertheless, Avner and I were forced to drop the idea.

I was in no great hurry to leave the foundation, but the failure to bring about a transformation of JPR left me feeling that I should perhaps seek a full-time role in publicly arguing the case for the European Jewish revival and changing the parameters of debate about Israel's impact on European Jewry. And in May 2005, the discovery that I might have prostate cancer made me think again about just how quickly I might want to move on. Tests soon revealed that I had no cancer, but my doubts increased about continuing to work with the Rothschilds.

*   *   *

Sipping an espresso at a café on the Rynek Glowny, Krakow's grand central square, in hot sunshine in July 2005, I was feeling a quiet sense of satisfaction that we had made a difference here in Poland supporting projects such as the Museum of the History of Polish Jews and the yearly Festival of Jewish Culture in Krakow, which I was visiting. I was just finishing Daphna Golan's *Next Year in Jerusalem: Everyday Life in a Divided Land*, in which she described her uphill struggle to get Israelis and the Israeli government to do something about the policies that abused the human rights of Palestinians and Palestinian-Israelis. Although she confessed that, ultimately, she failed, I still felt that she demonstrated just how much potential there was for achieving meaningful and lasting reconciliation with the Palestinians. The values for which she was fighting were ones that I had come to share, however belatedly.

I had been on a different journey, but at that moment I was inspired to think that perhaps my experience of Zionism and Israel was also worth recording because, in a small way, it was part of the picture that Daphna was painting – a damaged people's failure to face up to the injuries they had inflicted on another people and the attempt by some to rectify those mistakes.

10

OUT OF THE FRYING PAN, INTO THE FIRE

Judaism is not a religion of space and does not worship the soil. So, too, the State of Israel is not the climax of Jewish history, but a test of the integrity of the Jewish people and the competence of Judaism.

Abraham Joshua Heschel, 1969

By the summer of 2005 I knew that I was in a very different place from where I had been when I left JPR in 1999. I was troubled and heartened in turn by thoughts and conclusions which I needed to discuss publicly. Conversations with family members, old friends and acquaintances were often fraught, while I was drawn to others whose ideas and positions now seemed close to mine. I suppose I was living in a more edgy place, but cushioned to some degree by working in the discrete and very private world of Rothschild family philanthropy. Jacob generously imposed few constraints on my taking public positions. However, I recognised that there were limits and I had to operate within them.

Yet a consequence of my mental journey was that a position that had once represented sweet freedom became progressively more intolerable. The Israel grant-making programme failed to address the threat posed to democracy and civil society by the rise of a racist Zionist right. It failed to find creative ways to invest in Israeli-Palestinian reconciliation or to make working for the full equality of Israel's Arab citizens a top priority. I could do nothing to influence this situation and as part of an organisation that had the power to do something about these problems, but never exercised it, I felt as if I was complicit in condoning injustice. Finally, I felt that I was reaching the end of the road with respect to developing new initiatives in European grant-making. Most of the foundation's projected income was committed for the coming years with little chance of an increase in the capital endowment. Moreover, I could see that we had probably reached the limit of the trustees' understanding and appreciation of the work that we were doing in Europe.

With little opportunity to do new things, running the foundation thus became rather routine. With more time to reflect on the impact of our activities, I felt proud of how we had contributed to the rebuilding of Jewish life in Europe through the grant-making programmes I had put in place. But I was also increasingly conscious of the threats to that revival in the form of more widespread fears of antisemitism, the increasing tendency to equate severe criticism of Israel with antisemitism, a new defensiveness on the part of Jewish community leaders and a retreat from support for pluralism and multiculturalism. This confirmed my belief that what was now urgently needed was *advocacy* for the cause of Jewish cultural revival; that I should be publicly arguing the case for the future of European Jewry and for a Europe conducive to developing thriving Jewish and other minority communities.

At the end of June, I had a surprising call from Peter Levy. I was still unhappy that the plan to bring in the Rich Foundation to fund JPR's new direction had collapsed, but having worked closely with him for almost a decade and regarded him as a friend, I put aside my disappointment. Barry Kosmin was leaving JPR in September, he told me, and the trustees had begun a search for a new director. Would I be interested in putting my name forward? Nothing could have been further from my mind, but after much thought and consultation with family and friends, I eventually said yes.

Fundamental to my decision was the fact that JPR trustees had already decided that they wanted to make Europe their main area of policy research. I sensed the possibility to focus on multiculturalism, strengthening European civil society and introducing greater realism into relations between Israel and Europe's Jews. JPR had the potential to become a leader in developing ideas for creating the conditions in Europe in which religious, cultural and ethnic groups could maintain their distinctiveness within the framework of overarching common values. This was the public advocacy role I wanted.

I consulted with Avner and secured a commitment that the Rich Foundation would back me with a substantial multi-year grant. I would also bring to JPR a major $700,000 project, conceived and directed by Diana Pinto, on rediscovering a sense of belonging in Europe, to be funded by the Ford Foundation. Finally, Barry Kosmin had moved into the area of antisemitism and extremism and the trustees felt that the interests of JPR would be better served by not engaging in such polemics directly. Since I too wanted to distance JPR from the positions on antisemitism that Barry had been pursuing, I was happy to comply.

Nevertheless, I still had niggling doubts. Would I really be able to use JPR to achieve my aims? It might be a new challenge, but was it wise to go back, however positively I felt about my earlier tenure? I never completely resolved these doubts, but decided that it was worth taking a gamble. Towards the end of July 2005, Peter Levy told me that the inner group of trustees were enthusiastic about my return, but nevertheless wanted to conduct a search, using professional headhunters, to see who else might be available. This meant that nothing much would happen until the autumn.

*   *   *

A meeting of the Westbury Group was due to take place in September in London; the last to be held under my chairmanship. Its focus was partly on developments in the Middle East that affected Europe and I was to introduce a session on the centrality of Israel for the Jewish people. I decided to challenge the assembled foundation executives by opposing the concept. Most members of the group knew I thought that the threat of antisemitism was exaggerated, Israel's policies held dangers for European Jews and there was a need for greater European Jewish autonomy and assertiveness, but I had never addressed the issue of Israel's centrality before.

The ground had already been prepared the night before at the opening dinner of this two-day event when I chaired a talk by Avrum Burg, the former speaker of the Israeli Knesset and at one time a potential leader of the Israeli Labour Party. Burg had become a controversial figure for his severe criticism of trends in Israeli politics and society and of Zionist messianism. Confident, outspoken and charismatic, he summarised his views on these matters.

Opening my remarks the following morning, I suggested that the emotional, psychological and mythical links between Israel and Jews outside Israel were unsustainable no matter what resources were poured into artificially bolstering them by diaspora Jewish organisations and Israel. This was not an ideological or political statement but rather the inevitable consequence of the actions of a nation state and how those relate to people who had an ethnic, religious or historical link to it. Jews whose entire worldview was based on the notion of Israel's centrality might view this as a disaster and seek to counter it. But I argued that this development should be welcomed and encouraged, because it would lead to a more normal existence for Israel and for Jews elsewhere.

In essence, the notion of the centrality of Israel was a restatement of the Zionist case. I presented six propositions on which the idea of the centrality of Israel was based and then demonstrated how each was deeply flawed. (1) Jews were one people united around the central pillar – Israel. In reality, there were always differences, and there were more divisive ones now – over Israel, religious observance, who is a Jew. (2) There was an identity of interest between Israel and the diaspora: what Israel did was good for Jews everywhere. But on numerous occasions Israel had put national interests above those of Jewish communities in countries with which it had relations. (3) Because of Israel-diaspora unity, Israeli leaders could and did speak in the name of Jews everywhere. However, no Jewish community had given Israel a mandate for this and when practised it is used as a means of exporting Israel's internal crisis with the Palestinians and gaining diaspora Jewish support. (4) It was natural for Jews to manifest a form of unconditional national loyalty to Israel. And yet given how sensitive Jews have been to charges of dual loyalty, automatically labelling them antisemitism, Israel's uncompromising demand for solidarity from diaspora Jews had placed them in invidious positions. (5) Israel was the spiritual and cultural centre of the Jewish people. But while this sounded plausible, in Israel itself the Jewishness of Israeli youth was being questioned, rabbis and sages endorsed racism and religious leaders manipulated the Israeli political system. The frontier of the struggle for Jewish spirituality and culture was arguably in the Jewish diaspora where Jews sought to maintain their distinctiveness and embrace modernity, universal values, human rights and racial equality. (6) The State of Israel was a moral actor and entity, the concrete realisation of Judaism and Jewish values. The truth was more prosaic: states sometimes did moral things; sometimes they did brutal things; no state was a moral entity.

I called myself a Zionist for 40 years but I had concluded that Zionism had passed its sell-by date. Its worst features had come to the fore and could never be expunged. This was not a cause for despair. On the contrary, if Israel and Jews worldwide recognised that a relationship based on a spurious notion of centrality was untenable, it would permit a new beginning, a totally different kind of relationship – and this would be good for us all.

I never expected to convert anyone with this presentation. I simply wanted these influential people, who controlled $2–3 billion in charitable funds, to hear some radical thoughts about the role Israel actually played in Jewish life from someone who had been at the heart of the Jewish establishment for more than 20 years. But the reactions of the grant-makers and Jewish leaders present were sharp. Some were outraged and cried '*Gevalt!*' Others said Israel was the only safe haven for Jews; a glass half-full perhaps, but Israel inspired and was still the most exciting thing we had to offer. There was a moral reason for the basis of Israel, which is not the same as saying that Israel was a moral state. One or two colleagues argued that I had presented six straw men of absolutes, where absolutes didn't exist and that we had to delay facing the six 'questions' because global events posed such dangers for the Jewish people: the incursion of Islam into Europe; the spectre of terrorism; the fact that Israel was 'three minutes old' in the family of nations; its survival was still in question; we had to secure Israel's safety first.

The one person who breached this wall of denial was Avrum Burg. 'If I answer the "six questions" correctly,' he said, 'what's the next one? What kind of Jewish people do I want my children to be part of? A post-fears Jewish people. In the last couple of decades we've constructed our fears. Now we must be post-trauma, post-guilt feelings. We must help Jews and Israelis to trust the world and give up the claim to be the world's only victims.'

This was not the first time that I had heard an Israeli be far more willing to ask searching questions about Zionism and Israel than diaspora Jews. While arguments over these issues in Israel were often verbally violent, very radical views were openly expressed and debated in Israeli society. In the UK, while nothing prevented you from expressing similar opinions, they were not considered a legitimate part of intra-Jewish discourse. Establishment institutions and pro-Israel groups endeavoured to find ways to keep them out of the mainstream.

* * *

In October 2005 I was invited for an early afternoon interview with the headhunters about the JPR directorship, during which the senior partner appeared to fall asleep while I spoke. My words may have induced boredom, or he may just have had a good lunch. Soon after, I learnt something of the obstacles being placed in my path to the directorship. While some members of the JPR Board supported my return, a vociferous minority was bitterly opposed and supported the other leading candidate, Dr Emanuele Ottolenghi, a Middle East scholar at the Oxford Centre for Hebrew and Jewish Studies. Dr Ottolenghi was an unreconstructed Zionist with alarmist views on antisemitism. It followed that the principal objections to me concerned my very different views on these subjects. Two others were also in competition for the job: Dr Clive Lawton, a leading Jewish educationalist and former headteacher, and Simon Rocker, one of the *JC*'s longest-serving journalists.

On 30 November I was interviewed by the JPR selection committee. The eight-person panel gave me a thorough grilling. I made no attempt to deny or avoid discussion of my views on antisemitism or on Israel and Zionism, and I freely acknowledged that my unorthodox opinions on these topics were already well known. But I insisted that I had no intention of using JPR as a personal vehicle for propagating my political views but rather as a platform from which I would publicise and advocate the policies we devised and raise issues for discussion that flowed from JPR's research agenda. In the five-minute presentation I was asked to give about how I would develop and implement the European programme, all that I said in relation to Israel was: 'JPR would examine the impact of the conflict on Europe and European Jews, what Israel asks of Jews and what Jews ask of Israel, the kind of relationship a diasporic people's interrelated communities should have.'

Two members of the Board's selection committee took strong exception to my candidacy: Larry Levine, who jointly managed a financial services company with his brother Milton; and Dr Richard Bolchover, a former banker and head of Close Fund Management, an investment management company. Larry Levine quizzed me on whether I would make public statements as JPR director which reflected my personal opinions. Determined not to give hostage to fortune, I explained that whatever statements I made would be within a range of views that the trustees felt were acceptable for me to express. That did not mean every Board member had to agree personally with what I said, rather that, if they so wished, they would be able to say: 'I don't agree with Tony Lerman on this issue, but think it's right that he raised the matter for public debate.' If trustees felt I had overstepped the mark they would have every right to take me to task at a future Board meeting.

Dr Bolchover took a different tack. He questioned me on my Jewishness and how that influenced my views and the way I would run JPR. I answered by speaking about the diverse sources of my Jewish identity, which included Israel; how I saw social justice and equality as integral to what being Jewish is all about. As I expected, he pointedly drew a distinction between my views and those of other trustees like himself for whom the national element in Judaism and Jewishness – meaning Zionism and unequivocal support for Israel – was paramount. The implication was clear: the work of the JPR director had to be informed by these considerations, not the multicultural, 'leftist', pluralist stance he imputed to me. I simply responded that I had no objection to anyone deriving their Jewish inspiration from 'national' sources, but that I saw no reason why that had to be a qualification for the directorship of JPR.

Despite the lines of questioning designed to unsettle me, I thought the interview went reasonably well and I assumed that I would probably be appointed. But a few days later information was leaked to me that the trustees were divided and had proposed a compromise solution: I would be made director and Dr Ottolenghi would be appointed to serve under me as director of research. I could understand how a divided Board would reach such a conclusion, but it was a recipe for perpetual conflict and out of the question. By the time Peter Levy asked me to meet him at the Reform Club, I had already prepared my response. After he explained the Board's suggestion, I explained why it wouldn't work. In fact Peter seemed rather relieved and it was clear that he never really believed in the idea in the first place. He said he would go back to the Board and insist that there was only room for one of us at JPR.

The trustees met in December and after heated discussion a majority agreed to offer me the post. But the strength of feeling of those who objected could not be held in check. Three – Bolchover, Levine and Adrian Cohen, a lawyer at the huge city firm of Clifford Chance – simply got up and walked out. Impatient to tell the Jewish world, the three departing trustees leaked the decision of the Board to the JC, but they did not make it entirely clear what motivated them. All they told the paper was: "'The board of trustees, in making this appointment, have missed an opportunity to revitalise and regenerate the JPR and ensure it takes a path reflecting the concerns and aspirations" of Jewish communities in Britain and Europe.'

In mid January 2006, the *JC*'s influential weekly columnist, Geoffrey Alderman, in an article entitled 'JPR loses mind in choice of new head', launched an attack on me and the JPR Board. He purported to show that my views on antisemitism, and by extension on Israel and Zionism, were beyond the pale and that the JPR directors were stupid to have reappointed me. Much of his attack was based on misquoting and misrepresenting an article I had written on antisemitism for *Prospect* magazine in 2002, which was subsequently reproduced in a JPR book of essays, *A New Antisemitism? Debating Judeophobia in 21st-Century Britain* (2003). He concluded: 'Lerman is entitled to hold whatever questionable views he pleases on the nature of anti-Jewish prejudice ... The problem is (isn't it?) that as head of JPR no one is going to take him, or it, seriously any more.'

I was mystified by this attack. While sharp criticism was his style and he was entitled to express his personal views of my work, this seemed very personal and damning. It so happened that we agreed on things like the flaws of Chief Rabbi Jonathan Sacks and the failures of the Board of Deputies of British Jews. I was especially puzzled as to how he could square this attack on me with his position as chairman of the University of London's Academic Council, the most senior quality assurance committee of the federal university. Did he judge the work of academics unfavourably on the grounds of finding their views personally uncongenial?

Friends and JPR trustees were angry about the Alderman column, but there was little anyone could do. The damage was done. A letter from Margaret Harris, a professor at Aston Business School, Birmingham, was published in the paper. '[C]ould you remind your contributors and headline-writers that there is a difference between research findings and polemic? There is also a difference between reasonable criticism and personal abuse. It is a sad reflection on our small community that we have not yet learned the art of tolerant debate about issues on which there is a range of legitimate views.' I thanked her personally and she replied: 'The big danger now is of you and JPR losing credibility before you even start your job there because people think they know your views and know what JPR will be saying – and then they just pigeon hole them in the box marked "stuff I don't want to hear".' This proved to be very prescient.

Alderman's column came only days after a series of emails was sent to JPR, criticising comments I had made on BBC Radio 4's *Sunday* programme on 8 January and slamming JPR for appointing me director. Rabbi Sacks had publicly referred to a 'tsunami of antisemitism engulfing the world' and the BBC had invited me and Melanie Phillips, the *Daily Mail* columnist, to comment. The Boxing Day 2004 Indian Ocean tsunami was still fresh in people's minds and I thought Sacks's comments were an appalling exploitation of a terrible tragedy that had claimed the lives of over 230,000 people in 14 countries. Phillips, even more ready to exaggerate antisemitism than Sacks, was predictably delighted with his remarks. The emails falsely accused me of having 'a close association with CABU' – they presumably meant CAABU, the Council for the Advancement of Arab-British Understanding – and of legitimising the Muslim Council of Britain (MCB), which allegedly supported Holocaust denial and whose leader, Sir Iqbal Sacranie, had accused Sacks of exaggerating antisemitism in order to 'divert attention from Israel's policies'. I was 'undermining the Jewish community's standing in this country' by aligning myself with an 'anti-Israel organisation' and 'acting as [a] useful idiot for extremist Islamist ideology'.

These emails had clearly been centrally orchestrated since they all misspelled the CAABU acronym and all linked me with the alleged Holocaust-denying stance of the MCB. I could see how they were able to link me simplistically with Sacranie, since he had also criticised Sacks, but me and CAABU? An internet search revealed that a collective letter I had signed in the name of the JFJHR, published in the *JC* in October 2005, had been posted by CAABU on its website. The letter criticised the editor for pinning the blame for the collapse of the Oslo Accords on the Palestinians.

*   *   *

More than a month passed before I took up my new post. I had many loose ends to tie up at the foundation before I left and a scheduled trip to make to Israel. By the time I reached Ben Gurion airport at the end of January, I had put to the back of my mind the initial setbacks and was fully focused on seeing what response I would get from a range of Israelis to my plans for JPR and gauging informed opinion on the state of affairs between Israel and the Palestinians.

Avner Azulay organised a lunch discussion at a restaurant in the heart of Tel Aviv's business district with Zvia Greenfield, an orthodox Hebrew University academic and also parliamentary candidate on the list of the left-wing political party Meretz; Dr Sharon Pardo, head of the Centre for the Study of European Politics and Society at Ben-Gurion University of the Negev; Yedidya Stern, professor of religion at Bar Ilan University; Arik Bachar, the foreign editor of the popular daily *Ma'ariv*, and Dr Idith Zertal, one of the country's leading new historians. I explained to them what I intended to do and was pleased at the generally positive reception I received. Nevertheless, concern was expressed about antisemitism and Jewish official attitudes to Muslims in Europe. They acknowledged the growing divergence between Israeli Jews and Jews outside Israel as well as the problems of Israeli decision-making that failed to take into account the concerns of European Jews. But they also rightly thought that there was a woeful lack of involvement in EU institutions on the part of Jewish leaders in Europe – a situation extremely detrimental to the future of Jews in Europe and one which discouraged EU leaders and officials from challenging Israeli government policy on the occupation and peace negotiations.

Later that day, at a small dinner party Avner organised, I had the opportunity to discuss my plans with Avi Primor, the former Israeli ambassador to Germany and the EU; Akiva Eldar, a leading journalist and columnist on the daily *Ha'aretz*; Edualdo Mirapeix, the Spanish ambassador to Israel, and Aaron Ben-Zeev, president of the University of Haifa. Idith Zertal was there too.

Primor and Mirapeix immediately saw my ideas as potentially beneficial to both Israel and European Jews. But discussion moved quickly on to the issue of whether academics at Israeli universities who severely criticised Israeli policy and even challenged the state's ideology and legitimacy, should be free to do so. This was not an abstract question. Ilan Pappé, an Israeli anti-Zionist historian at the University of Haifa, who had become a hate-figure in right-wing Zionist circles in Israel, was facing censure for calling for a boycott of Israeli universities. Ben-Zeev believed it was right to curtail Pappé's freedom of speech for the greater good of the university and the state and called upon him to resign. Idith Zertal strongly disagreed and insisted that Israel should be able to tolerate the views of someone like Pappé, however offensive they might be to some. Forcing him out would only contribute to making Israeli society more repressive and illiberal.

The Zertal–Ben-Zeev exchange exemplified a perplexing confusion over the paths Israel could follow. The following day Peter Adler, a modern orthodox Jew from Australia who lived in a settlement on the West Bank, expressed how troubled he was that young people in the settler movement had become so radicalised and had lost respect for their leaders. Further bitter clashes with the authorities were inevitable. But he had no faith in the government of the prime minister, Ehud Olmert, and described him as 'worthless'. Reluctantly, he concluded that there would soon be a resolution of the conflict along the lines Barak had been pursuing at Camp David when he was prime minister. This surprised me. Was a new realism creeping into the settler movement? Remarkably, Peter Adler had reached the same conclusion as Idith Zertal, the radical historian, who also believed that Barak's parameters would provide the basis for a resolution of the conflict.

When I met with Fania Oz-Salzberger in her home town of Zichron Ya'acov in the hills overlooking the coastal plain, I was astonished at the transformation of a place I had known only as a backwater when I first visited Israel in 1964. Full of art galleries, good cafés, wholesome restaurants and specialist shops selling craft work, Zichron had caught the heritage bug and also become a middle-class dormitory town for people working in Haifa. Fania lectured in History at the University of Haifa and her optimism corresponded well to the image of Zichron. She thought Israel was showing a new maturity and strength. It had come through the second intifada and was more pragmatic and sensible in its relations with Europe.

I wanted to believe her, but when I met the human rights activist and academic Daphna Golan on the East Jerusalem Mt Scopus campus of the Hebrew University, I heard a different story altogether. She thought that the recent victory of Hamas in the elections in Gaza had thrown Israel into confusion and deep depression. Perhaps Israel's religious leaders were best placed to talk to Hamas, she thought, because they could speak the same doctrinal language. This was a very sad conclusion for someone who believed so strongly in the primacy of human rights. She feared greatly for human rights organisations, women's rights groups and women generally in a Gaza under Hamas's control.

In a café in Mishkenot Sha'ananim in Jerusalem, looking across to the walls of the Old City, I talked with Benjamin Pogrund, a former journalist who had been forced to leave South Africa in the mid 1980s because of his active opposition to apartheid. Deeply involved in Israeli-Palestinian dialogue and an indefatigable organiser of discussions aimed at achieving Israeli-Palestinian reconciliation, Benjamin still saw many possibilities for dialogue with the Palestinians. He had recently been sickened by a Palestinian torture case that was settled out of court for 2 million shekels and by the arbitrary arrest of a Palestinian friend for working in a clinic that was funded by Hamas. But he strongly believed that Israelis had travelled further down the road of accommodation with Palestinians – even Hamas – than Jews outside Israel.

One of my last meetings was with Varda Shiffer, who was working on a project aimed at helping the Bedouin communities in the Negev that were constantly under pressure from the state authorities. Varda was a founder member of the JFJHR. She no longer had any faith in the two-state solution. Israel had driven the Palestinians into the arms of Hamas. Harassment of the Palestinians would now intensify in the run-up to the elections. The Amona confrontation, in which 10,000 police, Border Police and IDF soldiers sent to destroy homes built illegally in a settlement on Palestinian land in the central West Bank clashed violently with 4,000 settlers and protesters, was racial in character, Varda said. The settlers and protesters were Ashkenazim and the police and army mostly Sephardim.

I returned to England at the beginning of February encouraged by the responses to my JPR plans, but I could see great difficulties ahead in crafting a meaningful programme of work on the impact of Israeli policy- and decision-making on European Jews. Despite some left-right coalescence around the Barak parameters, which I could not believe would lead anywhere, the atmosphere in Israel was confused and polarised. Finding the right partners with whom to work and influencing Israeli thinking would not be easy. Given the bitterness surrounding debate about Israel-Palestine among Jews in Europe, it would also be hard convincing people of the legitimacy of such a programme.

*   *   *

If I was to have no honeymoon period on my return to JPR, I was at least treated to a fine farewell reception by Jacob Rothschild in Spencer House, the private palace overlooking Green Park built by the first Earl Spencer, ancestor of Diana, Princess of Wales. Jacob expressed heartfelt thanks for what I had done. In turn I paid genuine tribute to his foresight in deciding to devote charitable funds to the cause of reviving Jewish life in Europe and to his generosity in giving me the chance to set up and run the European foundation. Privately, I wondered if he might be aware of the implications of Yad Hanadiv's failure to devote resources to the urgent task of strengthening democracy and civil society in Israel. Seeing that Sir Ronald Cohen (with whom I was at grammar school some 50 years back) and David Landau had come for my farewell bash, shortly before most people left I collared them and pleaded that, as trustees of the foundation, they should press Jacob and Ari Weiss to be far bolder in their grant-making in encouraging Israeli society to treat the Palestinians with fairness and respect. I knew that both of them were pronounced doves on Israel-Palestine, but in response, while they did not exactly shrug, they made it clear that they did not feel this was a task that the British Rothschild family foundation could take on. They were appointed to give Jacob support in continuing the tradition of Rothschild philanthropy, not to persuade him to follow some new course. I was disappointed, but I did not really expect them to say anything else.

11

CHARACTER ASSASSINATION AND SELF-CENSORSHIP

The reason they preferred him has to do with the traditional stand of the wealthiest and most assimilated circles in English Jewry ... These are people who don't like the Jews going out into the streets and causing a confrontation, because as they see it, that endangers their own status in general British society. Lerman's views are very convenient for them.

Professor Robert Wistrich, 2006

I had barely started work as director of JPR when a further crisis erupted early in March 2006. In his last year as director, Barry Kosmin had signed a contract with Profile Books to publish a book of essays on contemporary European extremism, which he was editing together with Dr Paul Iganski, a part-time JPR Civil Society research fellow. While the contract between the editors and Profile was confidential, JPR trustees had to approve the payment of £14,000 to the publisher. In exchange JPR would receive 2,000 copies, carry all the liabilities and yet have no control whatsoever over the content of the book.

During a meeting arranged at Iganski's request, he told me that he was fighting a losing battle with Kosmin concerning the academic quality, objectivity and credibility of the papers commissioned for the book. He was particularly uneasy because of what happened over *A New Antisemitism? Debating Judeophobia in 21st-Century Britain*, the 2003 collection of essays he edited with Kosmin, also published by Profile in association with JPR. He deeply regretted his involvement in that book because of its blatant bias and his inability to do anything about it. (Paul's feelings about the extremism book must have been affected by the fate of *A New Antisemitism?* after a libel action was brought against JPR, a fact I was told in early 2005 while still with the Rothschilds. In his contribution, Peter Pulzer, formerly Gladstone Professor of Government at Oxford University, falsely attributed antisemitic views in an *Observer* newspaper column to Christina Odone, the former editor of the Catholic weekly, the *Tablet*. Odone sued – she was not the author of the piece. JPR settled out of court, a large sum was paid and the book was belatedly withdrawn from sale.) After hearing Iganski's concerns, I discovered that

Kosmin had rushed to pay the £14,000 to Profile in July 2005 when many contributions were still outstanding. Knowing that he would be leaving JPR, he perhaps feared that the project would be cancelled.

After reading the contributions that had been submitted I shared Iganski's profound doubts. The JPR trustees agreed to seek cancellation of the project and Profile's managing director Andrew Franklin honourably returned most of the £14,000. He also decided to cancel the contract. I asked Iganski to remove the papers already posted on JPR's website. He told me that what I had asked him to do was the only correct and honourable course of action. He also told me that all the authors he had contacted were fine about this apart from Emanuele Ottolenghi who was trying to stir up media interest in JPR's withdrawal from the project – which explained why Amiram Barkat, a *Ha'aretz* journalist, contacted both Iganski and me about the book.

The cancellation of the book project triggered the resignation of a fourth trustee, Daniel Finkelstein, a leading journalist, former think tank head and Conservative Party strategist. In his resignation letter of 6 March, which he released to the *JC* (10 March), Finkelstein saw the cancellation as confirming his view that 'Mr Lerman intends to change the nature of JPR's contribution to the debate on anti-Semitism.' The linkage of 'JPR's name to the suggestion that the term anti-Semitism is being used much too loosely ... gives the impression ... that we believe the problem is exaggerated. This is not a view I share.'

The impact of this event was to add to the attempt to discredit me and JPR. In his reply to Finkelstein, Peter Levy pointed out that there was evidence that Finkelstein had informed others of his resignation a full three days before he informed JPR. Finkelstein responded stating: 'My first point is to acquit myself of any discourtesy.' But he then confirmed Peter's statement. Barkat, the *Ha'aretz* journalist, heard Finkelstein had resigned and asked him for a comment. 'I did not reply', Finkelstein said and continued: 'You now provide the additional information (which I did not know) that the source of information to this journalist claimed to have seen my resignation letter. This narrows down the identity of his source to one of the four people to whom I showed a draft. I am disappointed about this, and I apologise that you were contacted by a journalist before you were contacted by me. This, however, is very much a side issue and I do hope that we are not detained by it any further.' Would an experienced journalist and politician like Finkelstein really need four people to advise him on his draft letter?

Bad news usually comes in threes, so when Lord Weidenfeld, the veteran publisher and vice-president of JPR, wrote to Peter Levy on 28 March tendering his resignation too, it did not come as that much of a surprise. In his letter Weidenfeld alleged that I had not been very responsive when he tried to involve me in events which he thought could have been useful to JPR. He also emphasised that we did not share the same views on Israel just at a crucial time in Jewish history when unity of purpose and a common position was needed. His first complaint was puzzling. I had known George since the late 1980s and at his request had spent many hours over a period of five or six years, helping him plan the German-Jewish Dialogue colloquia he organised in Germany on behalf of the Bertelsmann Foundation, events attended by senior German politicians, academics, journalists and intellectuals as well as European, American and Israeli Jews. His second complaint exemplified the Jewish establishment's intolerance of dissenting views about Israel. Needless to say, the Weidenfeld resignation story also soon featured in the press.

It did not help that *Ha'aretz* published in both its Hebrew and English editions on 14 March a telephone interview the journalist Amiram Barkat conducted with me. He described JPR as 'a prestigious private think tank: four lords of Jewish descent – Rothschild, Weidenfeld, Kalms and Haskel – are on the honorary board of directors of JPR; and the British media and governing authorities place great weight on the position adopted by the institute'. This further illuminates Professor Robert Wistrich's absurd comment to Barkat (quoted above) that my appointment reflected the traditional pusillanimity of the 'wealthiest and most assimilated circles in English Jewry … Lerman's views are very convenient for them'.

Barkat tried to portray my critical approach to Zionism and Israel as anti-Zionism that condoned antisemitism. Although he quoted me accurately expressing sympathy for Palestinians who had lived in Palestine for many generations and could not accept that the Jewish claim to have the right to set up a state trumped Palestinian rights to the land, his choice of words ultimately made me appear extreme, uncompromising, deliberately setting out to attack the Jewish establishment at every opportunity, soft on antisemites and unfair on Israel. A mini-storm erupted. I had naively thought the interview would provide useful publicity for my JPR plans and had not expected a *Ha'aretz* journalist to portray me in this way. *Ha'aretz* gave me 500 words to clarify my views, but the damage had already been done. Edith Zertal congratulated me for my 'courageous thinking' while Rabbi Roberto Feldmann, emailing from Chile, was less charitable, accusing me of being 'either [*sic*] blind, a coward, or a pompous fool'. Professor Daniel Hochhauser, a consultant in medical oncology at University College Hospital, London, emailed this to Peter Levy: 'I doubt whether JPR will have any standing in the future as a result of this [interview] but I am sure Ken Livingstone is delighted. It is interesting that Mr Lerman can understand the resentment of the Iranian president, and gratifying that he does not regard it as being helpful. No doubt he respects the President's honesty in calling for Israel to be wiped off the map and for denying the Holocaust.' I had said nothing about Ahmadinejad in the interview.

Not all staunch Zionists felt this way. Giddy Shimoni, who taught me Jewish and Zionist history at the youth leaders' training institute I attended in Jerusalem in 1964–65, and was now a highly respected historian of Zionism at the Hebrew University, wrote to me: 'I was sorry to read the *Ha'aretz* article's rather distorted representation of your views on the so-called "New antisemitism" of the liberal-left. You did well to afterwards send *Ha'aretz* the brief statement of your views. I believe there is much validity in them and I hope there will be an opportunity for the academic community here to hear and discuss your perceptions of this important issue.' As long as people like Giddy understood the importance of giving due consideration to my ideas, I judged that I was following the right path. Nevertheless, my detractors immediately seized upon the interview as proof of what they had been saying about me. The behaviour of Felix Posen, a multi-millionaire philanthropist, was typical. Waving a copy of the *Ha'aretz* interview at a House of Lords lunch I was attending, he claimed in an audible whisper: 'This is the final straw. Tony Lerman can't carry on after this.' Posen was a long-standing patron of Robert Wistrich and had funded Barry Kosmin's new post at Trinity College in Hartford, Connecticut.

My suspicion was that the first three trustees to resign helped orchestrate the subsequent resignations and many of the attacks on me. And while my approach to antisemitism seemed to bother them most, I guessed it was my views on Israel and the link I made between Israeli policies and antisemitism that provoked them to act as they did.

I was dismissive of these early setbacks. The JPR trustees and my work colleagues were behind me and anxious to move on. We all thought – hoped? – that the initial bad press would abate and that JPR could reclaim attention on the strength of the quality of its work. It was a nice thought.

*   *   *

My friends in the JFJHR were very supportive, making it an important safety valve and an alternative means of pursuing some of my aims. But we were still struggling to reach a wider audience. One way of trying to get our message across was to fulfil our commitment to work with other groups. We saw potential rewards in creating a coalition and acting together.

Since we were all also connected with people from other human rights, peace and justice-promoting organisations, we decided to hold a public meeting which would promote the formation of a formal coalition between such bodies. But putting together a list of them proved difficult. However, one possible partner was Jews for Justice for Palestinians (JfJfP), an organisation set up in 2002, especially since some of our number were also JfJfP signatories.

At my 60th birthday party in March 2006 I talked about the idea with Jacqueline Rose who was in a group associated with the JfJfP, Writers Against the Occupation. We hatched the idea of arranging a JFJHR-Writers meeting to explore the possibility of developing a wider coalition focused on our common interest in Israel-Palestine. Speaking out together could make more impact and emphasise how the establishment bodies of the Jewish community, like the Board of Deputies, did not speak for all Jews.

A meeting between the two groups was arranged for 23 April 2006 and held at the obvious salon for such initiatives, the home of June Jacobs. Wearing JFJHR hats were Anne Karpf; Dr Brian Klug, academic philosopher and writer; Dr Tony Klug, veteran Middle East expert; Dr Edie Friedman, director of the Jewish Council for Racial Equality; Dr Anthony Isaacs, a General Medical Council panellist; Rabbi David Goldberg, former principal rabbi at the Liberal Jewish Synagogue in St John's Wood; Lady Ellen Dahrendorf, chair of the New Israel Fund, and myself. For Writers Against the Occupation were Jacqueline Rose; Lynne Segal, leading feminist and professor of psychology and gender studies at Birkbeck; Lisa Appignanesi, novelist and PEN activist; Leon Rosselson, folksinger; Ann Jungman, children's author and publisher; Susie Orbach, psychotherapist, psychoanalyst and writer, and Donald Sassoon, professor of comparative European history, Queen Mary, University of London. There was a lot of common ground, but not the immediate meeting of minds some of us expected. Nevertheless, we all agreed that a framework for the expression of alternative Jewish voices was necessary. The worsening situation in Israel-Palestine and the polarisation of debate in the UK made it urgent.

At a succession of meetings with an expanded group, we thrashed out a draft declaration of principles. The discussions were collegial, cooperative, engaged, alternately fascinating and frustrating, but always conducted in a positive atmosphere with a prevailing feeling that we could make a significant impact. The motivations of members of the group were varied. Some people were focused on the damage Israel was inflicting on itself. Others were more interested in the plight of the Palestinian people. We all felt the need for this initiative as Jews, but among us there were many different versions of what this signified: the link between Jewishness and universal human rights; concern for the future of the Jewish community; concern for Jewish dissidents who felt outside the community. No one advocated any form of anti-Jewish anti-Zionism that demonised the State of Israel and its Jewish population. Neither was there any vilification of other diaspora Jews who thought differently about Israel. Nobody sat in judgement on anyone else's Jewishness. On the contrary, this was an initiative designed to bring us closer to other Jews, not to distance ourselves from them; to demarcate a difference of opinion, but to say that there needed to be room for such differences among Jews and that there should be a space where they can all be expressed and not considered out of bounds. We certainly wanted to address the wider world, so that people would understand that to be Jewish is not synonymous with automatic support for everything being done by the State of Israel. But our primary audience was other Jews. Our message was: It's legitimate to hold dissenting views – join with us. By the end of June we had a draft text and were already turning our minds to precisely what we were going to do with it.

Perhaps recklessly we arranged to meet to consider this and other questions at the Everyman Cinema café in Hampstead on 17 July, before a Jewish Community Centre for London panel discussion on antisemitism taking place in the auditorium, in which I was a participant. There were journalists and activists milling around in the café and the lobby who would have had a professional interest in what we were cooking up, but fortunately they were oblivious to our presence.

A few months had passed since the mini-storm over my appointment, but I anticipated that some of the organised Jewish community's hostility towards me might surface during the panel discussion. I expected little sympathy from two of my three fellow panellists. I thought Daniel Finkelstein, who had become comment editor on *The Times*, would express polite disagreement, but that Dr David Hirsh, a sociologist at Goldsmiths, University of London, would be seriously unpleasant. Founder of the Engage website, set up to combat the academic boycott of Israel, Hirsh's site smeared dissenting Jews whose critical views on Israel were deemed antisemitic and some inflammatory and untrue things about me had been posted in recent months. The third panellist was a friend, Baroness Julia Neuberger, former director of the King's Fund, who broadly agreed with me on antisemitism and Israel. On hearing of my appointment in January she wrote: 'I'm absolutely thrilled … for all sorts of reasons that you can imagine all too well, and some you can only guess at … It will be great having you in that role.'

Things got off to a bad start when the chairman, the *Guardian* columnist Jonathan Freedland, flippantly referred to me as someone who didn't think there was any antisemitism. This was unwarranted and set the tone for the insulting comments that were shouted out from the audience as well as the angry questions that were put to me. The atmosphere was intimidating and I felt under siege. It made me think again about the many obstacles that I faced.

At least the earlier meeting in the café had gone well. Plans were already being laid to go public with the new initiative. The launch of the Lebanon War by Israel on 12 July confirmed how important it was to do this as soon as possible. It could not be before the late autumn at the earliest and in the meantime many of us were so appalled by Israel's action that we felt compelled to express our deep misgivings about the war. Twenty-four of us signed a letter that was subsequently published in the *Daily Telegraph* on 29 July. The letter expressed dismay at 'the human tragedies unfolding' and deplored 'the relentless bombardment of any civilians, Lebanese, Israeli and Palestinian, as well as the systematic destruction of civilian infrastructures. We believe', the letter continued, 'such actions, in flagrant violation of international law, can never be justified, regardless of the provocation.' We called on the British government 'to align itself with those countries demanding an immediate ceasefire, for the international community to intervene decisively to secure this on a long-term basis, and for a swift and complete end to Israel's nearly 40-year occupation of Palestinian territories, which remains key to a broader peace settlement between Israel and its neighbours'.

I thought that the letter was very balanced and that signing it was the least I could do. I did not believe that I was doing anything to compromise my position as director of JPR. But I was mistaken. I received a letter from Peter Levy in which he wrote: 'I was surprised you signed the ... letter – whatever your personal views I think as director of JPR you should not publicly align yourself at this time at least not openly.' At his request, we met, together with Simon Haskel, to discuss the issue. They both felt I should not identify myself publicly with letters or statements of a political nature, even in a personal capacity. I argued that what I had done was within parameters that I thought had been set when I took the job, but they disagreed. The question was not resolved. We agreed to differ. Nevertheless, it was clear that they had put me on notice.

The main consequence of this was to force me to reconsider my involvement with the joint JFJHR and Writers Against the Occupation initiative that by the autumn had acquired a name: Independent Jewish Voices (IJV). I knew that if Peter Levy and other JPR trustees objected to the *Telegraph* letter, how much more would they object to my involvement with IJV when it became public knowledge. After discussing with close friends what I should do, I concluded that I had no choice but to withdraw my name from the list of signatories. On 13 September I informed all the members of our group of how the trustees had reacted and the conclusions I had drawn:

> Initially, I had in mind to brazen it out. But as the weeks went by, I realised that if I persisted in my course of action, they would have cause to fire me, since it is certainly within their competence to determine whether the Director of JPR has licence to play a political role of this kind. Moreover, there is no doubt that my signing the declaration would have far more serious consequences for the image of JPR than my signing the Daily Telegraph letter ...

I continued to attend meetings of the steering group and offer advice, but I had to relinquish my former role. Everyone understood my position, but I found it difficult to adjust. I began having doubts about whether I had made the right decision to take up the JPR directorship. If I was forced to censor myself in this way, where would it end? How could I use JPR to open up discussion on these important topics if I was not in a position to make public my views? But friends reassured me that the role I was playing at JPR, a mainstream Jewish institution, was crucial.

*   *   *

You cannot influence opinion and policy-making by being shy and retiring. We hadn't yet fully formulated or announced our new programme, beyond the basic outline for change I had set out when I was appointed, but I lost no time in putting myself about both in the UK and on the continent. Between March and July 2006 I had a number of speaking engagements in Stockholm, Warsaw, Berlin and London. Although Israel-Palestine was not central to the questions I was asked to address, I found ways of introducing audiences to the link between the position of Jews in Europe and the policies of the Israeli government.

Speaking in March in Stockholm at an EU-funded international conference on 'The New European Cultural Landscape and the Jewish Experience' I argued that Europe faced a cultural crisis because it appeared to have lost confidence in multiculturalism and that this was mirrored by a similar crisis in the Jewish world. Jewish leaders were more concerned about preserving the 'purity of the tribe' than participating fully in society. And as Jews, we could not lecture to others on integration unless we had integration, coexistence and civilised discourse in Jewish organisational life, which meant facing up to the internal culture clash that turns so often around the issue of the Jewish connection to Israel.

In a lecture to the Central Council of Jews in Germany at the Leo Baeck-Haus in Berlin on 22 June, I addressed this more directly in comments on the so-called 'new antisemitism'. Part of the answer to the problem of antisemitism, I said, was not to see it as something to be dealt with differently from other racisms. The other key consideration was to acknowledge frankly that there was a direct link between anti-Jewish hostility in Europe and the intensification of violence in the conflict between Israelis and Palestinians. That meant first recognising that a significant part of anti-Jewish manifestations had more to do with intercommunal political and other differences than antisemitism in its traditional sense. Second, it meant realising that without a solution to the conflict based on respect for human rights and justice for Palestinians and

Israelis, anti-Jewish hostility would continue to plague the continent. It was very important that representative Jewish organisations and Jewish bodies concerned about Israel developed a more mature and objective attitude to the country, its government and the conflict. If they recognised the damage being done they could work actively to persuade the Israeli government to pursue a different path. I believed that this would help normalise Muslim-Jewish communal relations.

A month later, in the Barry Shenker Memorial Lecture I gave to the left-wing Zionist group Meretz UK, on the troubling connection between Israel and antisemitism, I returned to the theme and asked: Where did responsibility lie for the increase in manifestations of anti-Jewish hostility over the last five years? A very significant proportion of all the phenomena that have been interpreted as hostility to Jews over recent years was directly linked to the Israel-Palestine conflict. So, to what extent were Israeli actions responsible for provoking and legitimating antisemitism? Neither an attack on a graveyard in Marseilles nor the hurling of abuse at a devout Jew walking in the street could in any way be justified as a legitimate way of expressing anger at Israeli policies. But such acts nevertheless reflect the link between Israeli action and anti-Jewish hostility in Europe and elsewhere.

By and large, I argued, most Jews seemed to acquiesce in the Israeli government's proud claim to speak for Jews as a whole. They accepted the argument that all Jews had to show solidarity with Israel at a time when it was under mortal threat, and that only Israel could act as protector and refuge for Jews experiencing growing anti-Jewish hostility. Israeli and diaspora Jewish leaders could therefore hardly be surprised when Israeli actions provoked a backlash against Jews. Nor did it make any sense suddenly to deny the connection between the Jewish people and the Jewish state when Jews outside of Israel were implicated by default in the actions taken by the state. As Tony Judt put it in *Prospect* magazine in December 2004: 'It is the policies of Israeli governments in the past two decades, that have provoked anti-Jewish feelings in Europe and elsewhere.' I elaborated:

Israeli leaders, and many Jewish leaders, commentators, academics and thinkers outside of Israel, have in recent years embraced a form of Jewish particularism or ethnocentrism that sees the universalist impulses in the Jewish tradition as an aberration, a form of weakness. The enemy is always Amalek [the biblical, archetypal enemy of the Jews]; Palestinians are Nazis; the human rights movement promotes everyone else's rights at the expense of the rights of Jews; Israel and the Jews forever dwell alone, forever condemned to be victims. And if the world is so totally against us, there is no need to be shy in justifying brutal actions in the name of divine or tribal prerogatives, in the name of an interpretation of Jewish history that places the Holocaust at its absolute centre.

I therefore find myself reluctantly concluding that the intensification of anti-Jewish hostility, although certainly not deliberately incited by Israeli actions, serves to legitimate them nonetheless. And the fear and indeed panic which we have witnessed in some sectors of Jewish communities functions to justify and perhaps even fuel those very actions, because by accepting that those actions are necessary Jews validate the logic that says: 'They are harming our people in the Diaspora, therefore the world is truly against us and we must take even harsher action against our enemies here'.

Audiences abroad gave me a sympathetic hearing. Some in the UK did too, but an undercurrent of hostility prevailed. I kept hearing of muttering by communal leaders but at JPR we hoped the unpleasantness would eventually dissipate as we produced new work and organised new activities. I tried hard to believe this, but could not but find the whisperings demoralising.

* * *

In the first few months after the summer break, I was preoccupied with the fundraising dinner we were organising for JPR with Jim Wolfensohn as guest of honour. Jacob Rothschild was the host and delivered the tribute to his friend. The event was held in the ornate Dunbar Court in the Foreign & Commonwealth Office. Although some JPR supporters had absented themselves, it was clear that we still had a significant reservoir of support among the establishment.

In my brief speech I set out JPR's new programme with some caution, but did not avoid saying that we would be tackling difficult and controversial subjects: 'Also affecting us more and more is the fallout from the Israel-Palestine conflict and its impact on intensifying antisemitism. So how do we understand the nature of antisemitism today? And isn't it time that we asked what are the responsibilities that the interrelated communities of the Jewish people have for each other? Leaving others to answer these questions is not an option', I argued. 'We're deeply affected as individual Jews and as a group by these problems; we have to make a contribution to the debate about their solution.'

What I said seemed to go down well enough. I wasn't looking for a standing ovation or mass conversion. It was enough to feel that I had got my message across, reassured supporters that they were giving money to a good cause and had been honest about what we planned to do. The vibrations from the luminaries seemed positive.

At the dinner we distributed a small brochure outlining our programmes. It included the following:

> There is absolutely no doubt that the Israel-Palestine conflict is having a growing impact on Europe and its Jewish communities. Yet the degree of open and objective debate about this among Jews, between Jews in Europe and Israelis, and between Jews and the wider society has been very limited.
>
> The absence of a consensus on these issues is no reason to remain silent. Israel is a component of Jewish identity, fear of Middle East related terrorism is very high and Israel claims to speak and act on behalf of Jews everywhere. It would therefore be irresponsible to avoid serious discussion of the implications of policies and events.

A week or two later I received the following email from Amalie, Lady Jakobovits, wife of the late Chief Rabbi:

> On my return from America a few days ago I found your report entitled 'The Jewish future in Europe'. I just want to say how grateful I am that you keep me on your mailing list. Not only myself but every member of my family takes great interest in your reports and every line is carefully read.
>
> On page 6 I read the first two paragraphs [quoted above] with particular interest. Recalling as I do that when my late husband Lord Rav Jakobovits spoke these words some 20 years ago he was violently attacked by many individuals within the ranks of Our People in Israel and the Diaspora. How well do I remember him saying: 'Israel was meant to solve the Jewish Problem, sadly, oh so sadly it is now creating it.'
>
> With kindest wishes to you all.
>
> Shalom, shalom,
> Lady Jakobovits

Her words touched and encouraged me.

I felt very positive after the dinner and flew off with Kathy and our younger daughter two days later to be scholar-in-residence for ten days at the Institute for Human Sciences at Boston University, where I delivered a lecture on the revival of Jewish life in Europe. On my return I threw myself into JPR work. With the major grant we had received from the Ford Foundation, we launched the Europe-wide series of discussions on recreating a sense of belonging in the new Europe and we set about trying to secure funding for other projects we had planned.

12

'GUNNING FOR LERMAN'

To have such views expressed by the head of the JPR is obscene. It is symptomatic of an impotent communal leadership that it lacks the backbone to act against the chief executive officer of a publicly funded Jewish think tank who endorses the destruction of Israel as a Jewish state.

Isi Leibler, 2007

Late in December I began to prepare a paper I had been asked to deliver at a January 2007 conference on Jewish peoplehood being held in honour of my old friend and former teacher, Giddy Shimoni, who was retiring after many years as a professor at the Hebrew University of Jerusalem. The subject I was given originally, 'Contemporary left-liberal hostility toward Israel: self-hating and antisemitic?', contained a loaded question and was unworthy of an academic conference. It assumed that all 'left-liberal hostility' to Israel emanated from Jews and by only posing two damning explanations for its origins, 'self-hating and antisemitic', seemed to preclude free and objective enquiry. I was about to query this when I received an updated programme giving the title of my paper as 'The Jews and left-liberal critiques of Israel in the UK: the significance for Jewish peoplehood today'. The organisers had obviously come to their senses.

   The conference took place at the Hebrew University campus on Mt Scopus. It was open to the public and well attended, but the campus was virtually deserted for the winter break. Professor Michael Walzer, the liberal Jewish American political philosopher and prolific writer, delivered the opening address on the subject of Jewish peoplehood. I wrote in a diary note on the 8th: 'Walzer gave a very elegant lecture in praise of the perpetual anomalous state of the Jewish people. In retrospect, it was rather lightweight. Smart distinctions, which he then twisted back on themselves. But what did it add up to?' My thoughts partly stemmed from a deep unease about the concept of 'peoplehood'. I did not want to offend my friend Giddy Shimoni by mounting a full-frontal attack on the concept in my paper, so took a more oblique approach to criticising it, showing that the way it was being used did not fit the reality of the Jewish condition.

The recent provenance of the term 'Jewish peoplehood', I argued, suggested that it had come along exactly because we were finding it difficult to embrace the anomalies Michael Walzer had spoken about. He said the 'constant mixing of incongruous elements is our history', but some found it very hard to accept the 'incongruous element' of Jewish left-liberal critiques of Israel as part of Jewish history. The realities of current Jewish diversity suggested that no single definition of peoplehood would satisfy everyone. And for it to be useful, any concept of Jewish 'peoplehood' would need to accommodate left-liberal critics and four specific critiques.

Particularism versus universalism. The Jewish establishment had been joined by a significant sector of left-of-centre Jewish opinion in adopting a defensive/aggressive particularism in response to perceived threats to Jews and strong criticism of Israel. They displayed feelings of anger and betrayal towards former Jewish colleagues who were 'left-liberal' critics of Israel. The universalists criticised the particularists for ethnocentrism and having betrayed Jewish values. The criticism that left particularists levelled at 'left-liberal' critics of Israel had gone far beyond vigorous debate and sought to define such Jews as beyond the boundaries of the Jewish people.

Diversity of identity and opinion. This growing diversity meant that non-Zionist and even anti-Zionist groups that were expected to wither in the 1970s and 1980s now assertively claimed a place in the Jewish marketplace of ideas. But the establishment mindset remained as it was then: it saw them as a danger, sought to marginalise and ostracise them and prevent them from participating in communal debate.

The threat to an Israel-centric definition of peoplehood. Many left-liberal critics of Israel did not see Israel or Zionism as core components of their Jewish identity. The State of Israel and Judaism were not one and the same. Asserting this was seen as a threat to Jewish peoplehood by pro-Israel and pro-Zionist Jewish establishments.

Jews as subjects and not objects of history. 'Left-liberal' critics argued that Jews were responsible for their own fate. Others countered by saying that, as the new antisemitism proved, Jews were forever having to react to what was done to them. But if Jews were powerless, Zionism had to be judged a failure. In reality, as events since 1989 have shown, Jews have become the subjects and not the objects of history.

Of all the speakers at the conference, Professor Hedva Ben-Israel from the Hebrew University seemed to validate, albeit unwittingly, a significant part of my approach. One of Israel's leading historians of Zionism and nationalism, and a committed Zionist, Ben-Israel discussed the historical and ideological background to the current attempt to find a new concept that would express the unity of the Jewish people. Her key message was stark: 'all forms of Jewish existence continue to exist, and some extreme forms are getting stronger. The Jewish people is more split than ever on nationalism and Jewish universalism. History triumphed over Zionism and not the other way round.' The forthright and authoritative way in which she spoke presented a serious challenge to much of what was being said at the conference.

After the conference I noted: 'What is peoplehood anyway? Just another con-trick on the part of the Jewish Agency and Zionist bodies. As attachment to Israel declines and diversity gains pace, they have to find some other device to reinvigorate Zionism.' 'Peoplehood' was just a 'new' idea Zionists had appropriated to reassert their dominance of Jewish thinking about Jewish life.

At the same time as I was delivering my paper in the second-floor conference room in the Faculty Club at the Hebrew University, the Sassoon International Centre for the Study of Antisemitism (SICSA) was holding a panel discussion upstairs on 'Islam, British society and the terrorist threat'. The speakers were Robert Wistrich, recently appointed head of SICSA, Melanie Phillips, the *Daily Mail* columnist, and Isi Leibler, former head of the Australian Jewish community, now living in Israel and writing columns for the right-wing *Jerusalem Post*. All three were seen as outspoken apologists for right-wing Zionism and Islamophobia. I was aware of the event and found the line-up rather amusing given that they were all going to make roughly the same demonising comments about Muslims, but thought little more about it.

The university campus was eerily quiet once the conference ended. With all the cafés closed on Thursday evening, I subsisted on a packet of pretzels from a vending machine. On Friday I decamped to a hotel in West Jerusalem on Keren Hayesod Street, close to Café Paradiso, my favourite local eatery, and felt my anger at the way discussion of recycled Zionism hijacked so much of the conference dissolve in a bowl of hearty ribollita soup and a glass of Chilean wine. After being cooped up in the university campus hotel for three days, I needed air and exercise, so on Saturday I tramped the rain-sodden deserted streets of the semi-silent city. The rain had cleared by Sunday morning when I stepped out of my taxi to meet Dr Sharon Pardo of Ben-Gurion University at Café Lanver in Tel Aviv. We had first met when I was in Israel in January 2006 and were now making serious plans for a workshop jointly organised by his Centre for the Study of European Politics and Society (CSEPS) and JPR to discuss the impact of Israeli policy-making on European Jews. I left Israel late the following day, richer for the conference experience and the progress made with Pardo and, after discovering that my Israeli passport was out of date, sufficiently at ease to cope calmly with the need to spend almost an hour renewing it before boarding the plane back to England.

Before I had even settled at my desk on Monday morning, I discovered that the *JC* had published a story in which the chairman of the British Zionist

Federation, Andrew Balcombe, objected to my being invited to participate in a huge conference organised by the Mayor of London, Ken Livingstone, taking place on Saturday 20 January and titled 'A world civilization or clash of civilizations?' I was to speak about antisemitism at one of the many panel discussions being held. 'The ZF is ... upset that the only British Jewish representative is Anthony [sic] Lerman, executive director of the Institute for Jewish Policy Research', the *JC* reported. '"Tony Lerman's views on Israel are anathema to the vast majority of the UK Jewish community," Mr Balcombe complained. "But no doubt [they] will fit in with the views of the other 19 conference [speakers]. I am afraid the dice is loaded."'

Livingstone was a hate figure for the Jewish establishment, reviled for his unrelenting criticism of Israel and for his calling a Jewish *Evening Standard* reporter a 'concentration camp guard' when the reporter doorstepped him emerging from a party. (Livingstone did not know that the reporter was Jewish when he made the remark.) The president of the BoD, Henry Grunwald, had demanded an apology from Livingstone, but Livingstone refused. The argument between them had become bitter and remained unresolved.

The following day I received a curious email from Larry Levine, one of the three JPR trustees who walked out of the 2005 meeting at which my appointment was made, quizzing me about a speech I had given that had just come to his attention. I was supposed to have said that I was opposed to Zionism, which was guilty of ethnic cleansing; that I did not believe in a Jewish state, which must reject its ethnocentricity; that the Law of Return should be repealed, all Palestinian refugees allowed to return, the state should lose its Jewish character and just be a neutral civic society without ethnic identity. Larry wondered whether Jews living in the kind of state I envisaged would be able to do so free from persecution and whether this was a price worth paying. Given my views, he couldn't understand why I wanted to work in a Jewish think tank and suggested I would be better off working in a secular one. He feared that my directorship of JPR had the potential to harm the Jewish community and the Zionist cause.

It took me a minute or two to realise that Larry was referring to my presentation at the May 2005 JFJHR panel discussion at Hampstead Town Hall in which I suggested that a confederated Israel-Palestine might, in the long run, be the best way of containing and securing the national rights of Jews and Palestinians and protecting the human rights of all. It was clear from his comments that he had misunderstood and exaggerated my views and I found this very upsetting. I had known Larry quite well when I ran JPR in the 1990s and had regarded him as a friend. That he did not seem capable of talking to me face-to-face about his concerns was very troubling.

Perhaps I should have ignored his email or simply sent a perfunctory response. But instead I wrote him a long reply, which I copied – as he had copied his email – to Peter Levy and Simon Haskel. I wrote it as much for their sakes, to show that I was determined to fight any further attacks on me no matter from whence they came. I berated Larry for consorting with 'his friends ... who do not seem to like the true Jewish way of doing things, which is to engage in debate and argument. Instead they prefer the path of sending round insulting emails, whispering in little groups, trying to exert pressure on members of the JPR Board, in a rather pathetic attempt to shut me up.' I tried to rebuff all his distortions of my remarks. For example, I had not denied that Jews had national rights, nor was I ready to accept the persecution of Jews that he implied would occur in the kind of state I proposed. But I did not expect Larry to apologise. The only part of my response that I thought might have some effect was my expression of disgust about the campaign being waged against me and how he and his friends impugned my Jewishness.

> I'm astonished that you should wonder why I want to carry out my work in such a 'Jewish' environment as JPR. I've spent the last 30-odd years of my life working for the future of the Jewish people. I lived for three years in Israel, I served in the army, my oldest son was born there, I have family there, I visit quite often, I talk all the time with Israelis – of the left and right and centre. My views about Israel-Palestine are a direct expression of my concern for the Jewish future.
>
> Frankly, the people who are doing harm to the Jewish community and the Zionist cause are the snide emailers, the whisperers, cowards who never come directly to me with their complaints, the people who refuse to debate these matters openly, who refuse to face up to the truth of what's happening in Israel, who write columns and diaries and articles calling people like me 'self-hating Jews', who run off telling tales to bodies like the Jewish Leadership Council. These are the people who are harming Israel and endangering its future.

Peter Levy sent me a reassuring response: 'I have now read the speech and the exchange of emails. Not nice!! I also received similar expressions of concern from [Rabbi] Sidney Brichto. I must say it all seems well orchestrated bearing in mind it is historic [*sic*]. My inclination is to ignore the comments, it is clear that certain people for whatever reason do not hold the same views and are happy to put their own interpretation on what you said to satisfy their own ends.'

On Friday 12 January I checked the *JC* on the web to see if the Livingstone conference story was still alive and whether there were any more critical remarks about me. There was nothing on the home page. Instead, and impossible to miss, was an op-ed by Isi Leibler titled 'Enough of weak leaders!' Extracted from the presentation he gave at the panel in Jerusalem, it lambasted Anglo-Jewish leaders as 'trembling Israelites, grateful for the protection afforded them and desperate not to rock the boat', singling out Henry Grunwald for special opprobrium.

He then turned his attention to the phenomenon of 'Jewish, anti-Israeli activists'. This time it was my turn for the Leibler tongue-lashing, and worse:

> One of those who falls into this category is Antony Lerman, executive director of the Institute for Jewish Policy Research, a body funded by Jewish philan-thropists and purporting to be the premier think-tank of Anglo-Jewry. In his address to the Jewish Forum for Justice and Human Rights on March 21 2005, he publicly stated that in view of the fact that the State of Israel and Zionism have been 'failures' and that Israel 'perpetrates human-rights abuses', the Jewish state should be transformed into a bi-national state which would 'repeal Israel's law of return' and enable 'the right of return of Arab refugees'.
>
> Such views are now often expressed by left-wing Jewish fringe groups, but to have such views expressed by the head of the JPR is obscene. It is symptomatic of an impotent communal leadership that it lacks the backbone to act against the chief executive officer of a publicly funded Jewish think tank who endorses the destruction of Israel as a Jewish state.

It took a while before I fully grasped the comprehensive nature of Leibler's attack on me. He wasn't just presenting a distorted account of my views on Israel and Zionism; he was demanding that Anglo-Jewish leaders have me dismissed from my job.

Leibler was well-known for the aggressive, right-wing Zionist views he expressed in his regular *Jerusalem Post* column. Although I had never made any attempt to hide what I said at the JFJHR public meeting, before receiving the email from Larry Levine I had forgotten that my presentation had been posted on the JFJHR website. Leibler may have come across it on his own initiative, but I found this highly unlikely. It seemed too much of a coincidence that within days of each other both Larry Levine and Leibler could have independently discovered the text of my talk. What appeared more plausible was that, for reasons of political affinity, some of the people who had been attacking me in the UK had drawn Leibler's attention to my talk.

But it wasn't just the crudity of Leibler's personal attack that concerned me, it was also the cartoon by Krausz that accompanied the article. In it a man was depicted from behind, speaking at a lectern. The arm of someone out of the picture reaches towards the back of the speaker. In his hand is a thick red marker. On the speaker's back is a Star of David in black and overlaid on that, a swastika in red. It seemed to me that, in at least two ways, this cartoon could be taken to imply that I was an antisemite. The arm could be that of the anti-Israel Jewish critic perpetrating an antisemitic act by scrawling a swastika on the back of a Jewish speaker. Alternatively, the Jewish speaker could be me purporting to speak as a Jew but being outed as an antisemite by the hand reaching out and scrawling a swastika on my back. While it's true that the cartoon was ambiguous and lent itself to more than one interpretation, it was reasonable to read it as endorsing Leibler's criticisms of me and painting me as an antisemite.

I read the attack as possibly libellous and was encouraged to consult my friend Geoffrey Bindman, the eminent lawyer. He agreed and proposed that I seek counsel's opinion. Meanwhile, I was advised to draft a letter to the editor of the *JC*, pointing out the defamation and demanding an apology. Later that morning, I called Peter Levy who had known nothing about the Leibler article before it appeared. He said he was speechless and certainly sounded dumbstruck. But I could see that he was in a difficult position because he was chairman of both JPR and the Board of Directors of the *JC*. I told him what I was planning to do, making it clear to him that I was certainly angry and taking the matter very seriously.

When he called back an hour later, it was clear that he realised he faced a conflict between wanting to support me and JPR and fulfilling his responsibilities to the *JC*, should there be a libel action to defend. He also gave me more than just an inkling of the constant pressure he had been under from Jewish communal leaders arising out of my appointment. That was bad enough. This new furore appeared to be taking the pressure to another, possibly unresolvable level. It was not that Peter was unused to pressure or could not act decisively. But one of the things that made him stand out as a leader and philanthropist was his sensitivity – to the feelings of others, to conflicts which touched him personally, to the responsibility he felt for the Jewish community. And I felt that his sensitivity very understandably made it hard for him to see a way through this growing crisis. And this seemed to mirror my own position.

The pressure soon eased as a few days later I was sitting with Geoffrey Bindman in counsel's chambers hearing a very convincing explanation as to why the grounds for threatening libel action were extremely weak. Although Leibler's interpretation of my remarks may have been entirely wrong, they fell within the limits of acceptable opinion. Geoffrey had to agree. I abandoned the letter to the *JC* editor, David Rowan, and instead asked for and was given the right of reply. My article appeared the following week, titled by the editors: 'Don't slur me, Mr Leibler, engage with me'.

'Far from endorsing the destruction of Israel as a Jewish state,' I wrote, 'I'm for the reconstruction of Israel as a state in which Jewish values guide public behaviour and can be permanently sustained. The danger to Israel's existence comes not from critics outside who are concerned for the country's future, but from the many Leiblers inside Israel (and outside) who ... see salvation in waging war on their Jewish "enemies".' It was therefore necessary for concerned Jews to discuss the many possible futures Israel faces. But this was very difficult 'in an atmosphere coarsened by vicious language and reckless illustrations. Whatever the intention of the cartoonist, one interpretation of his cartoon that accompanied last week's article is that Jews like me, who make "addresses" criticising Israel, deserve to be branded as Jew-haters. Who would not be hurt by such an implication? Admitting Zionism's failures is not heresy. The future of the Jewish people is still a matter of debate. We are strengthened by engaging in it; fatally weakened by the people who level the slur of "self-hatred" at those who do.'

If I had any hopes that my article would be the end of the matter, I was soon to be disappointed. Another JPR trustee, Anthony Spitz, resigned. I was told that he did not want to make his resignation public, but it still found its way on to the front page of the *JC* on 26 January. The same story revealed that Lord Stanley Kalms had resigned from his position as honorary vice-president of JPR. The former Tory Party Treasurer and boss of Dixons wasted no time in rushing into print to justify his action. In an article published in the same edition of the paper he called my article of the previous week 'disingenuous' and endorsed Leibler's comment that my views were 'obscene'. He went on: 'When the previous executive director ... left the JPR and Antony Lerman was appointed, I admit I was unaware of his dangerous and unacceptable views, contrary to my concept of the diaspora – to support the State of Israel, warts and all.'

Meanwhile, I was also being further assailed, this time by Henry Grunwald, for participating in the Mayor of London's conference. He told a plenary meeting of the BoD: 'I was surprised that the director of JPR agreed to give a talk on antisemitism on *Shabbat*. That is something that should never have happened. If the JPR wants to be considered as part of the community, its director should not be speaking about that topic at that seminar on a *Shabbat*.' Though an orthodox Jew, he did not seem to be aware that there was no injunction against a Jew addressing a conference on *Shabbat*. When asked by the *JC* whether I had been approached by anyone prior to the conference not to take part, I replied: 'Absolutely not.'

Although Peter Levy still faced a conflict of interest as chairman of JPR and of the *JC*, I could not have asked for a stronger statement than the one he gave to the paper: 'Mr Lerman has the full confidence of the Board. There was no criticism [at the meeting of the JPR Board] whatsoever of Mr Lerman attending the conference on Saturday ... I am not concerned about the criticism of the Board [of Deputies].' Leibler's criticisms of me for something I had said about Israel prior to coming into office were unacceptable: 'Since he has been in office, he has not expressed any of his personal views on Israel.'

The paper's main leader on 26 January was headed 'Gunning for Lerman'. A strange concoction, it purported to support my right to express my 'views in a personal capacity and be judged in his day job by his institute's performance'. But it appeared to endorse Leibler's distorted representation of my views on Israel and took a sideswipe at the new programme I had devised for JPR, referring to the 'institute's insufficiently clear agenda'. And as if to rub salt into the wound, the first four letters the paper published were all extremely hostile to me. Responding to these multiple attacks became very time-consuming. They were upsetting too, but I felt that I had to maintain morale at the institute. Where I felt able to defend myself and seek redress, I tried to do so, and I made sure that I had a hand in drafting the letter of reply that Peter Levy wanted to send to Stanley Kalms.

I was particularly annoyed by the behaviour of the *JC* editor David Rowan. He had not been obliged to publish the inflammatory article by Isi Leibler. I wrote to him demanding corrections and apologies for his editorial, but he refused to concede that he had made any errors. I resolved to make a complaint against him and the paper to the Press Complaints Commission and I told him so. I knew that I could not do this without consulting Peter Levy, but David Rowan told him before I could. Peter soon called and sought to persuade me not to approach the PCC. My instant feeling was that he was putting the *JC* before JPR, but as we spoke I realised that this was unfair. If I went ahead, I would simply be making it harder to defend JPR because Peter was absolutely central to our effort to fend off those attacking me and the Institute and he had already proved his commitment to this end. I had to accept that his more realistic approach made more sense than my wish for redress, however hard it was to admit it.

Nevertheless, after my conversation with Peter I suddenly felt trapped and powerless. I had had my say in the *JC* but could do nothing about the continuing distortion of my views. And there was more than a whiff of a concerted campaign going on behind the scenes. This was more or less confirmed in the letter that Lord Kalms wrote, on 17 January, to Peter Levy and Lord Haskel, preparatory to announcing his resignation. After rubbishing my views Kalms revealed that several senior members of the community had contacted him that very week because of his connection with the JPR as its honorary vice-president and queried whether JPR intended to remedy the situation. He was also challenged as to whether he identified with my views and if not why was he adding his credibility and reputation to endorse me. Peter Levy replied: 'The question is: Does holding [strongly critical views on Israel] disqualify him from heading a Jewish think tank that develops policy ideas for Jewish communities? In my view, the answer is an unqualified no, and the JPR Board agrees with me on this. We will therefore be robustly defending our decision to appoint Tony as Director and rejecting all calls to have him dismissed.' He continued:

> Our resolve in this matter is strengthened by the deeply disturbing, underhand campaign that has been waged against Tony and JPR ever since the proposal to appoint Tony was discussed by the JPR Board. This campaign demeans our community, is decidedly un-Jewish and should be stopped. I have recommended to my colleagues that the JPR Board make it clear to the community and to those orchestrating this campaign that what is going on is very damaging. If we wish people to be tolerant towards us as Jews, we must be tolerant within our own community.

Kalms flatly denied any knowledge of such a campaign and claimed that he had merely been sent a copy of my speech. People in his circles were totally astonished that I could head JPR given my 'absolutely reprehensible' attitudes toward Israel. He linked me to what he called 'traditional self-haters', people like the MP Gerald Kaufman and the actress Miriam Margolyes, and in effect urged Peter Levy to have me dismissed.

This wasn't the first time I had encountered Kalms's crude, misplaced certainties about how to protect the sensitivities of the Jewish community. I could not help but be reminded of a meeting Peter Levy and I had with him in his Brook Street office on 17 November 2006 in which we sought his support for a project on monitoring EU policy-making on issues affecting Jews in Europe. There was only one 'interest' that European Jews needed to pursue in Europe, he said: Islam and Islamic fundamentalism. What JPR should be doing is fighting Islam, showing complete support for the two people who had stood up to Islam – Tony Blair and George Bush. Most Muslims didn't want to integrate, he said. Ultimately they would line up behind the fundamentalists. After making disparaging remarks about Islam he asserted that the problem was that what Muslims were doing in their schools, in their madrassas and in their mosques cannot be controlled. He wondered how it was possible that a situation had been allowed to develop here in this country where people can oppose the government and society and not be subject to any control.

Peter and I had no intention of following his advice and left as soon as we decently could. It was a demeaning experience. And it was deeply disturbing to think that some in high political circles would believe that his views were representative of Jewish views generally. For all I know, Peter may have heard it all before. (And I certainly found out later that we were not the first to have been given the benefit of Stanley's pearls of wisdom on Islam.)

The 2 February 2007 edition of the *JC* was again full of stories about 'the think-tank boss under fire'. In his regular monthly column Daniel Finkelstein argued that the blame for what had happened should be laid firmly at the door of the JPR Board, because they should have realised that the media would make my views 'the big story'. 'JPR chose someone with what many in the community (including, very strongly, myself) regard as utterly misguided and dangerous opinions. They can't, surely, have done it by accident. They can't, surely, have thought it wouldn't matter.'

The paper had received so much mail on the issue that it published an entire extra letters page devoted exclusively to 'Lerman: your views'. Of the twelve letters, seven were in my defence. And a story by Simon Rocker threw new light on high-level collusion in the campaign against me: 'The *JC* has learned that Mr Lerman's return to JPR was discussed early last year at the Jewish Leadership Council and some of its members privately expressed their concerns to Mr Levy. One JLC member confided: "The problem is that under its previous director, Barry Kosmin, JPR became the semi-official research wing of the community. It's nonsense that you can separate personal and institutional viewpoints."'

13

PRESSING ON

Jews for Genocide
[T]he British arm of the pincer of Jewish destruction.
> Melanie Phillips, 2007, descriptions of Independent Jewish Voices

[V]ocal post-Jewish minority ... I think is [a] truer description of these traitors
than Tony Lerman's self appellation as post-Zionist ... [T]hey need to be utterly
condemned because they have acted in a manner to deserve the biblical punishment
of 'being cut off from their people'.
> Rabbi Sidney Brichto, 2007

Newspapers cash in on the latest controversy, milking it for all its worth, and then move on when the story goes stale. The *JC* was no different. So I assumed the Lerman controversy was beginning to run its course as far as the editor was concerned. This was more than hunch, because I knew that Independent Jewish Voices was to be launched on Monday 5 February 2007 and that the paper, and probably the national press too, would be giving it publicity. Nonetheless, what had happened to me was central to what IJV was all about: the possibility for a Jew working professionally in the organised British Jewish community to speak out on issues of justice and human rights in relation to the Israel-Palestine conflict and not be treated as a traitor. It looked inevitable that my situation would be linked to the IJV launch, all the more so since I had agreed to write a piece on the significance of IJV for the *Guardian*'s Comment is free (Cif) website, which was running articles all week from signatories, observers and opponents. And since I was simply setting the IJV phenomenon in the wider context of recent developments in the Jewish world, and was not a signatory, I did not think it was necessary to 'clear' my contribution with JPR trustees.

The IJV steering group took a full-page in *The Times* to publish its statement of principles and the initial list of 139 signatories, and invited others to sign. A public 'Speak Out' was announced for Hampstead Town Hall on 19 February. The statement was published simultaneously on the *Guardian* website together with an article in the print edition by one of the key figures in IJV, the Oxford academic philosopher Dr Brian Klug.

The launch attracted wide publicity, especially because of the very well-known figures among the signatories: Stephen Fry, Harold Pinter, Zoe Wanamaker, Nicole Farhi, Mike Leigh, Jenny Diski, Professor Eric Hobsbawm and Professor Susie Orbach, among others.* On 5 February the *Guardian* put it in context: 'The emergence of the group ... comes at a time of ferment over attitudes towards Israel, stoked by the [1996] war in Lebanon and the bloodshed in the occupied territories. The question of whether radical opposition to Israeli policies necessarily amounts to anti-Semitism is central to the debate.' The reporter, Julian Borger, continued (albeit inaccurately summarising my views): 'The row was brought to a head in recent weeks by the resignation of board members of the Institute of Jewish Policy Research (IJPR) after it emerged that its director, Antony Lerman, had voiced support for the merging of Israel with the Palestinian territories into a single bi-national federation and a repeal of the "law of return" giving the right of anyone of Jewish descent to Israeli citizenship.' Borger, and Ned Temko previously in the *Observer*, linked it to developments in America: 'A parallel struggle is under way in the US where the American Jewish Committee published an article accusing liberal Jews such as the historian Tony Judt of fuelling anti-Semitism by questioning Israel's right to exist.' The article, in fact a lengthy essay, said that 'one of the most distressing features of the new anti-Semitism' was 'the participation of Jews alongside it'.

Coverage given to the launch of IJV in the *JC* on 9 February took everyone involved by surprise. The front-page banner headline read: 'The rebellion goes global'. Three more pages devoted to IJV included an unfriendly editorial; letters to the editor (all negative); a piece by a member of the initiating group, Anthony Isaacs, with responses by two critics, Emanuele Ottolenghi and Rabbi Sidney Brichto from the Progressive Jewish religious movement; a negative column by David Aaronovitch and extracts from Cif pieces and blogs. Quotes from my Cif piece were featured in the coverage: 'Can a Jew with radical thoughts about solutions to the Israel-Palestine conflict be head of an independent think tank whose work focuses on policy ideas which would benefit Jewish communities in Europe? One might hope that reasonable people will say "Yes" and, indeed, many have. But the fact that many haven't

---

* The people who devised the IJV statement of principles and together planned the launch of IJV were Dr Lisa Appignanesi, Sir Geoffrey Bindman, Lady Ellen Dahrendorf, Dr Edie Friedman, Rabbi David Goldberg, Dr Anthony Isaacs, Ann Jungman, Anne Karpf, Dr Brian Klug, Professor Francesca Klug, Dr Tony Klug, Antony Lerman, Professor Susie Orbach, Professor Jacqueline Rose, Leon Rosselson, Professor Donald Sassoon, Professor Lynne Segal, Gillian Slovo, Henry Stewart.

is more than a hint that Independent Jewish Voices is on to something.' I linked the creation of IJV to the split among Jews over particularism and universalism, with IJV standing for the reassertion of universal values and the Jewish tradition of social justice. I acknowledged that the issues had become so incendiary that even the head of a think tank found it hard to write about them objectively. I referred to having been subject to strong abuse but concluded: 'Most frustrating has been the way my views have been taken out of context, with critics taking off on flights of fancy to suit their preconceived ideas.'

Mercifully there were only three letters in the *JC* of 9 February relating to the Lerman controversy. One of those was from an Israeli, my friend Avner Azulay. His testimony was telling:

> I am an Israeli, a Zionist and a new member of the JPR Board. I made aliya in 1954 and served Israel for 33 years in the military, defence and security establishments. My children live in Israel and serve in the IDF.
>
> I have read the articles and letters about Tony Lerman's views. Frankly, I am more concerned about all those 'good Jews' who are burying their heads in the sand. Not one has said anything constructive. With all due respect to Lord Kalms and others, I don't see how they have contributed anything to Israel by walking out on JPR.
>
> These respectable gentlemen are so worried about the existence of Israel, but what have they got to say about the infringement of the civil and human rights of innocent Palestinians, the 'apartheid' procedures, such as separate roads for settlers and Palestinians, and the illegal expropriation of land? Have any of these concerned Jews in London or elsewhere once raised their voices against these excesses? Where are their Jewish moral values? Declining to attend a conference on Shabbat – is that what is going to save Israel?
>
> I am for two states for two peoples. Those who are driving Israel towards one state are those critics of Tony Lerman who choose to ignore what is happening and prefer to criticise and condemn some of his statements.

Supportive friends, including other Israelis, also wrote letters to the *JC*. I had many private messages of support, even though some felt they could not put their heads above the parapet and back me in public. After my *JC* article I decided to keep a dignified silence and was only enticed out of it momentarily when I agreed to write for the *Guardian* about IJV and the Comment editor, Georgina Henry, thought it essential that I referred to what had happened to me.

I had already made it clear to Peter Levy that I had no intention of resigning and that if trustees were unhappy it was up to them to take what action they saw fit. Throughout the whole controversy, I was determined not to make the same mistake I made over the *Jewish Quarterly* affair in the mid 1980s, when I allowed myself to be pressured to resign from the editorship. I always felt that I let down the many people who came to my defence. But I soon came to realise that the confidence I had in the strength of my position at JPR was misplaced. Soon after the IJV launch, my friend Tony Klug asked me whether I would agree to talk confidentially with Lance Blackstone, who was then chairman of the Kessler Foundation, the charitable trust that owned the JC. Lance met regularly with Peter Levy in his role as JC chairman and had information he thought I should be aware of. I naturally agreed. In two sympathetic calls Lance's stark message was that he thought I only had a 50–50 chance of surviving as director of JPR and he advised me to withdraw from public comment of any kind until the whole affair blew over. He saw it as a tactical withdrawal – retreating from this battle in order to be able to win the larger war. Peter was coming under a lot of pressure; and some trustees who had, until now, supported me, saw the article I had written about IJV as a step too far.

This was very disturbing. I could not afford to lose the support of my Board. There was certainly no point in taking on all the forces ranged against me and making success or failure in that battle determine my future. It would not help me introduce new ideas into public discussion and change people's thinking. But I had already more or less adopted the position that Lance was urging on me and had little room for manoeuvre.

It was always difficult to gauge fully the range and depth of what was being said – and potentially done – about me in Jewish leadership circles. But hard evidence of this emerged when I saw emails, written by people from those very circles, hinting at the existence of a concerted campaign to force me either to toe the 'communal line' or risk becoming so ostracised that my position at JPR would cease to be tenable. The first email dated back to 19 July 2006, after I spoke at the Jewish Community Centre's panel discussion on antisemitism at the Everyman Cinema. Stephen Pollard, editor of the JC at the time of writing, but then a columnist on the *Daily Mail*, was in the audience and reported to Jeremy Newmark, executive director of the Jewish Leadership Council (JLC), that I had given a terrible performance and implied that, in my answers to questions, I had confirmed the worst interpretations of my views on antisemitism. Had this distorted description of what I said simply been part of a personal exchange between Pollard and Newmark, it would mean little. But that same day Newmark forwarded Pollard's email to the key members of the JLC, Sir Trevor Chinn, Gerald Ronson, Lord Michael Levy and Henry Grunwald, telling them that I had not changed my tone despite various assurances that had been given in recent weeks.

Three of the recipients were among the most powerful people in the organised Jewish community: Sir Trevor Chinn, once one of the country's most prominent businessmen, former chairman of RAC plc and a hugely influential figure in the Jewish charitable field, especially for pro-Israel organisations; Gerald Ronson, chairman of the private international property development company Heron and of the Community Security Trust, the private charity responsible for the security of the Jewish community; Lord Levy, Tony Blair's Middle East envoy and former successful impresario, who played a leading role, principally as a fundraiser, in a number of major Jewish charities. And it confirmed Simon Rocker's report in the *JC* of 2 February that the JLC had discussed my position early in 2006. But more sinister were the references to various assurances given in recent weeks. Who gave these assurances? What business was it of Jeremy Newmark, feeding off tales told by Stephen Pollard, to expect that I should have changed my tone and to report on this to his bosses?

The second email was sent on 9 February 2007, just after the launch of Independent Jewish Voices. Its author, Rabbi Sidney Brichto, the director of the Israel-Diaspora Trust (IDT), was responding to emails from the Clifford Chance lawyer, Adrian Cohen, one of the three trustees who resigned and walked out of the JPR Board meeting at which my appointment was made, and from Jon Benjamin, secretary general of the Board of Deputies.

From: Sidney Brichto
To: 'Adrian Cohen'
Cc: 'Melanie Phillips'; MKay; rick haller; alan.melkman ... ; 'Jonathan Goldberg Q.C.; 'Geoffrey Goldkorn'; 'F.Hellner'; Mark G; [Jeremy Newmark]; stephenpollard ... ; Richard.Bolchover ... ; 'Larry Levine'; Daniel Finkelstein; 'dana brass'; George Pinto; 'Vernon Bogdanor'; 'David Rowan'; Lord Kalms; Felix Posen
Sent: Friday, February 09, 2007 9:39 AM
Subject: Re: More IJV nonsense debunked

...

What is interesting and should be promulgated widely by us is the truth that was expressed a number of times from a variety of sources in today's JC, which is that it was IJV who are seeking to stifle the free expression of mainstream Jewry and to suggest that Jews were not united in their support for Israel; so this vocal post-Jewish minority (I think this is truer description of these traitors than Tony Lerman's self appellation as post-Zionist) is seeking to misrepresent the situation by maintaining it is they who really speak for world Jewry. It wasn't enough for them that traitorous Jewish individuals were enabling Gentiles, in attacking Israel, to say, 'Look, this is what leading Jews, even Zionists are saying' but to go further by claiming, 'This is really what most Jews think but are afraid to say because of their fear of the heavy handedness of the Jewish establishment.' Why are they so desperate to disseminate such lies? Melanie

Phillips has been accused of hysteria, even by Israel's sympathizers, for writing about [IJV as] *Jews for Genocide*, but the behaviour of these Jews might make Melanie's critics rethink their criticism of her. It is hard for us Jews, whose love for our roots, our heritage, Jewish hopes and dreams, which is so deep in us, to believe that such Jewish haters could exist, but I am afraid they do. What is it that moves them – cowardice, a need to be loved by the Gentiles, alienation, an assimilation of antisemitic attitudes (of which I wrote about in my *Funny, you don't look Jewish*)? It has been said that some Jews in concentration camps began to believe that they had done something wrong in order to reconcile themselves to their situation and to relate to their persecutors. Could these Jews be suffering from the same pathology? But for whatever reason they need to be utterly condemned because they have acted in a manner to deserve the biblical punishment of 'being cut off from their people' because they have chosen to do this themselves.

As director of the IDT, a Jewish discussion-dining group, which brought together businessmen, politicians, professionals, philanthropists, academics, writers and Jewish communal leaders for confidential meetings at London clubs like the Athenaeum on issues affecting Israel and world Jewry, Brichto had a ready-made and generally very receptive audience for his views. In the past, as a Liberal rabbi without a congregation but holding a senior administrative post in the central organisation of the Liberal movement, Brichto had often crossed swords with the Jewish establishment, especially on issues of personal Jewish status. But in recent years he had become increasingly hawkish on Israel and the need for absolute communal solidarity and this had gone together with a growing antipathy to Islam and Muslims. We had been friends and had worked together when he was consultant fundraiser to JPR in the 1990s. He had intimate knowledge of my Jewish background. This made the farrago of nonsense and the language in his email quite shocking.

The fact that he copied this email to 20 people is no proof that they all agreed with him. But he knew he was addressing a broadly sympathetic audience. Sidney was someone who craved approval and attention. And here he was talking to the editor of the *JC*, the director of communications of the Community Security Trust, the associate editor of *The Times*, major Jewish philanthropists, a senior Oxford don, a rabbi, bankers, lawyers, newspaper columnists, the executive director of the Jewish Leadership Council – an influential group, without a doubt, and one containing five of the people who had resigned as honorary officers of JPR.

I was so desperate to remain positive that I don't think I ever properly faced up to the implications of these emails. But it was impossible to pretend that the events of January and February had never happened. Some of JPR's UK trustees were sufficiently troubled that they persuaded Peter Levy to write to me setting out the parameters within which he said I had agreed to operate in relation to public statements on anything political. He wanted me to consult more with the Board on anything I might say or write for public consumption, but I saw this as an unacceptable restriction and refused. I argued that I was already following the guidelines agreed when I was appointed and that should be sufficient. Peter clearly did not want a confrontation and declared himself satisfied that, essentially, we saw things in the same way.

At a particularly low point I wrote in my diary on 12 April: 'Now I just feel that I'm being muzzled, that the enemies are winning, ... that what I wanted to do – which was to make my voice heard through this platform – is out of reach.' This moment of hopelessness was one of a succession. Another occurred during and after the March Board meeting. Harold Paisner, senior partner in the major city law firm, Berwin Leighton Paisner, and a long-standing and extremely decent JPR trustee, had always been very supportive of me. The fallout from the affair was rather desultorily discussed at the meeting. Harold suggested that it might be a good idea if I explained my views on Israel-Palestine and Zionism to trustees, giving everyone a chance to discuss them. For a brief moment, I felt as if a great weight had been lifted from my shoulders and that JPR might embrace open discussions of alternative solutions to the Israel-Palestine conflict. But my hopes were immediately dashed when Peter Levy and Brian Smouha, the JPR treasurer, said that they felt such a discussion would not be helpful, and one or two other trustees expressed agreement. It was the first and last time that such a suggestion was made. After the meeting I thought to myself that if even JPR's trustees were not ready to talk about my views, how would I ever position JPR as an institution promoting open discussion and exploration of difficult issues, especially in relation to Israel-Palestine and relations between European Jews and Israel?

I threw myself into working on JPR's programme with as much enthusiasm as I could muster. But it became increasingly difficult. I wrote in my diary: 'Although I'm probably wrong about this, just feel that I'm not going to be at JPR that much longer.' The public furore over my views and stewardship of JPR and over the launch of IJV lasted two or three months, but eventually abated. Those who attacked me and JPR kept us in their sights, but moved on to other targets. I was left feeling as if I had been tried in the court of public opinion and found guilty. At some point the sentence would be carried out.

* * *

Outside of work, my involvement in other activities brought little relief from the intensified feelings of depression. I could no longer play a central role in

JFJHR. I was finding it hard to engage fully in running JPR. But it's also true
to say that somehow JFJHR had begun to lose its way. We had organised some
great meetings, but we all more or less acknowledged that raising our concerns
about Israel-Palestine and other issues through public meetings had only been
partially successful. So many of the original JFJHR friends had now become
active in IJV that there was little time to be heavily involved in both groups.
And I think many found IJV more fulfilling because it had a narrower, more
urgent focus. After deciding that I could not sign the declaration, I continued
to attend the steering group's meetings but became less active. I was left feeling
deeply frustrated and out of place.

Nevertheless, I had no intention of relaxing my efforts to bring to the
attention of the Jewish community and the wider world the negative impact
that continuing conflict between Israelis and Palestinians was having on
Europe's Jews and thinking of ways to change this situation. But talking
about these matters to a general audience necessitated performing a delicate
balancing act and demonstrating a nuanced understanding of how Israel's
actions could provoke antisemitism. This was the approach I took when I
spoke at Ken Livingstone's conference in January 2007. I acknowledged the
connection between Israel and antisemitism and said that 'Anti-Zionism and
hostility to Israel *can* be antisemitic if that hostility uses all the symbols of
the antisemitic figure of the Jew.' But I argued that there was a great danger
in automatically conflating what were two fundamentally different things.
As Brian Klug wrote in his submission to the 2006 All-Party Parliamentary
Inquiry into Antisemitism, if we conflate antisemitism and anti-Zionism,
'the credibility of those who seek to confront antisemitism is ... eroded.
It creates widespread cynicism, even among the liberal-minded, about the
subject. Moreover, people of good will who sympathise with the Palestinians
resent being falsely accused. This includes some British Jews who are living
in a state of discomfort, if not fear, because their political opinions about
the Middle East expose them to the taunt of "antisemitic" (or self-hating).'

Whenever I was asked to speak on contemporary antisemitism, I took the
opportunity to explain the Israel-antisemitism connection. A panel discussion
organised by the Faculty for Israel-Palestine Peace at Birkbeck on 14 May
focused on how the politicisation of discussion about antisemitism, through
the labelling of forms of criticism of Israel as antisemitic, was hampering
free and open consideration of current Jew-hatred. I outlined how Israeli
governments had successfully sought to control efforts to define and combat
antisemitism at the international level. Increasing acceptance of the so-called
'Working Definition' of antisemitism of the European Union Monitoring
Centre on Racism and Xenophobia had helped Israel in this regard. It had
led to a situation where 'We cannot discuss Israel-Palestine without getting

entangled in arguments about what critique of Israel is antisemitic; and we cannot discuss contemporary antisemitism without getting entangled in arguments about Israel-Palestine.' One of my conclusions was that the redefinition of antisemitism that had been taking place could alienate potential supporters of Israel, concerned for Israel's future but also conscious that there was good reason to criticise some of its self-defeating policies.

I spoke again at Birkbeck on 9 July at a conference on 'Antisemitism in English culture' and included in my remarks a passage on 'Jewish self-hatred'. The widespread use of this term, as if it were an academic category, to describe Jewish critics of Israel had become a major feature of the debate about the Israel-antisemitism nexus. This was not an issue I could approach entirely dispassionately. I became aware of the accusation that I was a 'self-hating Jew' quite soon after I was subject to public attack following my appointment as JPR director. Nor was it the first time I had attracted this libel. I had been charged with 'Jewish self-hatred' during the *JQ* affair in the mid 1980s (see Chapter 6). But I noted that from 2006 the use of the concept had become increasingly popular, with long, pseudo-scholarly articles on the subject appearing all over the internet.

For someone so involved in mainstream Jewish life, the idea that I could hate the Jewish part of my identity was simply absurd. Even so, I initially assumed that there were some Jews for whom the appellation was correct. But when an accusatory phrase is resorted to so readily in a bitter political argument, there are grounds for smelling a rat. As I read more on the subject, the murkier the picture became. The only serious book on Jewish self-hatred, Sander Gilman's *Jewish Self-Hatred: Anti-Semitism and the Hidden Language of the Jews*, was full of fascinating exegesis and analysis, but failed to clarify what Jewish self-hatred was all about.

Eventually I discovered a vein of scholarly analytical writing that cast doubt on the validity of the concept. The most comprehensive and influential piece was a definitive paper in the *British Journal of Social Psychology* (June 2005) by Dr Mick Finlay, 'Pathologizing dissent: identity politics, Zionism and the "self-hating Jew"'. I drew on this and on the work of historians such as Dr Steven Beller and Professor Shulamit Volkov for an article published in the *Jewish Quarterly* in the summer of 2008, 'Jewish self-hatred: myth or reality?' Referring to the prominent American psychologist, Kurt Lewin, who popularised the term and gave it theoretical underpinning, I quoted Finlay who wrote that Lewin's 'description of self-hatred is clearly a judgement about disloyalty and is a rallying call to American Jews. [He] concluded his paper ["Self-hatred among Jews"] by suggesting that Jews should be asked to sacrifice more for the group.' This same rationale, I noted, seemed to be underpinning the deluge of self-hatred accusations levelled at critics of Israel today. I concluded:

> The concept of the 'self-hating Jew' strengthens a narrow, ethnocentric view of the Jewish people. It exerts a monopoly over patriotism. It promotes a definition of Jewish identity which relies on the notion of an eternal enemy, and how much more dangerous when that enemy is a fifth column within the group. It plays on real fears of antisemitism and at the same time exaggerates the problem by claiming that critical Jews are 'infected' by it too. And it posits an essentialist notion of Jewish identity ...
>
> How much easier to dismiss [the] arguments [of dissenting Jews] by levelling the charge of Jewish self-hatred than by engaging with them.

Those using the accusation of Jewish self-hatred to denigrate Jewish critics of Israel were almost certainly not aware of the irony in Zionists choosing such a line of attack. It was well known that Zionism developed as a response to antisemitism and to the failure of emancipation and assimilation to overcome it. But that Herzl and other political Zionists, in order to justify their ideology, resorted to describing in antisemitic terms Jews who would not accept Zionism was less well-known.

Raising for discussion such controversial aspects of the history, politics and ideology of Zionism was part of my agenda to make it easier for people to understand the injustice suffered by the Palestinians. To look more closely at these imperfections I invited my friend Professor Idith Zertal, then based at the Institute of Jewish Studies at the University of Basel, to give a seminar in October 2007 on the work she was doing on the relationship between antisemitism and Zionism. Idith gave a historical overview of what she called the dense, twisted, pragmatic, relationship – both concealed and open – between antisemitism and Zionism. She illustrated how Zionism was nurtured and empowered by antisemitism, how it used it for its own ends, and mobilised it for the sake of the Zionist project. Indeed, in countries where there was no antisemitism, Zionism even served to inflame it. However, despite what she described as the disturbing, causal connection between Zionism and antisemitism, she stressed that there was no conspiracy between antisemites and Zionists. The early Zionists had seen the benefits of antisemitism. Herzl, for example, stated that it is 'anti-semites who will be our staunchest friends, and the antisemitic countries which will be our allies' (quoted in Richard Bernstein's *Hannah Arendt and the Jewish Question*, 1996). As Zertal notes in her book *From Catastrophe to Power* (1998), talk about 'transforming Jewish suffering into Zionist redemption reverberated in Ben-Gurion's statements throughout the 1930s and 1940s' (p. 314); and the Holocaust provided him with 'the object he needed for the complete realization of his concept of

"exploiting the Jewish tragedy" in the establishment of a Zionist Jewish state'
(p. 215). Zertal described the diaspora Jew as the first 'other' of Zionism,
against which Zionism defined itself.

Zionism as a whole was suffused with religious terms and ways of thinking,
she continued, which partially explained the success of the project. Zionism
thrived on Jewish troubles and needed Jew hatred. It was in Zionism's interest
that Jews outside Israel were discriminated against, as this legitimized claims
that Zionism was the only long-term solution to the Jewish question. This
fateful connection between antisemitism and Zionism could not be ignored,
she maintained. She concluded that the relationship between Zionism and
antisemitism was so interconnected that it seemed like a vicious circle. The
affinity in the outlook of antisemites and Zionists was equally disturbing, but
needed to be acknowledged.

For anyone who really wanted to listen, Idith Zertal's arguments made
it easier to understand why Israel used antisemitism for political purposes,
a point I had been making for some years. This was neither to say that a
conspiracy existed between Israel and antisemites, nor that Israel deliberately
incited antisemitism. Yet the intensification of hostility towards Jews
nonetheless served to legitimate Israel's aggressive and repressive military
and security policies.

I continued to argue that European Jews could help change Israeli policies
but not everyone regarded a more assertive European Jewish diaspora as a
good thing. Even those professing to appreciate the authenticity and autonomy
of European Jewish life, such as the Jewish People Policy Planning Institute,
which I had already encountered and found deeply deficient in its approach
to Europe, demonstrated this in strange ways. Its annual report on world
Jewry in 2007, which I critiqued in two entries on my director's blog early in
2008, made the underlying assumption that even though Jewish life outside
Israel might well continue for decades, it was fundamentally doomed. *Aliya*
therefore had to remain as the main option when Jews were faced with a stark
choice about their future. The JPPPI acknowledged that diaspora Jews were
becoming estranged from Israel but believed that the fault lay with Jewish
leaders who were not doing enough to counter unfair anti-Israel bias in the
Western media because of diaspora weakness and confusion. Developing ideas
to enhance Israel's centrality was how the JPPPI proposed reversing the process
of estrangement. But most Jews worldwide 'live in pluralist, multicultural,
secular states. Israel is an ethnonationalist or ethnoreligious state', I wrote.
'Isn't this fundamental cleavage bound to result in the eventual demise of the
political, ideological and psychological relationship between many diaspora
Jews and Israel?'

In a second blog entry I criticised the JPPPI report's section on 'The Jews of Europe 2000–2007', which used demographic decline to argue, erroneously, that European Jewry was becoming weaker and losing influence and that the current state of Europe was threatening to Jews. I concluded: 'There are some who see Europe, with its path-breaking forms of political organisation, as precisely the place where the diasporic Jewish future can be guaranteed, as long as Jews seize the moment and contribute to the further development of a pluralist and multi-identity continent.'

The JPPPI's senior research fellow, Professor Sergio DellaPergola, was considered to be the world's leading expert on Jewish demography and had been a major influence on Ariel Sharon's decision to disengage from Gaza through his analysis of the 'demographic threat' posed to Israel if it retained control of the Strip. He sent me an email on 6 February in which he took exception to my remarks (two of his senior colleagues had already posted critical comments on the blog): 'I read with some uneasiness the spirited and unrestrained prose against the JPPPI 2007 report in your blogs, and I think your arrows are not well directed. We have much more in common than things that divide us. Your polemic tone does not do much to change the status of European Jewry.' He had nothing to say on the substance of my critique so I replied the following day: 'I find the JPPPI Europe section deeply damaging "to the status of European Jewry". It reinforces negative stereotypes of Jewish life in Europe which you know perfectly well are repeated again and again in America and Israel. The interests of European Jewry are not best served by remaining silent on these matters.' I continued: 'my critique ... frankly deserved to be far more severe ... Not everything here in Europe is perfect, but we Jews who live here deserve a far more nuanced understanding of the complexities of the European situation from our colleagues in Israel and America.'

Perhaps unsurprisingly my reply seemed to rile Sergio even more. 'I think you have completely misread and misreported the intentions of those who work at JPPPI', he wrote to me on 9 February. 'Our prime goal is to let the Israelis understand that they cannot be any more self-centred and ignorant of the Jewish world out of Israel. We have appeared already four consecutive years in front of the Israeli Cabinet and we have stressed the insufficience of an Israeli approach only focused on aliya and antisemitism.' This sounded fine, but was contradicted by his prescription for change: 'We have supported the idea to create a Jewish international consultative body (whether a Second House or otherwise) where positions might be compared and topics of common or mutual interest might be elaborated.' He continued: 'Nothing of this is even remotely similar to the stereotype of Israeli colonial ethnocentrism of which you speak.' And yet the essence of this idea was to institutionalise diaspora subservience and impose a status on Jews in relation to Israel that most would reject.

His criticism then became more personal: 'I think these and other problems are worth discussing through a quiet confrontation of alternative ideas and positions. But I find the polemic tone a little troubling, as if the Israelis were your enemies. Frankly, your recent writings can be constructed as if you believe that Israel's existence is a nuisance and we would better dispose of it.' He continued: 'I truly dislike frontal attacks and delegitimation', when that is precisely what he had just indulged in.

The Israel-diaspora theme soon emerged again when the president of the WJC, Ronald Lauder, the billionaire American businessman and philanthropist, argued that Jews throughout the world must be given a say in the future of Jerusalem, and Moshe Kantor, a Russian oligarch domiciled in Geneva who was the new president of the European Jewish Congress (EJC), the regional affiliate of the WJC, went even further, saying: 'Israel's leadership should recognise that all the Jews in the world have the right to vote in Israeli elections.' Writing on my blog, I argued that 'Most Israelis would surely say an indignant "no". And I suspect that most Diaspora Jews – without the indignation – would agree.' I maintained that these proposals undermined Israeli sovereignty, but went even further: 'if Mr Lauder's proposal undermines it, Mr Kantor's destroys it completely. In fact, Mr Kantor's remarks are fundamentally retrogressive. By calling for Israeli voting rights for Diaspora Jews ... he also undermines the status of Europe's Jews, by calling into question their loyalty to their countries of citizenship.' But the truth is that such a diaspora Jewish role in the Israeli state's decision-making 'has absolutely no possibility of being realised – when real intervention, with dangerous consequences, takes place in exactly the opposite direction'.

Israeli leaders believed that Zionism gave them licence to claim that policies they pursued were undertaken in the name of the Jewish people, or for the Jewish people, 'even going to war', I wrote. 'As Ehud Olmert told an American audience during Israel's war with Lebanon in 2006, "I believe that this is a war that is fought by all the Jews".' 'Any Jew, Zionist or non-Zionist, affiliated or non-affiliated, politically engaged in relation to Israel or politically neutral can therefore be directly affected by Israel's policies', I continued. 'And this effect is intensified by the very public linking of the fate of the state of Israel with that of Jews worldwide, in which Israeli leaders indulge.' Fine if you were committed to support the State of Israel whatever its government did. But if, for example, you were a Jew whose identity was proudly rooted in the diasporic tradition, or a Zionist who was critical of the Israeli government, or just neutral about Zionism, you were obliged to take the 'rough' without a compensating 'smooth'.

Israel demonstrated that it had power to exert direct influence over the lives of diaspora Jews, and yet it took no responsibility for the outcome of that influence. It expected diaspora Jews to accept and support the policies it followed. So the key question was not whether diaspora Jews should have a say in any decision on the status of Jerusalem, or whether they should have the right to vote in Israeli elections, it's whether diaspora Jews could do anything about statements made by Israeli politicians and policies of Israeli governments that had a direct impact on their lives.

I remained optimistic enough to believe that, if conveyed using the right language, even conservative Jewish audiences could see the sense in greater realism and truth-telling about the relationship between European Jews and Israeli policy-making. And I was proven right when I invited Daniel Levy to deliver a public JPR lecture in April on 'The Israel-Palestine Conflict and the Jews of Europe'. A former adviser in the office of the Israeli prime minister Ehud Barak, Levy was a senior figure in a Washington DC Middle East peace think tank. He was also the son of the prominent Jewish leader Lord Michael Levy, which helped give Daniel a head start with any UK Jewish audience. We previously scheduled a call to discuss what he would say, but it was very economical. Within minutes it was clear that we were on the same wavelength. His message was exactly the one I had returned to JPR to help get across to Jews in Europe.

In his lecture Daniel spoke of Europe as a critical friend of Israel, not the antisemitic enemy. Describing himself as a strong advocate of 'Jewish glasnost', he warned that it was unhealthy to condemn outspoken criticism of Israel. He advised against closing down the debate within the Jewish community as this was a big 'turn-off' for the younger generation. Frank debate and diverse views should be welcomed. Jews should not feel that they either had to support Israel wholeheartedly or condemn it wholeheartedly. Equally, the accusation of antisemitism should not be cheapened by being used to shut down criticism of Israel. He also called for a more serious conversation to take place between Israel and diaspora communities in Europe, but its premise should not be obsequiousness. Israeli leaders needed to hear the concerns of the European Jewish community regarding the actions and language Israel adopted. Daniel concluded that the Jewish community should not be ashamed of standing up for Jewish values, declaring that it cared about Israel and its security as well as about universal human rights. In finding a solution to the peace process, offering dignity to both Jews and Palestinians was the most important factor.

This was a carefully crafted message from someone whose pro-Israel credentials could not seriously be questioned, but who held deeply critical views of Israeli policy and diaspora Jews' support for or acquiescence in it. He proved that it was possible to get Jews not only to listen to things they did not want to hear but also to show some understanding and sympathy for such views. I was delighted to see people enthusiastically clapping. These same people would have sat in stony silence had I said the very same things. And no one clapped more enthusiastically than Michael Levy.

In June 2008, when we honoured Bishop John Sentamu at a dinner, I felt able to insert into my speech a reference to our progress in making the impact of Israeli policy-making on the Jews of Europe an acceptable subject for the community's independent policy think tank to confront. We had extended the boundaries of debate to issues that were formerly taboo in Jewish communal circles, but it had been a painful struggle.

* * *

I never wavered in my conviction that the campaign against me was despicable and utterly unjustified. But conviction alone could not counter character assassination, misrepresentation and the erosion of support. Feeling that I was living on borrowed time, I put a brave face on what we were achieving, but recognised that it was only a fraction of what I had set out to accomplish. And on the specific issues of Israel, Zionism and the relationship between European Jews and Israel, while I felt encouraged and vindicated after Daniel Levy's success, I also knew that unless I could contribute to public debate with my own voice as director of JPR, my feelings of frustration would continue.

I thought a lot about my predicament and how to resolve it that summer while on vacation in Hania, Crete, where it was almost impossible not to shed cares and worries and dream about a better future. I mused about reducing my role at JPR to a half-time position and even discussed the idea with Kathy.

Some particularly illuminating and moving holiday reading also helped. S. Yizhar was the pen name of one of Israel's leading writers and politicians, Yizhar Smilansky, who was born in Palestine in 1916. His acclaimed 1949 novella, *Khirbet Khizeh*, which tells the story of the violent expulsion of Palestinian villagers by the Israeli army, was originally published just after the 1948 war but translated into English only in 2008. Given what it said about how the emerging new state was treating the Palestinians, this was not surprising. And yet this truth was being told to Israelis themselves immediately after the war. 'Yizhar was deeply disturbing,' I wrote, 'making a mockery of every Jew's protestation that no one knew what was going on at the time and compounding the guilt of the "Diaspora" for what has happened to Israel and the Palestinians since the establishment of the state of Israel.'

Woefully ignorant of Palestinian accounts of their experiences of 1948, the *naqba* (catastrophe) in their historical memory, I recovered a little ground by reading Ghada Karmi's memoir *In Search of Fatima*, her poignant, moving, sad, honest and angry account of an ultimately unequal struggle with her Palestinian identity. Forced to leave their home in Katamon, Jerusalem, in 1949, when she was nine, because of the danger to their lives, the Karmi family ended up in Golders Green via Syria. She was never at home anywhere, even after finally embracing the Palestinian political cause as her life's work. Dispossession, prejudice, rootlessness, misogyny – somehow she had to manage all these experiences at a time when no one fundamentally recognised that she and her family had any cause for dissatisfaction at all. Living among Jews in Golders Green and having Jewish school friends, it was not surprising that the Jewish experience of antisemitism eclipsed her own story, one that she could not yet fully articulate anyway and which would have been utterly rejected even had she been able to.

It was strange knowing that this person, who lived in exactly the same area as me when I was growing up, went to the same library, walked the same streets and went to the same shops and cinemas, had her life turned upside down by the very same force that attracted me and determined my life for many decades. What was for her an ill-wind bringing disaster, swept me to what I anticipated would be a brave new beginning.

14

THE SENSE OF AN ENDING

All journeys have secret destinations of which the traveller is unaware.

Martin Buber

Within days of returning to London, in September 2008 I was thrown into the maelstrom of the move to new offices. I had mixed feelings but was nonetheless hoping that our new modernised premises just north of Oxford Street by Oxford Circus would help secure the future for JPR. Together with the smooth transfer of the chairmanship from Peter Levy to Harold Paisner, the livelier, more efficient location heralded a new beginning, one that would help free me from a complicated past weighed down by history and memory.

There had been no new controversies in the previous few months, but we were still operating in an unreceptive environment and the mutterings and mumblings about me and JPR had by no means gone away. And they had an impact on anything we wanted to do that had a direct bearing on the British Jewish community. Fortunately, our premier project, the exploration of the sense of belonging in Europe, was not affected by the internal politics of British Jewry, but raising money for UK projects was becoming increasingly difficult. And I suspected that things were not going to get any easier. A book of essays, *A Time to Speak Out: Independent Jewish Voices on Israel, Zionism and Jewish Identity*, to which I had contributed, was about to appear. A review of the book in the *JC* on 19 September by Michael Pinto-Duschinsky was generally favourable, but published alongside three large photos of contributors, one of whom was me. The two others, Anne Karpf and Jacqueline Rose, had edited the volume with Barbara Rosenbaum and Brian Klug. I did not think it would help me or JPR to have my image thrust into the limelight once again. The fact that I was still not an IJV signatory was no longer of any consequence since my name was indelibly linked to the group.

Constrained to avoid public expressions of my views, I once again took the opportunity to make a symbolic stand by adding my name to the list of more than 200 signatories of an IJV-sponsored open letter, published in *The Times* on 19 November, drawing attention to the deteriorating conditions of Palestinian life under occupation and to increasing tension within Israel.

It quoted outgoing Israeli prime minister Ehud Olmert's Jewish New Year statement that the 'decision we must make is the decision we have refused to face with open eyes for 40 years ... We must reach an agreement with the Palestinians, the essence of which is that we shall actually withdraw from almost all the territories, if not from all the territories ... including in East Jerusalem.' With general elections imminent in Israel and the presidential election in America looming, the letter urged that maximum pressure be brought to bear on the peace negotiators to put the Olmert principles into practice. It concluded: 'We, Jews in Britain, affirm our opposition to the continuing occupation and call upon the British government to use its influence in Washington and the Middle East to bring the occupation to a rapid end.'

In the meantime the plan for a modest series of discussions with Dr Sharon Pardo's CSEPS at Ben-Gurion University was coming to fruition. They were to be firmly focused on civil society issues of common concern to European Jews and Israelis. We held the first workshop in November 2008 in London on the theme of 'European Jews and Muslims and Israel', with six Israelis and six Europeans. I spoke about European Jewish perceptions of European Jews and Israeli decision-making, grouping those perceptions under four headings: supreme loyalists who refused to question Israeli decision-making; critical loyalists who thought it was right to publicly question Israeli government policies; independents working to revive European Jewry who did not see Israel as the centre of the Jewish people and took a pragmatic approach to criticism of Israeli policies; separationists in the radical Jewish peace camp who wished consciously to disassociate themselves from the Israel that claimed to speak and act on behalf of all Jews. One thing all of these groups had in common was an understanding that Israeli decision-making and policies had a direct and indirect impact on Jews in Europe.

The loyalist tendency had been strengthened by fears of antisemitism, intensifying criticism of Israel and influential Israeli voices who were urging European Jews to take a stand against 'the Islamisation of Europe'. But many Jews needed no urging from Israel. There were plenty of Jewish commentators spreading a new cultural pessimism and arguing that European elites had abandoned the Jews for the Muslims. This 'unity' around the 'Muslim Question' was of no value for Jews in Europe, I argued. First, it bolstered Israel's own view of itself as protector of the Jewish people, a commitment it was in no position to honour. Second, it conflicted with the need to strengthen Jewish life in Europe and work with Muslims to build a tolerant society fit for our children to live in. Third, it encouraged European Jewish political leaders to present Jews as fearful victims, obsessed with the past, whose only priorities were commemoration, restitution and defence.

Sharon Pardo was even more critical of Israeli policy-makers and European Jewish leaders than I was, especially on the issue of dealing with antisemitism in Europe, which Israeli officials had taken upon themselves to discuss with EU officials without consulting European Jews. Pardo's view and the unanimity between most of those present were clear proof that I was right to be advocating a new form of dialogue between European Jews and Israel.

As we concluded the workshop and swapped ideas about the next steps, I suggested a joint JPR–Ben-Gurion University scholarly research project examining Israeli policy-making on antisemitism since the establishment of the state. Pardo politely acknowledged the need for such research, but clearly had no intention of embracing the project. I should have known better and I did not hold it against him. I knew the kind of pressures he and particularly his colleague Professor David Newman, who was closely involved in the workshop programme, were experiencing at Ben-Gurion for attempting to counter right-wing trends in Israeli politics and society.

*   *   *

My attitude to the future changed more decisively when I realised how naive I had been in judging that the 2007 controversy had done little long-term damage. I discovered that in small but debilitating ways, Jewish establishment organisations were being warned off working with us.

I had conceived of a project to bring together young, innovative thinkers and activists to rethink the concept of community. The aim was to break down the traditional barriers between those considered inside the Jewish community and those regarded as outside. I had in mind my own ostracism and the accusations against IJV and other dissenting Jewish groups that their supporters were Jews who had cut themselves off from the Jewish community. I asked Jonathan Boyd, a highly creative educationalist working in Europe, to chair this group, help choose its membership, work with it over a year and produce some findings and proposals. Jonathan accepted and began to discuss with various individuals their possible participation.

Among those we agreed he should approach was David Graham, an academic demographer, then working as a consultant to the BoD. On Jonathan Boyd's suggestion, we also agreed that someone from the Community Security Trust should be invited to join since a body concerned with security would naturally have a view on the community's boundaries. The CST had played a role both in vilifying me personally for my views and undermining the work JPR was doing. Nevertheless, I was not inclined to bear a grudge, so Jonathan Boyd met with Mark Gardner, the CST's director of communications, to discuss the idea. In the course of their conversation, Gardner asked Boyd who else was being invited to join the group and Jonathan told him. Shortly after their conversation, Jonathan learnt that the BoD had made it clear to David Graham that if he participated in this JPR initiative, he would no longer be asked to do any consultative work for them. So David Graham withdrew his name.

Something similar occurred when the Jewish Leadership Council decided to conduct a review of Jewish educational services in the Jewish community and engaged Professor Leslie Wagner, vice-chancellor of Leeds Metropolitan University, to carry it out. One of the people Wagner consulted about how he might conduct this enquiry was Professor Steve Miller, an outstanding social scientist and former pro-vice-chancellor of City University, who had worked very closely with JPR in the past and also been very supportive of me personally. Steve Miller suggested that, given JPR's expertise in this area, Wagner should consult us in the course of his enquiry. According to Steve, Wagner readily agreed to this suggestion. But when he outlined his proposals to the JLC, the JLC made it clear to him that on no account could he consult JPR.

Neither of these incidents was catastrophic, but they brought home to me how impossible it was to overcome the hostility of the Jewish establishment and how JPR would continue to suffer as a result. Finally, an incident occurred which became my tipping point. JPR continued a tradition of its predecessor, the Institute of Jewish Affairs, namely to invite the Israeli ambassador to address the Institute at least once during his tenure at the Court of St James. An invitation had therefore been extended to Ron Prosser to address JPR at Chatham House and he had agreed in principle. However, it proved extremely difficult pinning him down to a date. Eventually, an evening early in November was agreed, at relatively short notice.

Less than a week before the lecture, with invitations having long been dispatched by post and by email, and, if memory serves, an advert placed in the *JC*, Prosser cancelled. The excuse given was that the Israeli president, Shimon Peres, was coming to London and that Prosser had to be with him during his visit. But the explanation did not ring true. We had no conclusive proof, but there seemed little doubt that this was a snub. Someone must have finally warned Prosser not to be seen in the company of JPR and Tony Lerman. Within days we discovered that we were right. A chance encounter had taken place between the twenty-something son of JPR's director of fundraising, Judith Russell, and an official of the Israel embassy at a reception. During their conversation the young man asked why the embassy had cancelled the Prosser lecture and the official left him in no doubt that it was because the embassy had decided that JPR should be shunned.

Every former Israeli ambassador had addressed JPR and its predecessor. Prosser chose to behave in an undignified and insulting manner. Why? Because grandees of the Jewish community made it clear to him that shunning us would help bring about the demise of the director? Because I had raised for public discussion such issues as: legitimate demands for Palestinian national self-determination being best exercised within the eventual evolution of a federal or a confederal state; caution in how we assess the threat of antisemitism; Israel's responsibility for the rise in anti-Jewish hostility? The pettiness of this snub confirmed how far Israel's ministry of foreign affairs had strayed from a culture of civility.

In the weeks before this occurred, I had become increasingly depressed by the situation – withdrawn and grumpy at home, weighed down by feelings of despair at work. But in spite of these forebodings, I maintained a furious level of activity. We completed the move to Market Place off Oxford Street. In mid September I lectured on multiculturalism at an all-day Jewish educational event in Hackney. At the end of the month I made a memorable three-day trip with my two brothers to Ukraine to visit the town of Korosten where our paternal grandfather grew up before coming to England in 1901. In October I addressed the Glasgow Jewish Educational Forum on Jewish leadership and a few days later was at the launch of *A Time to Speak Out: Independent Jewish Voices on Israel Zionism and Jewish Identity* at London Metropolitan University. Then I flew to Stockholm to attend the Board meeting of Paideia, the European Institute for Jewish Studies. A week later I was speaking at the workshop we organised with Ben-Gurion University, the first major activity we had held at our new offices. And on 21 November I was off to Chartridge Conference Centre in Chesham for the first of two summative round-table discussions in our three-year project on restoring a sense of belonging in Europe.

*   *   *

It was 5.42 pm on Saturday afternoon, 22 November 2008, at Chartridge. We were talking about whether religion had a place in the *res publica*. I had just sent an email to the chairman, president and treasurer of JPR offering my resignation as director.

> With very great reluctance, I've come to the conclusion that it might be best for all concerned if I resign as Director of JPR.
>
> In all honesty I don't see any end to JPR's problematic image in certain quarters of the Jewish community while I am at the helm. This is damaging JPR's long-term prospects and its effectiveness. Short of me recanting publicly my views on antisemitism and Israel-Palestine, attitudes towards us won't change. With Harold [Paisner] taking over the chairmanship, there is an

excellent opportunity to rehabilitate JPR's image, but I believe that his potential effectiveness will be fatally compromised by me remaining in post.

It has been very difficult for me to acknowledge this reality because I personally believe that the task of JPR in these times is precisely to confront the negative trends represented by the people who have tried to undermine me and JPR. I hope you will therefore understand that I cannot lead JPR in that direction by remaining mostly silent on these matters. I genuinely believe that they are deeply damaging as far as the Jewish future is concerned and by not acting against them more openly and more determinedly, I personally feel that I am complicit in their continuation.

I had been thinking about the absurdity of the Prosser lecture affair and concluded that there was no longer any point in trying to work with integrity in a world sorely lacking moral scruples. Circumstances had become intolerable.

I wrote in my diary the following day: 'I suppose people will say that I was defeated. My detractors will see this as a victory for them. Of course, this will be hard for me to swallow. But in truth, I have felt defeated for more than a year. I knew that they had in effect "won" when for all the support that I was given by the [JPR] Board – and that was not total or unconditional – I realised that my freedom of action had been severely curtailed. My original plan to gradually introduce a more radical approach for JPR and for myself was no longer possible since I had to think at least twice about doing anything and 95 per cent of the time was forced to decide that I couldn't. As time went by this situation has made me feel increasingly hopeless ... I don't really care whether people will understand why I have done this, if it happens. I don't think I will ever be able to communicate what I have been going through. I'm perfectly capable of sounding and acting enthusiastic, enjoying convivial moments with members of the Board and colleagues at seminars and round tables. But inside I feel empty and often utterly desperate.'

I did not expect any of the honorary officers to persuade me to stay on. In what I believe was an attempt to protect me, they never fully told me what was being said about me and JPR in the establishment circles in which they mixed. So I assumed that my offer of resignation would come as a relief. I suppose that Simon Haskel's reply to me sums it up: 'It is probably for the best, but I am sorry that it has ended this way. JPR should now take this opportunity to renew itself with a new Director, a new Chairman and a largely new Board.' For Simon it had already 'ended', even though the opening sentence of my offer of resignation said '*might* be best' and '*if* I resign' – emphasis added.

By 30 November everything had been settled. At a meeting with the honorary officers we had all agreed that I should leave as soon as possible. There were expressions of annoyance at the way the community had treated me but more telling was the reaction of Brian Smouha, the treasurer, to my having signed the recent IJV advert in *The Times*. He was angry that I had gone against an undertaking not to go public on anything like that without clearing it with the Board. I explained to him, as politely as I could, that I had given no such undertaking. But Brian's demeanour made me aware more clearly than ever of the tensions among trustees over the problems we were facing and their perceptions of my role in creating them.

Fortuitously, there was a full trustees meeting scheduled for 1 December where my leaving arrangements could be approved. In a matter of hours I called as many trustees as I could to let them know about my decision. Feeling close to so many of them I wanted them to know from me in advance of the meeting what was about to happen. Most of the conversations were emotionally difficult. I felt that I was abandoning personal friends who had stood by me. But they were all sensitive to my position. I drafted a press release about the appointment of Harold Paisner as the new chair and my resignation. I included the sentence: 'JPR was Tony's conception and will always bear his imprint.' Brian Smouha objected and wanted it removed, and the others agreed.

The *JC* covered my departure in an unobtrusive little piece headlined: 'Divisive Lerman leaves JPR', gratuitously insulting to the last. Ruefully, I noted the contrast between that and the front page of 26 January 2007, which had devoted four columns to a story headlined 'Pressure grows on Lerman' alongside a large photograph of the then Israeli president Moshe Katzav who had recently been indicted on charges of rape and harassment.

Within days of my resignation being made public, a letter arrived at JPR for the new chairman. It was from David Hirsh, the Goldsmiths sociologist and founder of the Engage website, which continued to accuse me of denying the existence of antisemitism, being an anti-Zionist supporter of Hamas and believing that Israel should not exist. Hirsh was already putting himself forward for the directorship of JPR and cited the celebrity lawyer Anthony Julius in his support.

15
AFTERWORD

Peace is not an absence of war, it is a virtue, a state of mind, a disposition for benevolence, confidence, justice.

Baruch Spinoza, 1670

Half a century has passed since my first encounter with Jewish nationalism. Even though I am no longer a Zionist and it's almost 40 years since I lived in Israel, I forged a connection to the country that has an underlying permanence. I could take myself out of Israel, but I couldn't take Israel out of myself. In time the connection became a source of reflection and reconsideration. It influenced my general intellectual development, my thoughts about justice, human rights and universal values, my attitude to the future of Jewish life, the rights and wrongs and successes and failures of Zionism, the necessary preconditions for a just Israel-Palestine peace and much more. A new form of critical engagement with Israel and Zionism emerged driven by the questions I began to ask and the issues I faced in my professional role in Jewish organisations. So far I have found some answers, but many questions remain unresolved and new ones emerge all the time. The journey continues.

* * *

I chose to write this book in such a way as to allow the reader to understand what I experienced as it happened, with as little explanatory hindsight as possible. Naturally, I've had to provide some context and perspective, but I was determined not to pretend to an awareness of the implications of what I was believing and doing that I did not possess at the time. I could not see any other way of honestly conveying the nature of my journey, the way I came to hold certain views and then gradually and unsystematically to question and change them. But I also wrote the book to make sense of the experiences I went through and, ultimately, also convey that to the reader. Having reached the end of my story, for now, there remain some loose ends that need to be addressed if I am to 'make sense of it all'. To achieve this, context, perspective, hindsight and interpretation are all essential.

The Youth Movement, the Kibbutz and Zionist Myth-Making

Membership in Habonim was an intense experience at a formative time in my life and it had a lasting impact. I know many people who would say the same about their own involvement and who have warm and nostalgic feelings for the movement. Some say it 'made' them, transformed their lives and gave them goals they have pursued ever since. But I also know others who, while fondly remembering all the fun and the values of sharing, independence, freedom and self-reliance that they absorbed, came to reject Zionist ideology and criticise the way they were educated – some would say indoctrinated – to believe in it at such an impressionable age. In 2010, the internationally acclaimed film director Mike Leigh, a former member of Habonim, publicly announced that he had declined an invitation to attend various film events in Israel because of his feelings about what Israel was doing to the Palestinians. Interviewed by the *JC* (21 October) he said that he and his fellow former Habonim members had been 'duped by Israeli propaganda'.

As I learnt more about how Zionism achieved its ends and the history of the path Israel followed, it became clear that we were certainly not told anything like the whole truth about Zionist settlement in Palestine, the response of the indigenous Palestinian-Arab population, the actions of the Zionist leadership to create a Jewish state, the treatment of the Palestinians during the 1948 war and the national aspirations of the Palestinian people. But were we actually 'duped by Israeli propaganda'? When I was a member, was there a level of Zionist leadership in Habonim that knew the truth about what the Zionist movement felt it had to do to achieve Jewish statehood, but deliberately suppressed it and painted a sanitised picture of Israel instead? These ideological-political questions go hand-in-hand with the moral issue of whether it was right to seek to persuade 18-year-olds to conform to the strict ideological regime of the youth movement, which sought to reach into almost every aspect of a committed individual's life. While no one was coerced into subscribing to socialist Zionist ideology, could it not be argued that the systematic effort to change basic beliefs and attitudes was a form of brainwashing? And were we right to accept the movement's line that the most important thing about settling on a kibbutz was ideological self-realisation, or did the kibbutz see our presence in more prosaic terms? Answers to these questions must take into account that no one was forced to belong to the movement. At 18 you were encouraged to think about making a commitment to live in Israel, but at that age you are legally an adult responsible for the decisions you make about your life.

Nurtured in a mainstream orthodox Jewish environment, I was predisposed to accept the Zionist rationale for Jewish national self-determination in

Palestine. Longing for Jerusalem and the Land of Israel figured prominently in Jewish festivals and prayers. As a dispersed people we had experienced centuries of persecution, so why not overcome the problem permanently by returning to the historic homeland to become the majority once again? The genius of Zionism as a political movement lay in the simplicity of the idea.

Looking back, the late 1950s and early 1960s seem like an age of innocence in which Leon Uris's 1958 novel *Exodus*, a worldwide bestseller, and the subsequent 1960 film starring Paul Newman, popularised a positive image of Zionism and the story of the founding of the State of Israel for a generation. In a sense, the success of *Exodus* in defining how the world saw Israel was a reflection of the way, at the highest Israeli and Zionist political, ideological and military levels, messy historical reality had been successfully transformed into a myth that served the interests of Zionism. After 1948, the victors got in first with their histories. By the late 1960s the notion that the Arabs in Palestine had fled only at the urging of the Arab leadership had become commonplace. But the alternative Palestinian narrative of 1948 began to impinge on public consciousness in some circles and the Zionist movement was beginning to find it necessary to provide arguments designed to counter it.

In the Jewish milieu of my youth it was virtually impossible to know anything different, unless one deliberately sought out alternative information. It's true that not all Jews were suffused with enthusiasm for Zionism. But neither the Reform and Liberal synagogue movements nor the strictly orthodox were interested in any other narrative except their own specifically Jewish rationale for not accepting the arguments of the Zionists. Their opposition to Zionism was not because they recognised Arab nationalist claims to Palestine.

The years spent absorbing the Zionist arguments and only having them challenged by other forms of Zionism meant that when I finally went to live in Israel in 1970 I took everything for granted. It never occurred to me that, as a Jewish immigrant whose family was not from Palestine, I could be granted Israeli citizenship immediately, but a Palestinian born in Palestine, whose family was forcibly living outside Israel, had no right of return. I never questioned for one second whether it was right that I was immediately allocated a two-bedroom apartment in Jerusalem built by the state, whereas a Palestinian was not allowed to return to the house she had owned before 1948. When I went to live on Kibbutz Amiad in the Galil, I never bothered to wonder who lived on the land before the settlement was founded in 1946. For many years after, I remained completely oblivious to the fact that the population of the nearby Arab village of Jubb Yusuf had been forcibly driven out as part of General Yigal Allon's Operation Broom (*Mivtza Matateh*), the purpose of which was an attempt, in Allon's words (as quoted by the historian Benny Morris in *The Birth of the Palestinian Refugee Problem 1947–1949*, p.

121), 'to clear out the beduins encamped between the Jordan [River], and Jubb Yusuf and the Sea of Galilee' during the 1948 war. I was totally unaware of a people and a history the existence of which Israel and the Zionist movement had denied. They had been replaced with an image of bloodthirsty terrorists who had no rights to Palestine and only wanted to drive the Jews into the sea.

Wittingly or not, by becoming bearers of the Zionist story we played our part in perpetuating a false account of the conflict between Zionism and Arab-Palestinian nationalism and in the dehumanisation of the Palestinians. Once I came to understand more about what really happened to them, I felt angry and rather foolish that it had taken me so long. It's not that we consciously wanted to deprive them of their rights – it's hard to want to do that to people whose non-existence you accepted as fact. Nevertheless, since this was the consequence of our ignorance, we have to take our full share of responsibility for the Palestinians' plight. So while it is by no means wrong to see ourselves as having been duped in general, I do not believe that any of the layers of socialist Zionist leadership above us in the youth movement deliberately practised any deception. But more important, I cannot make that my principal conclusion since I would feel I was evading responsibility.

Who benefited from the emphasis on kibbutz as the highest expression of socialist Zionism?

By the time I went to live in Israel in 1970, mass *aliya* seemed to have more or less come to an end, but it was vital for the Zionist narrative of the developing state and its aim to achieve a Jewish majority in perpetuity to maintain the idea that only Israel offered a viable Jewish future. Although the state prided itself on its ability to absorb large numbers of immigrants, its handling of the process created ethnic tensions that had a negative impact on the social and political fabric of Israeli society and on its political direction.

The resources devoted to encouraging *aliya* to kibbutz were a cause of impatience and frustration within the mainstream Zionist movement by the late 1960s. More than lip service was paid to the notion of kibbutz as epitomising the ethos of the state, but in reality *aliya* to kibbutz came to be seen as benefiting narrow interests. State-building priorities were focused elsewhere, for example on industry, tourism, development towns, social and economic deprivation among the *mizrachim* (Jews from North Africa and the Middle East). In fact the kibbutz was already beginning to adjust to this new reality by moving into industrial production of various kinds. But this only reinforced the emphasis on the purpose of *aliya* to a kibbutz as a way of helping to make it economically and socially more viable. So while the youth movement still judged individuals according to their ideological commitment, the kibbutzim were more interested in numbers. The individual became a commodity.

Kibbutz members were ultimately more concerned with whether you worked hard and obeyed the rules. So while we were not exactly misled in relation to kibbutz ideology, there was a degree of duplicity on the part of those who were responsible for promoting it. Ironically, the relatively recent privatisation of life and work on kibbutzim, which has replaced the ideology of the dignity of labour, is an extreme version of what the small group of us advocated 40 years ago at Kibbutz Amiad and was regarded with such revulsion.

But what should taking responsibility for the dispossession and dehumanisation of the Palestinians mean? There is a difference, for example, between a former Habonim member who is an inactive yet self-identifying Zionist living in Manchester, an Israeli soldier harassing Palestinians at a West Bank checkpoint and a Jewish settler stealing Palestinian land and uprooting Palestinian olive trees. Yet all have been complicit in propping up an unjust occupation. In a context of what is still widespread Jewish denial, acknowledging the wrong is a step towards ending it.

From Zionism to Non-Zionism

In the light of these truths there could no longer be a viable socialist Zionism of any significance to the current politics of the State of Israel and indeed, to all intents and purposes, it is an ideology consigned to history. As I discovered, it was always flawed, so while I retain a residual degree of nostalgia for the interminable and intense ideological discussions we engaged in over its theory and practice, I do not regret its demise. Those who still think Zionism can be dressed up in socialist clothes – and there are some – are turning a blind eye to the dominance of the kind of Zionism that reigns supreme in Israel today and is highly influential among Jews elsewhere.

After 1967, the terms of debate about Zionism changed irrevocably. Success in the war was taken by religious Zionists as divine sanction to proclaim sovereignty over the entire Land of Israel and they sought to achieve this by establishing and expanding Jewish settlements in the occupied territories. Gush Emunim, the messianic, religious nationalist movement established in 1974, prepared the ground for the burgeoning settler movement. More than half a million settlers lived on the West Bank and in East Jerusalem in 2012. But this would not have been possible without all Israeli governments since 1967 having either actively promoted this kind of Zionism or been the witting or unwitting tools of the settlers and their political allies.

Settler Zionism is a form of xenophobic and exclusionary nationalism inspired by religious messianism. It claims that God promised Jews exclusive rights to the Land of Israel and that the Palestinians who have lived there for centuries have nothing more than squatters' rights. Some religious groups that originally opposed Zionism but subsequently embraced it, now explicitly support settler Zionism. And it's implicitly condoned by non-Zionist and even anti-Zionist religious groups that see their spiritual aims served by the state's continued hegemony over the Land of Israel. Like all nationalist ideologies, in its most extreme form Zionism is a continuous struggle to achieve the purification of the tribe.

Within the Zionist camp there *is* opposition to an unrestrained ethnocentric, colonising, supremacist form of Zionism. Such people would describe themselves as liberal Zionists. They support the national rights of the Palestinians and disapprove of the occupation of Palestinian land. But in supporting state policy to maintain a Jewish majority in Israel in perpetuity and rejecting the principle that Israel must be a democratic state of all its citizens, liberal Zionism has provided cover for many of the objectives of religious messianic Zionism and the legislative programmes of the illiberal, right-wing political parties in the Knesset. Liberal Zionism is therefore inconsequential as a restraining force on the right-wing government and the settler movement. When European Jews and Israelis discussed Israel's direction at the second Canisy round-table in 2004 (see Chapter 9), the idea that Israeli politics had become proto-fascist was seen by some as so controversial and unacceptable that the discussion came close to breaking up. Looking back, those who raised the alarm bell about incipient fascism now seem remarkably prescient. It's now routine for the political right and right-wing civil society groups to talk in terms of the nation, in effect, as an organic body. Even the most sober voices now describe the slew of anti-democratic, racist, anti-human rights legislation proposed and enacted, the absence of any serious political opposition to these developments in the Knesset, the institutionalisation of discriminatory policies on the local level, the continued treatment of Palestinian Israelis as second-class citizens and the nationalist-religious culture war against liberal secularism as akin to fascism. Had heed been taken of the warnings of Meir Pail, Tony Judt, Gideon Levy, myself and others, we could have been looking at a much brighter future for Jews and Palestinians today.

Zionist messianism and racist right wing parties still seemed relatively marginal when my views on Israel and Zionism began to change and they were not the primary or even the secondary cause. My questioning began because I felt that the Zionist 'revolution' was failing to live up to its ideals. It took me many years before I developed a consistent critique of Zionism and saw that the injustices and failures for which it was responsible stemmed from flaws in its fundamental premises. I had no 'Road to Damascus'-like conversion. I know people who have had such radical changes of heart and mind but I suspect that they are few and far between. Most of us who have been deeply engaged with Zionism and Israel and who developed doubts have found it hard to be so clear cut about what is wrong and what is right.

The number of Jews in diaspora countries expressing doubts about Israeli policies has increased substantially in recent years. Polling undertaken by JPR in 2010 revealed that a very large proportion of Jews in the UK believed that Israel was the ancestral home of the Jewish people, but that it had also made significant errors and that diaspora Jews should feel free to speak out in public about these matters. Nonetheless, most of these people probably do little more than voice their feelings with friends and family. When they do so, I'm sure that many are expressing a strong sense of confusion and uncertainty. And those who are in the process of changing their views are doing so hesitantly, performing a series of twists and turns as they try to hold on to cherished beliefs and feelings that seem to be negated by the new conclusions they are reaching. However, they should be reassured that acknowledging that far-reaching changes are needed if Israel is to be a truly democratic state with equal rights for all is not incompatible with support for Jewish national self-expression. Some of the most trenchant critics I know who advocate radical change in Israel are Israelis who still call themselves Zionists.

Having rejected the ethnocentricity of Zionism and the moral and practical implications of taking coercive, racist and illiberal measures to secure a state with a Jewish majority in perpetuity, I can no longer subscribe to a project the logical conclusion of which is to attain such a maximalist nationalist end. No people or state is obliged to follow a path laid down by the exponents of the most extreme interpretation of its national destiny. I became an Israeli citizen in 1970 and I intend to remain so. But it's not an act that requires endless repetition through an open-ended project of national self-realisation. So I see no incompatibility between being an Israeli and not being a Zionist, just as I am a citizen of the United Kingdom and can call myself British and English, but I'm not a British or an English nationalist. When Israel came into being it became possible for any Jew to cease to call himself a Zionist.

Demonisation

In some ways I felt as if all the experience I had acquired over the previous four decades had prepared me for the tasks I set myself when I returned to become director of JPR in 2006. But unbeknownst to me, from the day that I agreed to put my name forward in July 2005, I was on a collision course with forces in the Jewish community who were so opposed to my returning to lead what was regarded as its premier research and policy body – a status I had worked hard to achieve for JPR between 1996 and 1999 – that they were ready to begin a campaign against me that went on for more than three years.

I don't doubt that I made mistakes, but I do not believe for one second that any of the views I expressed, either before I became director or after, justified the way I was attacked and vilified. The very fact that I could meet with and amicably discuss my critical views on Israel and Zionism with staunch Zionists in Israel is surely proof that leaders of the Jewish community in the UK, as well as the US and elsewhere, should have been able to tolerate and engage with the ideas and issues I wanted to raise. The fact that they could not do this, but the very people they purported to protect by ostracising me could, shows just how dramatically so many Jewish leaders had cast themselves adrift from reality.

It did not take rocket science to understand why I was singled out for this treatment. The establishment could easily marginalise dissenting groups and individuals who felt it necessary to dissociate themselves from the organised Jewish community. They were seen as a threat, but not one that could storm the community's inner sanctum. But for someone who was at the heart of the community in a professional capacity for more than 25 years, was seen as part of the establishment, had an influential charitable role working for Lord Rothschild, a figure who represented the Jewish establishment *par excellence* – for someone like this to hold views usually associated with the marginalised, dissenting groups was an unprecedented danger, a traitorous act that simply could not be tolerated. Not all who thought this way went as far as those publicly demanding that I be sacked or wanting to see me excommunicated, cut adrift from the Jewish people. But clearly many in the establishment would have been delighted with such outcomes. The thought of engaging with me and my views was rejected out of hand. This left the field open for people to characterise my views on Israel, Zionism and antisemitism in ways that bore no relation to anything I had written or said. Yet it was impossible to refute these utterly false and contradictory characterisations in the brave new world of websites, blogs and instant comment. I would be less than human if I did not find this process of demonisation hurtful.

The attacks that I and others were subjected to were justified on the spurious grounds that we represent extreme danger to the Jewish people, infamously summed up in Melanie Phillips's disgusting phrase applied to Independent Jewish Voices, 'Jews for genocide'. It is quite shocking how Phillips and others appropriate the language of the antisemites and how their views can be applauded by audiences of seemingly moderate Jews apparently convinced that they are acting in the best tradition of defending Zionism and the State of Israel.

Before the state was established, in the years when the chill winds of Nazism and fascism were blowing through the Jewish communities of Europe, Jewish non-Zionist and anti-Zionist groups in Palestine, with small memberships but headed by influential figures such as the philosopher Martin Buber, the first chancellor of the Hebrew University in Jerusalem, Judah L. Magnes, and the philosopher Ernst Simon, were active in arguing for ways in which the Yishuv could fulfil the aims of national regeneration without establishing an exclusive Jewish state and by sharing the land with the Arab population. Rather than argue for these Jews to be excommunicated from the Jewish people or condemned as self-hating, 'In the eyes of some of the leaders of the Zionist mainstream, including Ben-Gurion, these "peacemakers" were the guardians of a clear, if not pure, moral seal, and those Zionist leaders engaged in a constant dialogue with the "peacemakers"', wrote Uriel Aboluf in *Eretz Acheret* (online) on 4 November 2010. 'Although they were perceived as non-Zionists (even at times as anti-Zionists) and although their solutions appeared useless, they were never excluded from the public discourse.' 'Exclusion from the public discourse' does not mean literally preventing people from speaking or writing. It would have been impossible to do that in the 1930s and it's impossible to do that now. What it does mean is to define the views of dissenting Jews as beyond the pale and therefore to be treated with contempt. Phillips and others have done this with considerable success.

A Jewish leadership with a sense of history, vision, courage, openness and justice would now be following in Ben-Gurion's footsteps and 'engage in a constant dialogue' with Jews who are currently being branded as anti-Zionists, delegitimisers and self-haters. Sadly, this is not the temper of Jewish leadership today.

The tone set by such leaders makes it even more difficult for the many Jews who wish Israel would change course for its own sake and would like to speak out, but remain silent because they believe that they will be consorting with Jews who have 'cut themselves off from their own people', that they will have to deny and repudiate what they once believed in. By writing this account I have tried to show that Jews can liberate themselves from both of these false notions. It is a mistake to demonise dissenting Jews; they care, but care differently. Entering into dialogue with them is a constructive act; it will not make you unclean. A discourse through which we make judgements about each other on whether or not we love Israel, or define ourselves as Zionists, is a trap. It sets up false opposites. The absence of love is not hate. The person who isn't a Zionist does not, a priori, wish to destroy Israel or subscribe to anti-Zionism. Those who wish to interrogate Jewish dissenters in this way and counter what they wrongly assume is Jewish hatred and delegitimisation of Israel and Zionism by holding events entitled 'We Believe in Israel' are relegating Judaism to being a subsidiary of Zionism. It makes Judaism less important than Israel. But Judaism, Jewishness, Jewish identity and Jewish ethnicity are much more than Zionism. As one of the leading

Jewish theologians and philosophers of the twentieth century, Abraham Joshua Heschel, wrote: 'The state of Israel is not the climax of Jewish history.'

Addressing Diaspora Jews

Having decided in the late 1970s that I would not be returning to live permanently in Israel, as a matter of principle I made a decision not to join any of the worthy UK incarnations of Israeli-based peace, human rights, philanthropic or political groups such as Peace Now or Meretz, for two reasons. First, I would be contributing to the perpetuation of a form of Israel-diaspora relations I rejected – an absolute identity of interest between Jews definitively making homes outside Israel and Israeli Jews continuing to live in their nation state. And I thought this was damaging to the future of Jews outside and inside Israel because it implied that Palestinians in Israel would never have full equality and citizenship since they are not Jews and that this therefore radically reduced the possibility of achieving reconciliation with the Palestinians. Second, I do not think that, with their current outlooks, these organisations can do much more than apply sticking plaster. They are not vehicles through which diaspora Jews can seriously influence Israeli policies. In effect they have provided cover for Israeli governments to exploit their self-serving perception of the state's connection with Jews worldwide in order to bolster Israel's legitimacy.

I decided that the role I could best play would be outside any such formal structure trying to influence diaspora opinion. It was necessary for Jews to acknowledge that they did not feel it was right simply to accept the impact of Israel's policies but to go further, expressing their firm and determined opposition to those policies. And, if they wish to express themselves politically within Jewish frameworks, rather than exclusively through non-sectarian political, human rights or justice-promoting organisations, that had to be done by working through their own, independently created, autonomous diaspora groups. Israel, for fear of losing the crucial moral legitimacy and public relations advantages it received from its connection with the Jewish diaspora, would then come under far more pressure to change its policies. Israel has only been able to strike out on its own on the understanding that diaspora Jews were tacitly or openly backing whatever it chose to do. And its room for manoeuvre would be constrained even more were diaspora Jews to embrace fully Palestinian rights to justice, equality and self-determination, both as something inherently due to the Palestinians and as something fully consonant with Jewish values.

One of the things preventing this is the language in which the relationship between the Israeli state and Jews living outside of Israel is couched. Both for

Jewish Zionists of whatever stripe and for Jewish critics of Zionism, when this relationship is discussed the term 'Israel-diaspora relations' is almost always used. I myself have used it very often throughout this book. But folded into this phrase is the unacknowledged assumption that when we speak of Israel, we speak only of Jewish Israel, of Israel as a Jewish state, of Jewish-Israelis. I cannot recall any discussions in Zionist circles today, or in the past, where Palestinian-Israelis are an integral part of the Israel-diaspora narrative. It is true that in some liberal Zionist frameworks, the problems faced by Palestinian-Israelis, still more commonly referred to as the 'Arab minority', are taken seriously, but the issue is dealt with as a separate matter; perhaps impinging upon, but still external to Israel-diaspora relations. Decades of this kind of narrative demonstrate the power of a particular semantic framework to influence an entire mindset, shared probably by the great majority of Israeli and diaspora Jews, in which Israel's Palestinian citizens are written out of the national script, excluded from discussions that relate to and influence the overall direction of the state. What reinforces the problematic nature of this state of affairs is that the term 'Jewish diaspora', as meaning Israel's diasporic hinterland, has never been accurate because so very few Jews at the time of the establishment of the state could formally trace their ancestors directly back to living in the area of what became Mandate Palestine. Experts in diaspora studies nevertheless agree that Jews around the world clearly manifest the attributes of a diaspora, but they derive that from common religious, historical, cultural, ethnic and national attributes, developed over centuries in the countries where they have lived, that have nothing to do with Israel. But since 1948, the issue of what exactly is the 'diaspora' in 'Israel-diaspora relations' has become even more complicated. First, because it marked the 'formal' birth of an Israeli-Jewish diaspora that has grown to a size in excess of 1 million, and second because it also marked the 'formal' birth of an Israeli-Palestinian diaspora. While the first group is recognised by the state as fully part of the Israeli national family, the second is not. Once we acknowledge this reality, we see the fundamental illegitimacy of the exclusionary Israel-diaspora narrative and how continuing to use it constitutes a barrier to Palestinian rights to full equality within Israel and to self-determination.

Explaining the inherent dangers for Jews in Europe and for Israel in the current state and conceptual framework of Israel-diaspora relations and in the policies being followed by Israeli governments; alerting people to the fact that antisemitism in Europe was being exacerbated by Israeli policies towards the Palestinians; arguing that a resolution of the Israel-Palestine conflict will only be achieved if it is based on universal human rights values; emphasising that what Palestinians want is an acknowledgement and implementation of their rights, not gifts of so-called 'painful compromises' on the part of the

Israelis for good behaviour – addressing Jews in Europe, and especially in the UK, on these key issues has been the focus of what I have done on the issue of Israel-Palestine since 2000. It was in this area that I believed I could make a unique contribution, being passionately committed to the revival and continuation of a thriving Jewish life in Europe.

I am doubtful about what I was able to achieve, especially once I became a demonised figure. And yet, I see grounds for hope. With respect to Jewish attitudes to the Israel-Palestine conflict, a significant line was crossed when Mick Davis, the chairman of the United Jewish Israel Appeal (UJIA), the main and largest pro-Israel body in the UK, openly criticised the Netanyahu government during a public discussion moderated by the *Guardian* columnist Jonathan Freedland. Davis warned that Israel could become an apartheid state if a two-state solution failed to materialise. If such views are now being expressed by the head of the UJIA – and closer to the heart of the Jewish establishment you cannot get – anything is possible in terms of a broader sea change in the public expression of what we already know is widespread private uncertainty and doubt about Israel's path. However, the forces of right-wing Zionism, in thrall to a propagandistic pro-Israel narrative, demonstrate a tenacity, activism and degree of uncompromising commitment that is currently more than equal to the efforts of those seeking to marshal the doubters into an effective movement.

In any event, what Mick Davis has said does not go far enough. It hardly meets the legitimate needs of the Palestinians for a true understanding of what they have lost and what they are entitled to. And it's a change that may have come too late. Support for a two-state solution is rapidly becoming a mantra that majorities on both sides say they support, in theory, but either doubt that it will ever come about or are not prepared to make the sacrifices needed for it to happen.

In truth, any final settlement predicated on a version of two independent states looks increasingly anachronistic. The reality of West Bank settlements, expropriated Palestinian land, Jews-only roads, Israel's proclaimed need for a permanent security presence along the Jordan, as well as the actual and planned Jewish settlement in and round East Jerusalem only supports my contention that the area of Mandate Palestine west of the Jordan river is today virtually one state – one undemocratic and repressive state, with which the dominant authoritarian forces in Israeli politics and society are increasingly comfortable. I fail to see how East Jerusalem could ever become a viable autonomous capital of a Palestinian state given the way Jewish control of the entire Jerusalem urban area is being consolidated. Yet to reach my preferred option of a confederated Israel-Palestine state would almost certainly require first implementing some interim version of a freely negotiated two-state arrangement.

There is no point in getting fixated on plans that once looked or sounded good. Whatever the challenges facing Palestinian society in the West Bank and Gaza, it is what happens in Israel, with its vastly superior power, that counts. And it may well be that social and political trends, not just the facts on the West Bank and East Jerusalem ground, are leading to a complete disintegration of the two-state idea. The dominant political and religious forces clearly reject the 'two states for two peoples, land for peace' formula that held sway during the period of the Oslo Accords. A fundamental shift has taken place in Israeli politics and society towards the authoritarianism of a state like Russia, which rejects European democratic norms and multicultural-ism, or Singapore, in which prosperity achieved through hi-tech, cyber-savvy scientific prowess in a globalised world is prized above fundamental freedoms. In this new atmosphere, Israel's relations with the Palestinians and its other Arab neighbours have been relegated to the status of a regional problem to be managed, not resolved. The struggle for Palestinian rights, for a peace with justice, may well be forced to shift to fighting for equality, citizenship, democracy and human rights within the de facto one-state framework, since the possibility of anything other than a Bantustan-type Palestinian entity or entities will be out of the question. Is it possible to see this as the beginning of a new road rather than an end of all hopes for Palestinian self-determination?

Owning the Past to Claim the Future

I have come a long way from the young, idealistic socialist Zionist of the late 1960s and yet I still feel close enough to that past to be able to understand and empathise with people who are bound up in the Zionist idea. For me, understanding and empathy are key ingredients both for developing dialogue within a group and between groups defined as being on opposing sides. As Spinoza wrote, 'The endeavour to understand is the first and only basis of virtue.' If we can't understand the motivation of the other 'on our side', we'll never understand the motivation of the other 'on the other side'. This doesn't mean understanding all to excuse all. On the contrary, it should help make clear where lines need to be drawn between a discourse that is acceptable and one that is not. Anything that states or implies destruction of the other or denial of their human rights is unacceptable, but even then, that doesn't necessarily mean that there are no conditions in which people who hold to such positions can be brought into discussion and dialogue.

But if we are driven only by depressing and intolerable day-to-day realities, if we are wedded to the clauses of a solution to the conflict that are frozen in time, the future is truly hopeless. There has to be a way of both acknowledging harsh realities and rising above them to chart a way forward towards an eventual just solution to the conflict. And given the fact that peace plans have spawned a peace process industry that feeds off itself and in which no 'practical' proposal ever really dies but just enters a half-life, I believe that it is essential to begin with a set of principles. In my view, it is only through this gateway that the fight for rights and a just peace within the repressive, de facto one-state framework, if it comes to that, may discover a new road that could lead to genuine national self-determination for Palestinians and the reaffirmation of national self-determination for Jews.

My conclusions about what those principles should be were shaped by the journey I have described in this book. And a key part of that journey was retaining links with the past. I don't feel that I had to jettison everything I experienced in order to take the key step towards realising that there will never be peace and reconciliation unless and until Jews living in Israel and elsewhere understand and accept the legitimacy of the narrative and the aspirations of the Palestinians. On the contrary, I think what held me back for so long from being able to take that step was indeed the feeling that I had to see no legitimacy whatsoever in the position that I held. The key moment came when I realised that finding a way through the thicket of injustice past and the awful inevitability of future injustice required three essential elements. First, Jews and Palestinians need to acknowledge that there is a set of universal human rights values which they hold in common and to which they must adhere, that supersede history and memory and offer an ethical and fair guide to achieving justice and human rights for all. Second, in that context, the sum of a people's suffering, the harsh facts of history, the injustices experienced and meted out, the inescapable but unassailable ancestral claims and the role of the imperatives of competing religious beliefs, all have to be brought into the open and taken into account. Third, for peace and justice to prevail, if we must have nationalism, there needs to be a commitment on both sides to detoxify and transform it into civic patriotism, not crank it up in pursuit of a mythical homogeneity.

The Israel-Palestine conflict may look like a matter of irreconcilable polar opposites. It has certainly been exploited as such by some Israeli and Palestinian leaders to serve the interests of extremists on both sides. It can be used by the stronger for foisting an unjust solution on the weaker or by either side in justifying an armed struggle until ultimate victory. But there are numerous signs that at root this is not the irreconcilable conflict it has so often been made out to be: for example, joint struggle against the occupation, Palestinian-Jewish coexistence, movement of popular opinion towards compromise positions, numerous Israeli-Palestinian dialogues. None of these have been perfect; many such initiatives have met barriers that could not be overcome. Nevertheless, they are points of light, part of the penumbra of 'acts of kindness' that are a counterweight to the headline grabbing acts of violence and bloody destruction. It may be very difficult, but there is something there that can be harnessed. As Palestinians and Jews are diasporic peoples used to managing multiple identities and facing societies that have problematised their core identities and made it difficult to sustain them, there is surely still great untapped potential for empathy with the experience of the other. There may be many good arguments for the continued involvement of the major powers in seeking a solution, but as time goes by they are wearing thin, and anyway these countries increasingly have other bigger issues to worry about and are deliberately downgrading their engagement. If there is to be any lasting just reconciliation, tapping into the internal resources of the two peoples must offer at least the possibility of a way forward.

An experience that profoundly influenced these thoughts occurred in the early 2000s when I was a member of a confidential Christian-Jewish-Muslim dialogue group trying to find ways of discussing the Israel-Palestine conflict in a constructive manner. There was a superficially amicable atmosphere, but for much of the time there was no meeting of minds over the hard issues. On one occasion the discussion degenerated into particularly harsh exchanges about the legitimacy of the state of Israel with arguments about the validity of UN resolutions being flung back and forth. I remember playing my part in the flinging and getting quite angry that my arguments were not accepted by some in the room. The excellent moderator made us take an extended break. When we returned, he insisted that we approach the problem from the point of view of values that we held in common. As we spoke, it very soon emerged that there were indeed many such values, a great deal of them linked to human rights. When the moderator coaxed us to shine the spotlight of these values on some of the core issues of the Israel-Palestine conflict, such as Palestinian refugees, the right of return, the legitimacy of the State of Israel, the status of Jerusalem, it was remarkable how much agreement then emerged. We weren't a large group, perhaps about 15 people. But what has stayed with me ever since is an especially sharp memory of a liberal Zionist rabbi, a Palestinian activist and academic, a hard-line Islamist and I reaching some extraordinary common positions on the core issues being discussed. Perhaps the emphasis on values opened us up to an understanding of the innermost feelings of the other.

In so far as my personal and political journey has brought me to believe that justice for both peoples is attainable without unbearable sacrifices, it has only been possible because I have not disowned my past but taken responsibility for who I was.

ACKNOWLEDGEMENTS

I am indebted to many people for the inspiration and guidance that have been crucial to me in writing this book. Many of those mentioned in the text had a significant influence on the development of my ideas and the book could not have been written without them.

At over 200,000 words, the original manuscript was unwieldy to impose on friends to read, but all gave generously of their time. My brothers Steve and Michael Lerman kindly corrected faulty memories about my early years. Jacqueline Rose read the entire original draft and was wonderfully encouraging in her comments and advice and in her championing of the book. Richard Kuper also saw its potential and crucially helped to bring it to the attention of Pluto. Ann Jungman read a considerably slimmer manuscript and had some immensely constructive thoughts on improvements I could make. Avner Azulay and Diana Pinto also gave me valuable, positive feedback, and Geoffrey Bindman's comments on specific sections were extremely helpful. Peter Levy and Harold Paisner read the last five chapters and I am grateful for their tolerant and open-minded response. My heartfelt thanks to all of them.

I owe special thanks to my partner Kathy for the many discussions we had about all kinds of aspects of the book and for her close reading of the final manuscript. Most of all, I owe a huge debt to Barbara Rosenbaum who was enthusiastic and encouraging about the project from its very beginning in March 2009. Despite her own heavy workload, she helped to sustain me during the writing process and she then applied her brilliant editorial skills to the text, discussing it with me for hours over coffee at the Literary Café or the Yumchaa. Although the final version of the book is entirely my own responsibility, it could not have reached this stage without her indispensable straight talking, her passion for what I was trying to achieve and her constancy.

In the end it is a publisher who makes the crucial judgement about whether a manuscript becomes a book and I am very grateful to Roger Van Zwanenberg, chair of Pluto, for recognising its worth even before it was cut to size. I have also benefited greatly from the close support and enthusiasm of David Shulman, assistant commissioning editor, and from all the other Pluto staff responsible for getting my book into print and publicised.

Finally, my loving thanks are due to all those in the Lerman household who lived through the last few years as I worked on the book. Kathy, Ben, Rachel and Emma helped sustain me with their love and encouragement. And their expectation that I would always be ready to sustain them with their favourite dishes helped me to keep a grip on the really important priorities of life.

SOURCES FOR CHAPTER HEADING QUOTATIONS

Ch. 1: Chaim Nachman Bialik's poem, 'Techezakna', 'Strengthen the hands' (1894), originally titled *Birkat Haam* ('The people's blessing), anthem of the Zionist youth movement; Ch. 2: Tony Judt, 'Kibbutz', *The Memory Chalet* (Vintage Books 2011), pp. 92–3; Ch. 3: Thom Gunn from his poem 'On the move', *The Sense of Movement* (Faber & Faber 1957); Ch. 4: *'V'shavu banim l'gvulam!'*, from Jeremiah 31:17, printed in the Immigrant's Document; Ch. 5: included in *Encounter with Martin Buber* (1972) by Aubrey Hodes; Ch. 6: Bernard Kops, letter to the editor of the *Jewish Chronicle*, 2 August 1985, and Sir Alfred Sherman, letter to the editor of the *Jewish Chronicle*, 2 January 1987; Ch. 7: Aviezer Ravitzky, from notes taken by the author of a speech given at the American UJA-CJF General Assembly, Jerusalem, November 1998; Ch. 8: Sir Nigel Rodley, elected UK member of the UN Human Rights Committee, speech at the launch of the Jewish Forum for Justice and Human Rights, 2 October 2003, and Roger Cukierman, President of the Conseil Représentatif des Institutions juives de France, November 2002; Ch. 9: Dr Adel Manna, Director of the Centre for the Study of Arab Society in Israel, 'The long journey to two demands', bitterlemons.org, edition 41, 11 November 2002, and Martin Buber, 'Nationalism' (1921), in *Israel and the World: Essays in a Time of Crisis* (Schocken Books, 1963), p. 219; Ch. 10: Abraham Joshua Heschel (1907–1972), *Israel: Echo of Eternity* (New York 1969); Ch. 11: Robert Wistrich, in Amiram Barkat, *Ha'aretz*, 14 March 2006; Ch. 12: Isi Leibler, 'Enough of weak leaders', *Jewish Chronicle*, 12 January 2007; Ch. 13: Melanie Phillips, 8 and 19 February 2007, online diary, melaniephillips.com and *Jewish Chronicle*, and Sidney Brichto, email, 9 February 2007; Ch. 14: attributed to Martin Buber but unsourced; Ch. 15: Baruch Spinoza, cited as from the *Theological-Political Treatise*, 1670.

NOTE ON SOURCES

My book is based largely on memory, diaries that I kept intermittently over 45 years, letters, newspapers, notebooks that I kept during the years 1999 to 2009, published and unpublished writings as well as some other documentary material that I used mostly to check on factual information and dates.

I found a number of books and articles very useful as a means of jogging my memory or providing important background information. And there were also various works that significantly influenced my thinking and others I refer to in the narrative. I have pulled together a selection of all of these.

Books and Articles

Aboluf, Uriel, 'On the Jewish state as an alien state', *Eretz Acheret* website, http://www.acheret.co.il/en/?cmd=articles.455&act=read&id=2438, 4 November 2010.

Avineri, Shlomo, *The Making of Modern Zionism: The Intellectual Origins of the Jewish State*, London, Weidenfeld & Nicolson, 1981.

Avishai, Bernard, *The Tragedy of Zionism: Revolution and Democracy in the Land of Israel*, New York, Farrar Straus Giroux, 1985.

Avnery, Uri, *My Friend, The Enemy*, London, Zed Books, 1986.

Bernstein, Richard, *Hannah Arendt and the Jewish Question*, Massachusetts, MIT Press, 1996.

Brook, Stephen, *The Club: The Jews of Modern Britain*, London, Constable, 1989.

Buber, Martin, *Israel and the World: Essays in a Time of Crisis*, New York, Schocken Books, 1963.

Finlay, W.M., 'Pathologizing dissent: identity politics, Zionism and the "self-hating Jew"', *British Journal of Social Psychology*, 2005, 44, 201–22.

Gilman, Sander, *Jewish Self-Hatred: Antisemitism and the Hidden Language of the Jews*, Baltimore and London, Johns Hopkins University Press, 1986.

Golan-Agnon, Daphna, *Next Year in Jerusalem: Everyday Life in a Divided Land*, New York, the New Press, 2005.

Iganski, Paul and Kosmin, Barry, eds, *A New Antisemitism? Debating Judeophobia in 21st-Century Britain*, London, Profile Books in association with JPR, 2003.

Jay, Martin, 'Ariel Sharon and the rise of the new anti-Semitism', *Salmagundi*, 137/8, winter 2003.

Judt, Tony, 'Goodbye to all that', *Prospect*, December 2004, 105.

——, *The Memory Chalet*, London, Vintage, 2010.

Karmi, Ghada, *In Search of Fatima: A Palestinian Story*, London, Verso, 2002.

Karpf, Anne, Klug, Brian, Rose, Jacqueline, Rosenbaum, Barbara, eds, *A Time to Speak Out: Independent Jewish Voices on Israel, Zionism and Jewish Identity*, London, Verso, 2008.

Kashua, Sayed, *Let It Be Morning*, London, Atlantic Books, 2007.

Khoury, Elias, *Gate of the Sun*, London, Harvill Secker, 2005.

Laqueur, Walter, *Young Germany: A History of the German Youth Movement*, New York, Basic Books, 1962.

Lerman, Antony, 'Fictive anti-Zionism: third world, Arab and Muslim variations', in Robert S. Wistrich ed., *Anti-Zionism and Antisemitism in the Contemporary World*, London, Macmillan in association with the Institute of Jewish Affairs, 1990.

——, 'The Palestine Liberation Organisation and the "Peace Process"', William Frankel ed., *Survey of Jewish Affairs 1990*, Oxford, Basil Blackwell, 1990.

——, 'Sense on antisemitism', *Prospect*, August 2002, 34–8.

——, 'A framework for considering European Jewry's challenges', *Journal of Jewish Communal Service*, 132–5, vol. 79, no. 2/3, winter/spring 2003.

——, 'Israel-Palestine uncensored: what future for the two peoples?', panel presentation, Jewish Forum for Justice and Human Rights, 21 March 2005, Hampstead Town Hall, unpublished.

Litvinoff, Emanuel, *Journey Through a Small Planet*, London, Penguin, 2008.

Luyendijk, Joris, *People Like Us: Misrepresenting the Middle East*, Berkeley, Soft Skull Press, 2009.

Marqusee, Mike, *If I am Not for Myself: Journey of an Anti-Zionist Jew*, London, Verso, 2008.

Morris, Benny, *The Birth of the Palestinian Refugee Problem 1947–1949*, Cambridge, Cambridge University Press, 2004.

Pappé, Ilan, *Out of the Frame: The Struggle for Academic Freedom in Israel*, London, Pluto, 2010.

Ravitzky, Aviezer, *Messianism, Zionism and Jewish Religious Radicalism*, Chicago, University of Chicago Press, 1996.

Rose, Jacqueline, *The Last Resistance*, London, Verso, 2007.

——, *The Question of Zion*, Princeton, Princeton University Press, 2005.

Sabbagh, Karl, *Palestine: A Personal History*, London, Atlantic Books, 2006.

Scham, Paul, Salem, Walid, Pogrund, Benjamin, eds, *Shared Histories: A Palestinian-Israeli Dialogue*, Jerusalem, Panorama and Yakar, 2005.

Shapira, Anita, *Berl: The Biography of a Socialist Zionist. Berl Katznelson 1887–1944*, Cambridge, Cambridge University Press, 1984.

Raja Shehadeh, *Palestinian Walks: Notes on a Vanishing Landscape*, London, Profile Books, 2007.

Wistrich, Robert S., *Anti-Zionism and Antisemitism in the Contemporary World*, London, Macmillan in association with the IJA, 1990.

Yizhar, S., *Khirbet Khizeh*, London, Granta, 2008.

Zertal, Idith, *From Catastrophe to Power: Holocaust Survivors and the Emergence of Israel*, Berkeley and Los Angeles, University of California Press, 1998.

——, *Israel's Holocaust and the Politics of Nationhood*, Cambridge, Cambridge University Press, 2005.

Zertal, Idith and Eldar, Akiva, *Lords of the Land: The War Over Israel's Settlements in the Occupied Territories 1967–2007*, New York, Nation Books, 2007.

GLOSSARY

(Founding date of organisations, where known, in parentheses)

aliya	Jewish immigration into Israel
asefa	Meeting or assembly
Ashkenazi	A Jew of central or Eastern European descent
Bet Midrash	A study hall and synagogue (literally 'house of learning')
Betar	Hebrew acronym for Joseph Trumpeldor Alliance (1923), revisionist Zionist youth movement
B'nei Akiva	Hebrew for Sons of (Rabbi) Akiva, a religious Zionist youth movement
botz coffee	Finely ground roasted coffee made in a cup or glass with boiling water (literally 'mud' coffee)
challah	Bread baked specially for *Shabbat* or festivals
cheder	School for Jewish religious instruction, usually outside primary or secondary school hours
Galil	Hebrew for Galilee
gazoz	A carbonated drink flavoured with a thick, sweet syrup
gizbar	Treasurer
Ha'aretz	Israeli daily broadsheet newspaper
Habonim	The Builders (1929), Zionist-socialist youth movement
hachshara	Agricultural training farm for *olim*
Haganah	Clandestine defence organisation of the Yishuv (1920)
haredi (*haredim*)	Strictly orthodox Jew (pl.), literally 'devout'
Hashomer Hatzair	The Young Guard (1913), Marxist-Zionist youth movement
Hehalutz	The Pioneer (1880s): an association of pioneers preparing for *aliya*
kibbutzim	Plural of kibbutz
Kinneret	Hebrew for Sea of Galilee
Labour Alignment	The alliance of Mapai (the mainstream Labour Party that governed Israel in coalition until 1978) and Ahdut HaAvoda formed in 1965
madrich (*madrichim*)	Guide (guides) in the youth movement
mazkir	National secretary (youth movement); general secretary (kibbutz)
Meimad	Medina Yehudit (Jewish State, 1999), a left-wing religious Zionist political party in Israel
Mizrachi	Religious Zionist party (1902)

Mizrachim	In modern Israeli usage, it refers to all Jews from North African and West Asian countries, many of them Arabic-speaking Muslim-majority countries
oleh (*olim*)	Jewish immigrant (immigrants) into Israel
Palmach	Elite fighting force of the Haganah (1941)
Palmachnik	Member of the Palmach
sabra	A Jew born in Israel, or before 1948, in Palestine
Sephardi	A Jew of Spanish, Portuguese or North African descent
Shabbat	Saturday, the Jewish sabbath
shaliach (shlichim)	Emissary (pl.)
Shoah	Hebrew for Holocaust (though not an exact translation)
shtetl	A small Jewish town or village formerly found throughout Eastern Europe
Tiveria	Hebrew for Tiberias
United Synagogue	Mainstream British orthodox Jewish denomination the spiritual head of which has the title of Chief Rabbi
Westbury Group	Association of international Jewish philanthropic foundations (2001)
Yad Hanadiv	Rothschild family philanthropic foundation (1958) for Israel-based charities, known in Israel as *Keren Rotchild* (Rothschild Fund)
yerida	Jewish emigration from Israel
Yishuv	The Jewish community in Palestine before the establishment of Israel
yeshiva	Jewish religious seminary
yored (*yordim*)	Jewish emigrant (emigrants) from Israel

INDEX